Edinburgh German Yearbook

Edinburgh German Yearbook

General Editor: Peter Davies

Vol. 1: Cultural Exchange in German Literature
Edited by Eleoma Joshua and Robert Vilain

Vol. 2: Masculinities in German Culture
Edited by Sarah Colvin and Peter Davies

Vol. 3: Contested Legacies:
Constructions of Cultural Heritage in the GDR
Edited by Matthew Philpotts and Sabine Rolle

Vol. 4: Disability in German Literature, Film, and Theatre
Edited by Eleoma Joshua and Michael Schillmeier

Vol. 5: Brecht and the GDR: Politics, Culture, Posterity
Edited by Laura Bradley and Karen Leeder

Vol. 6: Sadness and Melancholy in
German Literature and Culture
Edited by Mary Cosgrove and Anna Richards

Vol. 7: Ethical Approaches in Contemporary
German-Language Literature and Culture
Edited by Emily Jeremiah and Frauke Matthes

Vol. 8: New Literary and Linguistic Perspectives on the
German Language, National Socialism, and the Shoah
Edited by Peter Davies and Andrea Hammel

Vol. 9: Archive and Memory in German
Literature and Visual Culture
Edited by Dora Osborne

Vol. 10: Queering German Culture
Edited by Leanne Dawson

Vol. 11: Love, Eros, and Desire in Contemporary
German-Language Literature and Culture
Edited by Helmut Schmitz and Peter Davies

Vol. 12: Repopulating the Eighteenth Century: Second-Tier
Writing in the German Enlightenment (Forthcoming 2018)
Edited by Johannes Birgfeld and Michael Wood

Edinburgh German Yearbook

Volume 10

Queering German Culture

Edited by
Leanne Dawson

 CAMDEN HOUSE
Rochester, New York

First published 2018
by Camden House

Camden House is an imprint of Boydell & Brewer Inc.
668 Mt. Hope Avenue, Rochester, NY 14620, USA
www.camden-house.com
and of Boydell & Brewer Limited
PO Box 9, Woodbridge, Suffolk IP12 3DF, UK
www.boydellandbrewer.com

ISSN: 1937-0857
ISBN-13: 978-1-57113-965-8
ISBN-10: 1-57113-965-6

This publication is printed on acid-free paper.
Printed in the United States of America.

Edinburgh German Yearbook appears annually.
Please send orders and inquiries to Boydell & Brewer at the above address.

Edinburgh German Yearbook does not accept unsolicited submissions: a
Call for Papers for each volume is circulated widely in advance of publication.
For editorial correspondence, please contact either the General Editor,
Professor Peter Davies, or the editor(s) of individual volumes, by post at:

Edinburgh German Yearbook
German Section
Division of European Languages and Cultures
59 George Square, Edinburgh, EH8 3JX
United Kingdom

or by email at: egyb@ed.ac.uk.

Contents

Introduction   1
Leanne Dawson

Part I. Queer Histories and Archives

From Brooklyn to Berlin: Queer Temporality, In/Visibility,
and the Politics of Lesbian Archives   21
Leanne Dawson

"Die zarte Haut einer schönen Frau": Fashioning Femininities
in Weimar Germany's Lesbian Periodicals   57
Cyd Sturgess

Based on a True Story: Tracking What Is Queer about Queer
German Documentary   83
Kyle Frackman

Part II. Queering the Other

The Culture of Faces: Reading Physiognomical Relations in
Thomas Mann's *Der Tod in Venedig*   111
John L. Plews

Seeing the Human in the (Queer) Migrant in Jenny Erpenbeck's
Gehen, Ging, Gegangen and Terézia Mora's *Alle Tage*   153
Nicholas Courtman

The Transgressive Representations of Gender and Queerness in
Fatih Akin's *Auf der anderen Seite*   177
Sarra Kassem

Part III. Queering Normativity

Bitter Tears and Pretty Excess in Fassbinder's *Die bitteren Tränen der Petra von Kant* and *Die Sehnsucht der Veronika Voss*   199
    Lauren Pilcher

Mothers, Masculinities, and Queer Potentials: Jonathan Franzen's Rereading of Thomas Brussig and Phillip Roth   217
    Gary Schmidt

Notes on the Contributors   235

Introduction

Leanne Dawson, University of Edinburgh

Issues concerning LGBTQ+ and other traditionally marginalized identities are in the cultural and political mainstream in the German-speaking lands and beyond as I write this introduction in the summer of 2017. One reason for this is that Germany has become the twenty-third country to legalize same-sex marriage, a move that Angela Merkel voted against, and which came into force on October 1, 2017. This means that those who enter into gay marriage will have a more normalized status in German law and society, in line with the recent trend in the Western world of granting rights relating to family and finances (adoption, pensions, and suchlike) to same-sex couples. This focus on marriage equality has come under fire from many queer activists, who disagree with both a heteronormitization of queer subjects and the vast resources, both time and finances, that have been poured into a cause that most benefits middle class or above, white, cisgender, same-sex pairs while the lives of the most vulnerable LGBTQ+ subjects (trans people, queers of color, queers living in poverty, many of these identities intersect) remain under threat every day.

Indeed Germany's vote for same-sex marriage happened at a time when minorities and other underprivileged groups were being attacked elsewhere. Across the Atlantic, the President of the United States of America, Donald Trump, used Twitter to voice his intent to reinstate the ban on trans people serving in the military.[1] Less than three weeks later, racial tensions exploded at a "Unite the Right" rally in Charlottesville, Virginia, where white supremacists, mostly men, carried both the flag of the Confederate States of America and the Swastika and not only chanted National Socialist slogans such as "Blood and Soil" (from the German, Blut und Boden), but also uttered anti-gay slurs about "fags," demonstrating a hatred for those who are not straight and white.[2] Since then, debates about the removal of racist Confederate-era monuments have foregrounded questions relating not only to the discrimination against certain identities in sociopolitical reality, but also to the ways in which these identities are remembered.

This book's three parts, entitled Queer History, Queering the Other, and Queering Normativity, are somewhat inspired by the aforementioned pressing issues, although there have long been questions about how LGBTQ+ people are treated (whether othered or normalized) and how our culture is remembered. Queers—and other marginalized groups— have often been erased from or re-written in history, a fact that renders important not only the preservation of our lives but also questions of agency, which are raised throughout the book's first part. As the white supremacist coupling of racism and homophobia makes clear, otherness in terms of ethnicity, gender, sexuality, and so on, have often been conflated, making pertinent the examination, in part two, of queerness in relation to ethnicity, perceived foreignness, or migrant status. Finally, the exploration of norms such as white hegemonic masculinity and essentialist ideas relating to sexuality—as we see in the final part of this book—may help us to destabilize them.

Queer History and Language

This introduction aims to provide an overview of queer history and culture, predominantly German—although authors and artists from other German-speaking lands in Europe, as well as some US culture, are included—to set the scene for the subjects dealt with in the rest of the volume: LGBTQ+ archives, physical and digital; literature, in the form of novels and the vessel of the periodical; and film, both narrative and documentary. The treatment here is necessarily abbreviated, although endnotes accompanying both this introduction and the following essays offer a range of recommendations for further reading about LGBTQ+ history, literature, film, and other arts.

First, the important matter of language: the term "queering" is used in the title of this book, incorporating queer both as an umbrella term for LGBTQ+ identities and as a verb to acknowledge that mainstream culture—from which LGBTQ+ people have often been excluded or erased— can be rendered queer through against-the-grain (re)readings of texts and histories, by foregrounding silenced voices and LGBT identities. As an inclusive word for a wide range of identities and theories, the term queer is not intended to erase the identities included under the umbrella but rather incorporates an ambiguity not present in definitions such as lesbian or gay, although these certainly continue to be valid and are of use when no ambiguity is desired.

German language and culture have played pivotal roles in both the understanding and the representation of non-normative genders and sexualities. The term "homosexuality," coined in 1869 by Karoly Maria Kertbeny, was first brought to public attention in Carl Westphal's *Die conträre Sexualempfindung* (Contrary Sexual Feeling) in 1871, the same year that Paragraph 175 of the German Penal Code was introduced. Paragraph 175 was a law that criminalized sex acts between men; sex acts between women were not eventually included due to unresolved debates, in 1907, about how female sexuality should be defined. As Alice A. Kuzniar notes, discourse on the term homosexuality arose—and continued for the subsequent twenty years—exclusively in a German context, and she claims that this can lead to speculation "about the cultural legacy enabling this discourse."[3] The term homosexual was then popularized by sexologists such as Karl Heinrich Ulrichs, Johann Ludwig Casper, Richard von Krafft-Ebing, Albert Moll, and Magnus Hirschfeld, "and not imported in the English language until the translation of Krafft-Ebing's *Psychopathia Sexualis.*"[4] While "the concept of homosexuality arose to signify a psychopathology, a medical association that explains the gay community's abandonment of the term for self-designation," which has been seen in recent years, it is only after the word "homosexuality" was coined did the expression "heterosexuality" enter psychological/psychoanalytic discourse.[5] In *The History of Sexuality*, French historian of knowledge and power Michel Foucault, who would go on to profoundly inspire queer theory in the 1990s, contrasts the "homosexual," as an identity, with the act of "sodomy." "The nineteenth-century homosexual became a personage, a past, a case history, and a childhood, in addition to being a type of lie, a life form, and a morphology with an indiscreet anatomy and possibly a mysterious physiology."[6]

The term "sexual inversion" was also used by psychiatrist and psychologist Krafft-Ebing, as well as other sexologists, to refer to homosexuality; the invert was considered to, perhaps inherently, possess supposedly reversed traits of what we now call gender, meaning the male invert would be stereotypically feminine and attracted to men, while the masculine female invert would desire women. Unlike many of his contemporaries, Magnus Hirschfeld, founder of Berlin's Institut für Sexualwissenschaft (Institute of Sexual Research), concerned with both sexological research and homosexual rights, argued in his study *Die Homosexualität des Mannes und des Weibes* (The Homosexuality of Men and Women, 1914) that those without "inverted" gender could also be homosexual. He coined the term "transvestite" and it is thought that he performed the world's first gender reassignment surgery. Rosa von Praunheim's film *Der Einstein des Sex* (The Einstein of Sex: Life and Work of Dr. M. Hirschfeld, 1999), would go on to combine fiction and the reality of the Jewish sexologist.[7]

Homosexual groups in Germany around the time that Hirschfeld was conducting research included the Deutscher Freundschaftsverband (DFV, German Friendship Association), which began in Berlin in 1919 to work towards civil rights for homosexuals, although the leaders clashed and split and the Bund für Menschenrecht (BfM, Federation for Human Rights) was subsequently created. The latter was led by Friedrich Radzuweit, who advocated for a "homonormativity" with the aim of incorporating supposedly respectable homosexuals discretely into "the social fabric" via a rejection of gender nonconformity and the extremely problematic Greek pederastic ideal—I turn to this shortly in relation to German-language literature—and a push for same-sex couples to enter monogamous long-term relationships, which we may consider in relation to the move towards normalization of the more conservative and respectable same-sex couple in contemporary society.

After the First World War, Berlin was a cosmopolitan city with a range of cafes, bars, and balls contributing to a queer subculture, where both gender and sexual experimentation and homosexual lifestyles were accepted in certain circles and which contributed to a substantial queer artistic output. At this time, a decision was made to repeal Paragraph 175, although the rise of the National Socialist German Workers' Party then prevented this from happening. After Adolf Hitler's appointment as chancellor, the queer culture that flourished in the Weimar period began to wither and, in 1935, the Nazis expanded Paragraph 175. Widespread prosecutions and social persecutions of homosexuals occurred, with thousands dying in concentration camps after being arrested and forced to wear the pink triangle as a sign of their supposedly deviant sexuality. Although not covered in this book, Rob Epstein and Jeffrey Freidman's 2000 documentary film *Paragraph 175* is a German, British, and American co-production detailing the lives of gay men at this time. Their female counterparts, lesbians, always absent from Paragraph 175, were mostly arrested for being *Asozial* (antisocial), as women under National Socialist rule were supposed to focus on *Kinder, Küche, Kirche* (children, kitchen, church), meaning lesbian sexual transgression was foregrounded as a social one. While homosexuals were being killed, their culture was also being destroyed: the contents of Hirschfeld's Institute of Sexology library, for example, were removed and burned in Berlin's Bebelplatz Square on May 10, 1933, in a symbolic attack by Nazi officials. This horrific time in German history highlights the danger of being othered, which is pertinent not only with regard to the National Socialism of twentieth-century Germany, but also what is happening in the USA and elsewhere today.

In 1950, after the end of the Second World War, the German Democratic Republic abolished the Nazi amendments to Paragraph 175, then reformed it in 1968 and repealed it in 1988, while the Federal Republic of Germany modified Paragraph 175 in 1969 by introducing an age of consent of twenty-one for sex between men before lowering this to eighteen in 1973, then finally repealing the paragraph on March 10, 1994, when the country's legal age for male homosexual sex was lowered to fourteen, bringing it in line with that of heterosexual sex. Many reformers, however, long believed that decriminalizing sex between consenting men of legal age was not the same as accepting homosexuality, and culture after the Second World War prioritized a masculinity based on family values relating to marriage and fatherhood, a move away from the militarized masculinity of times past, but still foregrounding heterosexuality and normative masculinity.[8]

This conservativism in Germany and beyond gave rise to a range of countercultures throughout the 1960s and '70s, including the Student Movement, the Civil Rights Movement, Second Wave Feminism, and Gay Liberation. 1969 is a key year in queer culture: on June 28, the Stonewall riots started outside of the eponymous Stonewall Inn in Greenwich Village, New York City, when patrons decided to fight back against yet another police raid at the mafia-run bar and the continued persecution of LGBT people. Indeed the bar was primarily frequented by those queers already most at risk of attack, including butch and femme lesbians, drag queens, trans people, sex workers, many of them people of color, as well as the homeless youths who slept in the park located just outside of the establishment on Christopher Street. The effects of the riots would be felt around much of the Western world and are often credited with kick-starting rights for gay people in modern society, highlighted in the prominent use, in both Germany and Switzerland, of the name "Christopher Street Day" in place of (Gay) Pride for such events as Christopher Street Day Cologne, CSD Hamburg, and CSD Zurich. This not only underlines the significance of the Stonewall riots in relation to gay rights, but also the importance of remembering queer history. German director Roland Emmerich's *Stonewall* (2005), an English-language US film depicting the pivotal time in history, has been widely criticized for—among other things—whitewashing the riots, underscoring the importance of both remembering and fairly representing LGBTQ+ history.

The 1980s saw an AIDS crisis in Germany, the USA, and other countries; a crisis that was made worse by the unwillingness of Ronald Reagan's administration—leading the most powerful and influential country in the world—to acknowledge or address the issue, as it considered HIV/AIDS a gay disease and therefore not a pressing matter.[9] The result was lesbian, gay, bisexual, and trans people uniting in a way they had not done before and have not done since in order to both care for and speak up with those who were HIV-positive, appropriating the term "queer" to encompass the identities of the LGBT+ people involved in the grassroots activism. The term "queer" had entered the English language in the sixteenth century to mean strange or eccentric and by the twentieth century was used as a derogatory term for gay people in general, but especially men perceived as "effeminate."[10] More recently, it is increasingly used by LGBT+ people to signify not only an identity but also a political stance: to highlight a queer politics that stands in opposition to normalization; a response to a shift towards mainstream liberal conservativism, with queer politics rejecting causes such as same-sex marriage.

Indeed, recent decades have seen massive steps towards rather conservative gay rights, including in the German-speaking lands, such as the Eingetragene Lebenspartnerschaft, a form of civil partnership, which was introduced in Germany on August 1, 2001 (2007 in Switzerland, 2010 in Austria, and 2011 in Liechtenstein), some sixteen years before the legalization of same-sex marriage, which arrived rather late in comparison to the rest of Europe. Same-sex adoption was legalized in Germany in 2005, expanded in 2013 to allow those in same-sex relationships to adopt a child already adopted by their partner, and full adoption rights equal to those of heterosexuals have been introduced alongside the legalization of same-sex marriage. Since 2013 there have been some adoption rights in Austria, while Switzerland passed a bill, which came into law at the start of 2018, expanding their adoption laws. In Liechtenstein, however, such rights have been categorically denied.[11]

Queer Culture on Screen, Page, and Stage

LGBTQ+ cultural representation, language, and politics are, as we have witnessed, incredibly bound together, but in this section I home in on some key movements and trends in gender and sexuality predominantly in LGBTQ+ German-language film and literature to set the scene for the rest of this volume. As Alice A. Kuzniar explains in *The Queer German Cinema*, German films produced since the Weimar era have "played a leading, innovative role in the annals of gay and lesbian film, with the tantalizing sexual intelligibility and gender instability of figures from the 1920s screen anticipating the queer sensibilities of the 1990s," with the New Queer Cinema movement.[12] Early examples of Weimar cinema include the silent films *Michael* (Carl Theodor Dreyer, 1924), *Geschlecht in Fesseln* (Sex in Chains, dir. William Dieterle, 1928) and the Austrian-directed *Die Büchse der Pandora* (Pandora's Box, dir. G. W. Pabst, 1929). The Marlene Dietrich and Josef von Sternberg collaboration introduced a range of gender queerness coupled with a blatant female sexuality to the big screen, including one of the first-ever talkies, or sound films, *Der blaue Engel* (*The Blue Angel*, 1930), which was shot simultaneously in German and English, and *Morocco* (1930), made in Hollywood. Like *The Blue Angel*, *Morocco* features Dietrich playing a tuxedo-wearing cabaret singer—with the tux a signifier of lesbianism at that time—but while the former film shows her as a heterosexual *femme fatale*, a queer sexuality is hinted at in *Morocco* when she both flirts with and kisses a woman in her audience. Although overshadowed by *The Blue Angel* at that time, the first German-language sound film with a pro-lesbian storyline was *Mädchen in Uniform* (Girls in Uniform, dir. Leontine Sagan, 1931), which also employs the trope of cross dressing and the staged performance to explore lesbian desire.

Jumping forward to the next most important period with regard to LGBTQ+ representation in German-language film, New German Cinema of the 1960s and 1970s was inspired by Italian Neorealism, British kitchen-sink drama, the French New Wave, and Hollywood genre movies. It saw filmmakers sever ties with much of what had gone before the world wars, both artistically and politically. A group of filmmakers signed the Oberhausen manifesto, which declared, "Der alte Film ist tot. Wir glauben an den neuen" (the old cinema is dead, we believe in the new cinema). New German Cinema productions featuring LGBTQ+ themes and characters include *Der junge Törless* (Young Törless, dir. Volker Schlöndorff, 1966) and *Jagdszenen aus Niederbayern* (Hunting Scenes form Bavaria, dir. Peter Fleischmann, 1969). The queer works of Rainer Werner Fassbinder, New German Cinema's most well-known filmmaker, include a film analyzed in Lauren Pilcher's essay in this book, the lesbian drama *Die bitteren Tränen der Petra von Kant* (The Bitter Tears of Petra von Kant, 1972). Indeed Fassbinder explored a range of LGBT identities onscreen, including working-class gay struggles in *Faustrecht der Freiheit* (Fox and His Friends, 1975) and trans representation in *In einem Jahr mit 13 Monden* (In a Year of 13 Moons, 1978). While Fassbinder often adapted his own plays for the screen, his film about a bisexual sailor, *Querelle* (1982) was based on Jean Genet's 1947 novel, *Querelle de Brest*.[13]

Although there has been a transnational turn in Film Studies in recent years, the Dietrich and von Sternberg collaboration shows us that cinema has long been transnational.[14] Films that portray more recent queer relationships between foreigners and migrants include the English- and German-language *Salmonberries* (dir. Percy Adlon, 1991), starring lesbian singer k. d. lang as an androgynous Alaskan woman who desires a female East German immigrant—played by Rosel Zech, who had earlier appeared in some of Fassbinder's films—and *Kleine Freiheit* (A Little Bit of Freedom, 2003) by Kurdish director Yüksel Yavuz, focusing on a relationship between two illegal immigrant boys in Germany. Popular German-Turkish director Fatih Akin's work includes *Auf der anderen Seite* (The Edge of Heaven, 2007), the focus of Sarra Kassem's essay in this volume, about a Turkish-German lesbian relationship, where one of the lovers is killed and returns to her mother, briefly, as a ghost.[15] Indeed, I have noticed a trend of representing the feminine woman who desires queerly as a ghost in recent German transnational film. Ghosts return in Christian Petzold's *Gespenster* (Ghosts, 2005) about two girls living on the periphery of society, which is part of the Berlin School, a movement that emerged in the early twenty-first century. Prolific queer feminist transnational filmmaker Monika Treut's *Ghosted* (2009) is a German-Taiwanese love story in which one of the characters is a specter.

While there have been lesbian ghosts on the German screen in recent years, which is also tied to the important theme of memory in the German national context, the trope of the lesbian vampire is longstanding, with films such as *Wir sind die Nacht* (We Are the Night, dir. Dennis Gansel, 2010) and *Vampyros Lesbos* (dir. Jesús Franco, 1971), a West German-Spanish horror film made in Turkey. Recent queer German horror has included *Cannibal* (Marian Dora, 2006) and *Rohtenburg* (released in English as *Grimm Love*, dir. Martin Weisz, 2006), inspired by cannibal killer Oliver Hartwin's internet search for a willing victim to be eaten and the young man who volunteers.

Returning to Treut: her other work includes documentary *Gender-nauts: A Journey Through Shifting Identities* (2000), which focuses on trans, non-binary, and genderqueer subjects in the San Francisco Bay area. Along with Elfi Mikesch, who also worked on *The Einstein of Sex*, Treut had made *Verführung: Die grausame Frau* (Seduction: The Cruel Woman, 1985), before later shifting her focus to a more normalized lesbian representation in *Von Mädchen und Pferden* (Of Girls and Horses, 2014).[16] A more normalized homosexuality is also seen in recent films with gay male protagonists, such as *Sommersturm* (Summer Storm, dir. Marco Kreuzpainter, 2004) and *Freier Fall* (Free Fall, dir. Stephan Lacant, 2013), which has been compared to Academy Award-winner *Brokeback Mountain* (dir. Ang Lee, 2005), a film that is said to signal the end of the aforementioned New Queer Cinema.

In the significantly older art form of German-language literature, there is, of course, a much longer tradition of representing same-sex desire, homoeroticism, and genderplay. The term homosexual can be problematic when used to describe people from a time before sex acts were grouped together and conceived of as determining a sexual identity, as outlined earlier in relation to Foucault. Same-sex desire and relationships were, however, represented in medieval times in works such as Ulrich von Liechtenstein's *Frauendienst* (Service of the Lady), a collection of poetry considered autobiographical in which the male protagonist travels to Vienna pretending to be Venus, the goddess of love, and Dietrich von der Glezze's work from the thirteenth century, *Der Borte* (The Belt), which employs crossdressing and same-sex physicality to satisfy material desires.

The Age of Enlightenment frequently focussed on Classical Greece and Rome in the arts, especially literature, some of which foregrounded the Greek tradition of male friendship bordering on the homoerotic as well as the appreciation of the nude male form. In *Outing Goethe and His Age*, Kuzniar makes clear that Johann Wolfgang von Goethe's—the most famous German-language author's—christening of the 1700s as "the Century of Winckelmann," alongside it being named "the Century of Frederick the Great" by Immanuel Kant, references two well-known figures in gay history.[17] Indeed, Johann Joachim Winckelmann, the author of *Gedanken über die Nachahmung der Griechischen Werke* (Reflections Concerning the Imitation of the Greeks, 1755) and *Geschichte der Kunst des Altertums*

(History of Ancient Art, 1763) features in the writings of Goethe, who was fascinated both by Winckelmann and the aforementioned classical Greek culture. Some of Goethe's prose and poetry, such as *Faust* (parts one and two, published in 1808 and 1832 respectively) and the *Römische Elegien* (Roman Elegies, 1795; full version 1914) include homoerotic imagery and desire. Homosocial bonding, at that time, was apparent in texts such as Jakob Michael Reinhold Lenz's *Die Soldaten* (The Soldiers, 1776) and there was gender crossing, for example in the work of Achim von Arnim and Joseph Eichendorff, while Friedrich Schlegel's *Lucinde* (1799) sees characters swap gender positions during intercourse. Going beyond homo-eroticism to "the earliest known novel that centers on an explicitly male-male love affair" by Augustus, Duke of Saxe-Gotha-Alternburg's *Ein Jahr in Arkadien: Kyllenion* (A Year in Arcadia: Kyllenion), set in Greece, appeared in 1805, just at the end of the Enlightenment.[18]

Moving forward into the twentieth century, the Weimar period was pivotal with regard to non-normative gender and sexuality in German-language literature, just as it was with film. At this time, same-sex desire between women became more visible. The Mann family foregrounded queerness: Erika Mann acted in *Mädchen in Uniform*; the literature of Klaus Mann openly dealt with homosexual characters and themes; while the work of their father, Nobel Prize winner Thomas Mann, is famously homoerotic. Although it appeared before the Weimar era, Thomas Mann's *Der Tod in Venedig* (Death in Venice, 1912), details the obses-sion of a male protagonist, often thought to represent the author, with a fourteen-year-old boy.[19] Adolescence is explored in relation to lesbian sexuality in both a 1930 play and a subsequent novel, *Das Mädchen Manuela* (The Child Manuela) by Christa Winsloe, which served as the basis for the film *Mädchen in Uniform*, and these themes also feature in Maximiliane Ackers' novel, *Freundinnen* (Girlfriends, 1923).[20] Lesbian desire is tied to childhood experience in Anna Elisabet Weirauch's three-part lesbian Bildungsroman, *Der Skorpion* (The Scorpion), the first vol-ume of which was published in 1919, the same year as what is considered to be the world's first pro-gay film, *Anders als die Andern* (Different from the Others, dir. Richard Oswald) was released. It was co-written by Oswald and Hirschfeld, who also features onscreen and helped to fund it via his Institut für Sexualwissenschaft. The other two volumes of *Der Skorpion* were published in 1921 and 1931 and not only detail lesbian culture during that period, but also reference theories by some of the aforementioned sexologists.[21]

Queer Theory

Since German unification in 1990 there has been a proliferation of queer themes and authors; not only in fiction, but also theoretical texts. Indeed, beyond grassroots activism, queerness has also taken hold within the academy of the German-speaking lands, including sociologist Sabine Hark's work on gender and lesbianism, Lann Hornscheidt's analyses of queer linguistics, and the German literature scholar Andreas Kraß's work with queer theory. In 2006, Antke Engel founded the Institute for Queer Theory as a hub for academic discussion, with board members including Hark as well as US-based queer theorists such as Judith Butler, Lisa Duggan, and Jack Halberstam. This American contingent is significant, for a large number of key queer theoretical texts originate from there and, as is often the case in queer studies, Anglo-American and French theory dominated in the scholarship submitted for consideration for this volume.

French existentialist philosopher Simone de Beauvoir published *Le Deuxième Sexe* (The Second Sex) in 1949, just four years after the end of the Second World War. Beauvoir was inspired by the horrific National Socialist treatment of Jews, who were abused and killed because they were othered.[22] She noted that women, too, were othered and relegated to a second, inferior, position in society via a binary system where the first position is powerful, as is the case in patriarchy, or neutral, for example, the term mankind is used to refer to humans in general. Beauvoir's text went on to inspire second-wave feminism in the 1970s and early 1980s as well as queer theory in the 1990s. Unlike the two positions of Beauvoir's binary, queer theory tends to foreground an entire spectrum of—often shifting—identities. This was partially inspired by the grassroots activism during the AIDS crisis, where lesbian, gay, bisexual, and trans people united and reclaimed the term "queer," which defies the more rigid categorization of lesbian, gay, bisexual, and trans (LGBT).

Eve Kosofsky Sedgwick discusses the spectrum in her works, including *Between Men: English Literature and Male Homosocial Desire* (1985) and *Epistemology of the Closet* (1990), claiming that the binary limits the context of the understanding of sexuality, that there is rather a spectrum of same-sex bonding and desire, coining the term "homosocial" for certain same-sex relationships that are neither romantic nor sexual.[23] Judith Butler has, alongside Kosofsky Sedgwick, been hailed as introducing queer theory to the world. Butler credits Beauvoir's seminal 1949 statement, "one is not born, but rather becomes a woman,"[24] as an insight into gender as a process, a becoming. Butler's book *Gender Trouble: Feminism and the Subversion of Identity* (1990) is her attempt to unsettle established notions of gender identity, subjectivity, and human agency via the concept of gender performativity.[25] *Gender Trouble* was, however, much criticized for being too theoretical and not showing enough understanding of the dangers of lived reality. Her later works respond to this by dealing with the politics and realities of LGBTQ+ people, such as intersex issues and gay marriage, before examining livable lives and (de)humanization in relation to ethnicity, citizenship, and war.[26] Putting theory into practice, Butler refused the Zivilcouragepreis (Civil Courage Award) at the 2010 Christopher Street Day Parade in Berlin because the event had become too commercial and was ignoring the problems of racism and the double discrimination facing gay and trans migrants.

A focus on temporality, particularly a move away from a straight and linear heteronormative lifestyle with a fixation on the future, has been the biggest trend within queer theory for over a decade, with this queer rethinking of time influenced by both the AIDS epidemic and the aforementioned normalization of the gay subject. Queer temporality emphasizes a focus on the here-and-now; or a blending of past, present, and future; or life lived in rapid bursts (such as the drug addict or the criminal), rather than a steady progression towards the future via pro-duction (capitalism) and reproduction, which often includes martyrdom of the self in the present. J. Jack Halberstam's *A Queer Time and Place: Transgender Bodies, Subcultural Lives* (2005) declares that "queer uses of time and space develop, at least in part, in opposition to the institutions of family, heterosexuality, and reproduction."[27] Halberstam's queer life is "unscripted by the conventions of family, inheritance and child rearing"; it rethinks the "adult/youth binary," for Halberstam argues that "queer subcultures produce alternative temporalities by allowing their participants to believe that their futures can be imagined according to logics that lie outside of those paradigmatic markers of life experi-ence—namely, birth, marriage, reproduction, and death." In the queer context, young, untimely deaths and the fear of a death sentence via sexual acts result in a "constantly diminishing future," without norma-tive life markers such as marriage and parenthood, which "creates a new emphasis on the here, the present, the now."[28] Other significant work on temporality within queer studies includes writing by Lee Edelman (2004), Elizabeth Freeman (2007), and José Esteban Muñoz (2009).[29] Although not covered in this volume, other key contributions to queer theory include Sarah Ahmed's work on the politics of emotion (2004) and queer phenomenology (2006). More recently, debates surrounding gay marriage and adoption have led to a—much critiqued—scholarly exploration of queerness in relation to normativity (Robyn Wiegman and Elizabeth Wilson 2015).[30]

Queering German Culture: Structure and Content

To structure this volume I employ something of a queer temporal-ity, which shifts back and forth in time, rather than delivering a straight importance with the associated notion that this equals progress, for we know this to be false. I have used the overarching themes of Queer Histories and Archives, Queering the Other, and Queering Normativity.

Part 1: Queer Histories and Archives

The volume opens with my own essay on archives to underline the importance of LGBTQ+ representation and remembrance and their importance, in relation to the arts, for the other essays in this book. "From Brooklyn to Berlin: Queer Temporality, In/Visibility, and the Politics of Lesbian Archives" considers the historical, cultural, and sociopolitical significance of the Lesbian Herstory Archives in New York City and Spinnboden Lesbenarchiv und Bibliothek (Lesbian Archive and Library) in Berlin. Here, I employ a range of ideas from feminism (the Beauvoirian binary), queer theory (Halberstam's queer temporality), and archive studies (Jacques Derrida) to deliver a comparative analysis of the two archives, which were conceived of and founded during second-wave feminism and which continue today long after the dawn of queer theory and activism. I examine how the archives, as both bricks and mortar and living spaces, blur binaries and boundaries to queer the cities in which they are located, while considering the importance of temporality and in/visibility in both the archives' local urban and digital contexts. I turn to archives beyond the physical space of a building, including online material and film; this can be both physically and digitally located in archives, while the content of a film can itself constitute an archive. Films and online content not only reach a wider audience than the bricks and mortar archive, but play a significant role with regard to visibility.

Cyd Sturgess's "'Die zarte Haut einer schönen Frau': Fashioning Femininities in Weimar Germany's Lesbian Periodicals" continues this theme of remembering lesbians and other queer women in the past. Sturgess's work examines the two most widely distributed journals for women who desired women in the interwar era, *Die Freundin* (The Girlfriend) and *Frauenliebe* (Women's Love), alongside two of the largest emancipation movements for homosexual citizens, the aforementioned Bund für Menschenrecht and the Deutscher Freundschaftsverband, in relation to early theories of homosexuality. Academic interest in female masculinities—which have been foregrounded in much queer theory, most notably in work by Halberstam—has led to a significant historical focus on the nineteenth-century invert, so Sturgess's essay attempts to open up a plurality and to rethink relationships between femininity, agency, and desire to problematize the representation of feminine women as passive objects of masculine desires—recalling Beauvoir's binary—and the notion that authentic lesbian desire is tied to masculine embodiment; an oscillation that emphasizes the fragility of the binary.[31]

Gay experiences of a past time and place come to the fore again in Kyle Frackman's "Based on a True Story: Tracking What Is Queer about Queer German Documentary," which focuses on *Unter Männern— Schwul in der DDR* (Among Men: Gay in the GDR, dir.Ringo Rösener and Markus Stein, 2012) and what Frackman calls "a kind of fraternal twin production released in the following year," *Out in Ost-Berlin—Lesben und Schwule in der DDR* (Out in East Berlin: Lesbians and Gays in the GDR, dir. Jochen Hick and Andreas Strohfeldt, 2013). Both films engage with history, while themselves becoming artifacts. Frackman's essay interjects itself into scholarly discussion about queerness in relation to German documentary, to explore the former film as a collection of different memories of and reflections on GDR history and demonstrate the significance of LGBTQ+ individuals having a forum where they can write their own history, including that of filmmaker Rösner, whose personal biography connects the other sections of film together, combining public and private. Weaving together threads of memory, the film can be read as multiple layers of queerness, both blatant, such as the gay men featured, and the less obvious, like the form of the film and the presentation of East Germany, which Frackman reads via Elizabeth Freeman's engagement with historiography and history itself.

Part 2: Queering the Other

This section opens with John Plews's essay "The Culture of Faces: Reading Physiognomical Relations in Thomas Mann's *Der Tod in Venedig*," which focuses on the extremely controversial practice of assessing character according to facial and cranial features; this also relates to the notion that foreignness and sexuality is written on the body and a—decidedly unqueer—essentialism. Mann's 1912 novella includes a consideration of the human form in relation to Ulrich and Hirschfeld's theory of the Uranian or third sex, which combines an androgynous mix of the effeminate and the exaggeratedly masculine via textual references to boys and men as Greek sculptures with skin that has the quality of marble. This draws on the tradition in German literature of coupling Greek references with homosexuality. In the Venetian setting, Aschenbach's idea of the foreigner posing a danger or threat to national or personal interests exposes a paradox. According to Plews, the use of physiognomy highlights the double bind of homoeroticism underpinning art discourse and the homophobic economy of symbolic recognition. He compares an interest in men with the interests of men, while offering comment on the medicalization of "queer" bodies. The inclusion of Plews nods to *Queering the Canon: Defying Sights in German Literature and Culture* (1998), a book edited by Plews and Christoph Lorey, which queered German history and thought, film, and literature.[32]

Continuing our exploration of queerness, the foreigner, and border crossings with a more contemporary theoretical reading, Nicholas Courtman's essay "Seeing the Human in the (Queer) Migrant in Jenny Erpenbeck's *Gehen, Ging, Gegangen* and Terézia Mora's *Alle Tage*" engages sociopolitical reality alongside the literary representation of the queer migrant in the two texts to consider crossing of various types, including migration and non-normative sexuality. Erpenbeck's work centers on a retired East German professor who befriends refugees at Berlin's Oranienplatz, predominantly Muslim men of African descent displaced by the Libyan war of 2011, while *Alle Tage* is about the aftereffects of the conflicts in the former Yugoslavia on, and through, a woman who flees to Berlin. Courtman's essay considers dehumanization via the state's treatment of refugees and undocumented migrants, exploring a relationship between Butler's theory of normative violence and cultural intelligibility and how norms define who is recognized as a subject capable of living a life that counts. Like some other essays in this book, Courtman's draws on theories of queer temporality. He considers "natural" temporality and heteronormative affiliations, versus a queer temporality beyond heterosexual conventions, for instance those of marriage and child-rearing, to examine the intersection of sexuality, migrant experience, and the important question of visibility to argue that existing criticism has obscured the double displacement of the queer migrant.

Migration and queer subjectivities come to the fore again in Sarra Kassem's "Transgressive Representations of Gender and Queerness in Fatih Akin's *Auf der anderen Seite*." Akin's film is divided into three parts to explore the interconnections between the lives of six people, including a Turkish prostitute living in Germany, the prostitute's asylum seeker daughter, and the daughter's middle-class white German girlfriend. Like all the other essays in this volume, Kassem's considers the importance of representation and in/visibility; here, alongside questions of community and the appropriation of urban space. Starting with Melanie Kohnen's lament that, although there has been an increase in queer characters onscreen, the mainstream tends to present queer *white* identities, the essay builds on, first, Gayatri Gopinath's argument that there is an absence of diasporic queer female subjectivities in cinematic texts and, second, Butler's concept of gender performativity and work on unlivable lives to discuss the way some human lives are valued more highly than others and to question the resulting dehumanization.[33] Kassem explains how the film plays on the victimization of women, engaging primarily with queer lesbian subjectivity to highlight how the lesbian refugee is habitually excluded from cinematic texts.

Part 3: Queering Normativity

Lesbian relationships on screen are also a key focus of Lauren Pilcher's "Bitter Tears and Pretty Excess in Fassbinder's *Die bitteren Tränen der Petra von Kant* and *Die Sehnsucht der Veronika Voss*," which considers the representation of a highly stylized femininity and how this intersects with aesthetics of race, class, and sexuality, which are usually controlled for viewing pleasure. Pilcher argues that the gender performativity in both Rainer Werner Fassbinder films is key to assessing the queerness of his engagement with representations of otherness and their relationship to visual pleasure. She takes as a starting point feminist film scholar, Laura Mulvey's 1975 theory, which argues that narrative cinema reinforces patriarchal subjectivity by either demystifying or fetishizing the female as passive object of the gaze in order to minimize castration anxiety, a visual construction of pleasure that perpetuates the oppression of women.[34] Pilcher reads this alongside Butlerian gender performativity and a theatrical femininity to argue that, in many of his films, Fassbinder's looking relations expose the performativity of gender in ways that destabilize conventional visual pleasure, for the construction and deconstruction of otherness on the cinematic screen rejects a strict binary division between subject and object.

Binaries and spectrums are examined again in Gary Schmidt's essay in this volume, which moves from Fassbinder's cis femininity to explore normative masculinity and sexuality. Schmidt's "Mothers, Masculinities, and Queer Potentials: Jonathan Franzen's Rereading of Thomas Brussig and Phillip Roth" argues that the increasing fluidity of gender identities has been accompanied by a re-evaluation of hegemonic masculinities. It combines Freudian psychoanalysis with Kosofsky Sedgwick's continuum of male homosocial desire and Butlerian performativity in order to explore three novels: Brussig's *Helden wie wir* (Heroes Like Us, 1997), Roth's *Portnoy's Complaint* (1969), and Franzen's *Purity* (2015), which have both the meaning and valorization of manhood at stake, according to Schmidt, who argues that masculinity is renegotiated in relation to femininity (the overbearing mother) and non-hegemonic forms of masculinity (the male homosexual) in those texts which associate hypersexual heterosexual masculinity with mental illness or perversion. This is certainly a welcome change from the earlier focus on a medicalization and pathologization of the homosexual.

This volume, therefore, examines LGBTQ+ representation in the German-speaking lands and beyond from the early twentieth century to the present day. It considers a range of sexual identities, from those that could clearly be labeled gay or lesbian to more ambiguous queer desires, a spectrum of gender including a hyperbolic masculinity and femininity of cis characters and gender "inversion," and how these intersect with other identities, such as that of the parent, the criminal, and the foreigner. It illuminates queer history and sociopolitical reality, alongside current cultural output in order to consider both the heteronormitization of LGB subjects and the queering of LGBT+ and straight ones, at a complex time in which LGB people are rapidly receiving more rights and recognition than ever across swathes of the Western world while otherness in the form of queer sexuality or gender is being demonized in those very same places.

Notes

[1] On July 26, 2017, Trump tweeted, "After consultation with my Generals and military experts, please be advised that the United States Government will not accept or allow Transgender individuals to serve in any capacity in the U.S. Military." He followed this with another tweet: "Our military must be focused on decisive and overwhelming victory and cannot be burdened with the tremendous medical costs and disruption that transgender in the military would entail."

[2] The rally in question took place on August 11–12, 2017.

[3] Alice A. Kuzniar, *Outing Goethe and His Age* (Stanford, CA: Stanford University Press, 1996), 4.

[4] There is more information on Karl Heinrich Ulrichs, in the context of lesbian periodicals, in Cyd Sturgess's essay in this book.

[5] Kuzniar, *Outing Goethe and His Age*, 4–5.

[6] Michel Foucault, *The History of Sexuality, Volume 1: An Introduction* (London: Allen Lane, 1979 [1976]), 43.

[7] Rosa von Praunheim's work has continually foregrounded LGBTQ themes, including *Nicht der Homosexuelle ist pervers, sondern die Situation, in der er lebt* (It Is Not the Homosexual Who Is Perverse, But the Society in Which He Lives, 1971), *Horror Vacui—Die Angst vor der Leere* (Horror Vacui, 1984), *Ich bin meine eigene Frau* (I Am My Own Woman, 1992), *Männer, Helden, schwule Nazis* (Men, Heroes, and Gay Nazis, 2005), a documentary which investigates gay men who have extreme right-wing and Nazi beliefs, as well as *Ein Virus kennt keine Moral* (A Virus Knows No Morals, 1986), about the AIDS epidemic.

[8] Robert G. Moeller, "Private Acts, Public Anxieties, and the Fight to Decriminalize Male Homosexuality in West Germany," *Feminist Studies* 36 (2010): 528–52. Furthermore, Kyle Frackmann's essay in this book, on queer documentary about East Germany, expands on life in the GDR.

[9] HIV and AIDS have since moved from being considered a "gay disease" and have become associated with Black people and drug users, too, with this link to otherness and the underprivileged resulting in a continued stigmatization of the disease. Homosexuality, like HIV, is sometimes considered to be catching. In recent years, however, the greatest increase in HIV transmission in the Western world has been as a result of heterosexual sex.

[10] The etymology of the term "queer" is sometimes attributed to the German *quer* and, although this has been called into question, the words are visually similar, and translations of *quer* include cross and across, so it is clear why they may be linked, even if erroneously.

[11] During Prince Hans-Adam II's New Year's Day interview in 2016, Liechtenstein's head of state opposed the adoption of children by same-sex couples in his country.

[12] Alice A. Kuzniar, *The Queer German Cinema* (Stanford, CA: Stanford University Press, 2000), 1.

[13] Jean Genet, *Querelle de Brest* (Décines: *L'Arbalète,* 1947). This was first published anonymously.

[14] The meaning of transnational cinema is often disputed, but research on transnational film includes: production, distribution, and exhibition, that is, the movement of both films and filmmakers across national borders and the reception of these beyond the country of production; transnational film as a regional phenomenon, that is a focus on film cultures and national cinemas, which invest in a shared geopolitical boundary and/or cultural heritage; and works on diasporic, exilic, and postcolonial cinemas, which, through their representation of identity, aims to challenge the Western neocolonial construct of nation and national culture and, by extension, national cinema as Eurocentric in narrative and aesthetic formations and ideological norms in Will Higbee and Song Hwee Lim, "Concepts of Transnational Cinema: Towards a Critical Transnationalism in Film Studies," *Transnational Cinemas* 1, no. 1 (2010): 2–21; here, 9.

[15] There has been a definite shift from 1980s German directors' representations of immigrants as unhappy victims to more playful and parodic representations of immigrants by Turkish, and other, directors working and/or living in Germany, such as *Lola + Bilidikid* (Kutluğ Ataman, 1999).

[16] For an overview of Treut's career, see Leanne Dawson and Monika Treut, "Same, Same but Different: Filmmakers Are Hikers on the Globe and Create Globalisation from Below," in "The Other: Gender, Sexuality and Ethnicity in European Cinema and Beyond," ed. Leanne Dawson, special issue, *Studies in European Cinema* 11, no. 3 (2014): 155–69.

[17] Kuzniar, *Outing Goethe and His Age.*

[18] George Haggerty and Bonnie Zimmerman, "German Literature," in *Encyclopedia of Lesbian and Gay Histories and Cultures* ed. Haggerty and Zimmermann (London: Routledge, 2000), 612.

[19] John Plews's essay in this book focuses on Mann's *Der Tod in Venedig* (Berlin: S. Fischer Verlag, 1912).

[20] Christa Winsloe, *Das Mädchen Manuela* (Leipzig: E. P. Tal & Co, 1934).

[21] Radclyffe Hall's infamous British lesbian novel, *The Well of Loneliness* (London: Jonathan Cape, 1928) was written around this time and helped to popularize the ideas of those sexologists who argued that homosexuality was inherent. The book was the subject of an obscenity trial in that year, and because of this, it is arguably the best-known piece of lesbian literature.

Continuing lesbian themes, Ingeborg Bachmann, in works such as *Ein Schritt nach Gomorrha* (A Step Towards Gomorrah) considered another mode of living (Ingeborg Bachmann,"Ein Schritt nach Gomorrha," in *Das dreißigste Jahr* (Munich: Piper, 1961). Bachmann influenced writers such as her fellow Austrian, the Nobel Prize–winner Elfriede Jelinek, whose work includes *Krankheit oder Moderne Frauen* (Illness or Modern Women, first published in the avant-garde journal *Manuskripte* in 1984), which continues the aforementioned association between lesbian sexuality and the vampire.

[22] Simone de Beauvoir, *The Second Sex* (1949; New York: Vintage, 1997).

[23] Eve Kosofsky Sedgwick, *Between Men: English Literature and Male Homosocial Desire* (New York: Columbia University Press, 1985) and *Epistemology of the Closet* (Berkeley: University of California Press, 1990).

[24] Beauvoir, *The Second Sex*, 249.

[25] Judith Butler, *Gender Trouble: Feminism and the Subversion of Identity* (London: Routledge, 1990).

[26] Judith Butler, *Undoing Gender* (London and New York: Routledge, 2004); *Bodies that Matter: On the Discursive Limits of "Sex"* (London and New York: Routledge, 1993); *Frames of War: When Is Life Grievable?* (London: Verso, 2009).

[27] Judith Halberstam, *A Queer Time and Place: Transgender Bodies, Subcultural Lives* (New York: New York University Press, 2005), 1. Please note that Halberstam now goes by the name of J. Jack.

[28] Halberstam, *A Queer Time and Place*, 2.

[29] Lee Edelman, *No Future: Queer Theory and the Death Drive* (Durham, NC: Duke University Press, 2004); Elizabeth Freeman, ed. "Queer Temporalities," special issue, *GLQ: A Journal of Lesbian and Gay Studies* 13, no. 2/3 (2007); José Esteban Muñoz, *Cruising Utopia: The Then and There of Queer Futurity* (New York: New York University Press, 2009).

[30] Sarah Ahmed, *The Cultural Politics of Emotion* (Edinburgh: Edinburgh University Press, 2004) and *Queer Phenomenology* (Durham, NC: Duke University Press, 2006); Robyn Wiegman and Elizabeth A. Wilson, eds., "Queer Theory without Antinormativity," special issue, *Differences, A Journal of Feminist Cultural Studies* 26, no. 1 (2015).

[31] Gilles Deleuze and Félix Guattari, *A Thousand Plateaus*, trans. Brian Massumi (London: Continuum, 2004).

[32] Christoph Lorey and John Plews, eds., *Queering the Canon: Defying Sights in German Literature and Culture* (Rochester, NY: Camden House, 1998).

[33] Melanie E. S. Kohneh, *Queer Representation, Visibility, and Race in American Film and Television: Screening the Closet* (London: Routledge, 2015).

[34] Laura Mulvey, "Visual Pleasure and Narrative Cinema," *Screen* 16, no. 3 (Autumn 1975): 6–18.

Part I.

Queer Histories and Archives

From Brooklyn to Berlin: Queer Temporality, In/Visibility, and the Politics of Lesbian Archives

Leanne Dawson, University of Edinburgh

> *The strongest reasons for creating the archives was to end the silence of patriarchal history about us—women who love women. Furthermore, we wanted our story to be told by us, shared by us and preserved by us. We were tired of being the medical, legal and religious other*
>
> —Joan Nestle, Co-Founder of the
> Lesbian Herstory Archives

> *There is no political power without control of the archive, or without memory*
>
> —Jacques Derrida, theorist of the archive

POST–SECOND WORLD WAR culture is fixated on memory and, by association, the archive, which collects, preserves, and houses documents or artefacts to be used by researchers and laypeople to confront, understand, and share the past. The range of archives in Germany and the United States of America, the two countries housing the lesbian archives I explore in this chapter, is too large to detail here, but both countries have archive cultures.[1] US archives focusing exclusively on LGBTQ+ subjects include: the ONE National Gay and Lesbian Archives (Los Angeles); the June Mazer Lesbian Archives (Los Angeles); the Archive at the Lesbian, Gay, Bisexual and Transgender Community Center (New York City); the Gay, Lesbian, Bisexual and Transgender History Museum (San Francisco); the Gerber/Hart Library and Archives (Chicago); the Barbara Gittings Gay/Lesbian Collection at The Independence Branch Library (Philadelphia); the Jean-Nickolaus Tretter Collection in Gay, Lesbian, Bisexual and Transgender Studies (Minneapolis), while Germany's queer archives include the Centrum Schwule Geschichte (Gay History Center, Cologne) and the Schwules Museum und Archiv (Gay Museum and Archive, Berlin).

Such archives house information while offering us an opportunity to think critically about systems of oppression and the interlocking mechanisms of the personal and the political.[2] A link between archives and non-normative sexuality makes sense, for as Laura Doan and Sarah Waters suggest, "retrospection is a condition of homosexual agency,"[3] and Heather Love locates queers among the "groups constituted by historical injury" for whom "the challenge is to engage with the past without being destroyed by it."[4] The archive may be a site of melancholy, and the LGBTQ+ archive houses the lost and sometimes scared and scary lives of queers, but I argue that this situation exists alongside a more positive space in LGBTQ+ repositories.[5] I do this through an investigation of two lesbian archives that have been shaped by transnational lesbian and gay, feminist, and queer movements: Spinnboden Lesbenarchiv in Berlin, which advertises itself as "the largest collection of testimonies and traces of lesbian existence"[6] in Europe, while crisscrossing the Atlantic to consider the oldest and largest historical lesbian collection in the world, the Lesbian HerStory Archives (LHA) in New York City.

This essay delivers the first analysis of the two archives alongside each other. Both were conceived of and founded during second-wave feminism and continue today long after the dawn of queer theory and activism. I employ a range of ideas from feminism (Beauvoirian binaries), queer theory (Halberstam's queer temporality), and archive studies (Derrida), interwoven with a brief history of these archives, not just the history contained within each repository, but also their archivists, collections, and physical homes. I examine how the archives, as both bricks and mortar and living spaces, blur binaries and boundaries to queer the cities in which they are located, while considering the importance of temporality and the interplay of visibility and invisibility in their local urban (physical) as well as digital contexts; I turn to archives beyond the space of the building, including film—both in and as an archive—and online material, which not only create a wider reach, but play a significant role with regard to LGBTQ+ visibility.

Indeed these lesbian archives became important to me because of the questions of passing and lesbian in/visibility I deal with professionally, in my academic research, and personally, because of my femme lesbian identity. To pass is to be read as a norm or the dominant group, whether with or without intention. It was used in relation to light-skinned Black people perceived as white in the US during slavery and was later employed for gays and lesbians who, to apply an essentialist notion, did not look like homosexuals, before referring to trans subjects who pass as cisgender.[7] In my research, I frequently explore the concept of passing in relation to the femme subject. The term "femme" was taken from the French for woman and first used in the lesbian context in 1940s US working-class bar culture to describe feminine women who partnered with masculine or butch women (the Black equivalents were "fish" and "stud," respectively, although only the former is still used in the lesbian context today),[8] and whose heteronormative appearance meant she often passed as straight despite a lesbian or queer desire.[9] There is an invisibility surrounding sexuality and intimate life in general, and this problematizes the recording of LGBTQ+ history.[10] Passing and queering are both pivotal to this chapter, for the archive simultaneously works with and against the silence of the "closet," that is not being "out" as LGBTQ+.[11] Indeed heterosexuality maintains its privilege partially through the closet, which helps to mute LGBQ sexualities, and "passing demands quiet. And from that quiet— silence,"[12] which queer archives can cleverly subvert.

Such questions of in/visibility are key to my work on the femme subject and one reason why I am interested in queer archives. The Lesbian Herstory Archives were co-founded and housed by a working-class Jewish femme lesbian, Joan Nestle, who continues to be on the committee of "archivettes" today, over forty years later.[13] My research on the lesbian archive was inspired not only by Nestle's work to preserve lesbian history and make lesbian lives and culture visible, but also by an increasing interest in lesbian and queer sites in relation to sociopolitical change and community-building that grew out of my work as Chair of the Scottish Queer International Film Festival (SQIFF), which has not only changed the LGBTQ+ cultural landscape in Scotland, but also convinced me to write about the significance of the sight/site of lesbianism beyond page, stage, and screen.

Feminism—Lesbianism—Queerness

This essay combines sociopolitical reality, past and present, with feminist, queer, and archive theory, so it is important to set the scene, for this book will be of interest to scholars from a range of fields. In 1949, French existentialist philosopher Simone de Beauvoir published *Le Deuxième Sexe* (The Second Sex), inspired by her abhorrence of the National Socialist treatment of Jews, whose form of otherness led them to be abused and killed.[14] Indeed the complexities of "passing" meant that Jews had to wear the Star of David under National Socialism, in order to be recognized as such. Beauvoir noted that women, too, were othered in society; that man was the subject, the absolute, and woman was the object/other and considered lacking or less than. Beauvoir outlined a binary system of subject-object, in which the first position is considered the most important or neutral and the second position is other or negative. Examples of this include man-woman; white-Black; Aryan-Jewish; heterosexual-homosexual; and, more recently, cisgender-transgender. As part of the man-woman dyad, onto which active-passive, public-private, and logic-emotion have been mapped—all of which are of significance to the lesbian archives in this chapter—men were traditionally located in the public sphere to work and appropriate space outside of the home, while women were expected to stay indoors, run the household, and raise children.

Second-wave feminism, partly inspired by Beauvoir's aforementioned text, happened in the 1970s and early 1980s; this helps us to contextualize the archives at issue in this essay, as the LHA and what would go on to become Spinnboden are located in 1970s Western countries and cultures, which were relatively liberal—although with traumatic pasts and inegalitarian presents—leading to prominent feminist movements in each. That the term "lesbian," rather than queer, is used in the names of both LHA and Spinnboden is a sign of the times in which they were founded, during second-wave feminism and before the queer movement and the dawn of queer theory, with the latter's focus on a spectrum of identities with fewer labels and categorization and more fluidity.

Lesbianism remains the oldest word still in use for women's same-sexual relationships and, according to Terry Castle, refers to those "whose primary emotional and erotic allegiance" is to other women.[15] The "L" can frequently get lost within LGBTQ+ culture, politics, and theory; one of the pro-feminist reasons for L being situated in first position in the acronym is that gay men, as men, are located above lesbians within patriarchal society's hierarchies. To counteract some issues with language, that is naming, visibility and power, the LHA has always archived work according to first name, circumnavigating the problem that surnames are often passed to women from men (fathers and husbands) in patriarchal society and that many collection contributors opted to use only their first name for the sake of anonymity to avoid punishment for their supposed sexual and social transgressions. Furthermore, the Brooklyn-based archives employ herstory, rather than history; originally coined in 1970 by Robin Morgan, in the term "herstory" the three letters also used as the male possessive adjective "his" are replaced by the female possessive "her" as a political and social statement, which highlights ongoing issues relating to terminology.[16]

Second-wave feminism achieved many things for women, such as improved political and social rights, but one of the criticisms leveled at it, especially in more recent years, is that it was not sufficiently intersectional. Second-wave feminists sometimes failed to consider how identity is an intersection of gender, sexuality, ethnicity, class, religion etc., so middle-class white feminists in the West often spoke up, wholesale, on behalf of all women. The movement could be rather proscriptive, as lesbians were frequently encouraged to follow feminist dress codes, which would erase strongly gendered styles, such as butch and femme, from lesbian communities.[17] During this time, the feminist "Sex Wars" were happening, with a key event being the "Towards a Politics of Sexuality" conference at Barnard College in 1982, which debated—among other things—femininity and the femme within patriarchy, with Joan Nestle arguing for freedom of gender and sexual expression.[18] To demonstrate the significance of archives, audio recordings of the 1982 debates can be listened to at the LHA, where the tapes are housed.[19]

Throughout her life, working-class Jewish femme Nestle has high-lighted problems of in/visibility and passing (Judaism will come to the fore shortly in the German/archival context). Nestle's aim to create a space for all lesbians, past and present, in order to honor history and pro-mote visibility is especially generous as she is giving a home to those who attempted to refuse her right to be recognized as a lesbian because of her femme aesthetic and ability to pass as straight. Nestle makes clear, "I have worked very hard to make clear that what I write about as Joan Nestle, the femme, is not in any way an official voice of the archives, but as an archi-vist I have also made clear that the lives of all lesbian women are worthy of being documented."[20] When Nestle has presented on the archives, her talks have been dedicated, she has written, to "lesbians who had sat next to me on the bar stools of the Sea Colony, a working-class lesbian bar of the late fifties and early sixties. I always wanted to remind the progres-sively younger women in our audiences of the generations before them, of the different language and style of an earlier courage. I would say, 'I am a femme of the fifties.'"[21] Nestle's work on the archive increased the visibility of the femme subject, while offering a more inclusive type of lesbian space, which foregrounds co-existence in a location that is simul-taneously queer and homely. The rejection of a highly gendered aesthetic, such as that argued during the Sex Wars, was also happening across the Atlantic and is exemplified by texts such as Verena Stefan's 1975 novel *Häutungen* (Shedding), hailed in Germany as the lesbian bible among a sea of German-language feminist literature of that time.[22]

As the 1980s progressed, there was a cultural shift from feminism, which was often considered proscriptive, to a focus on a spectrum of identities via the queer movement. The latter was inspired by the AIDS epidemic and lack of government response to this by the Reagan admin-istration in the USA, while the West German government was led by Helmut Schmidt's Sozialdemokratische Partei Deutschlands [Social Democratic Party of Germany]. The epidemic saw LGBT people caring for the sick, leading them to unite in a way they had not before and have not done since. At this time, the term "queer" was re-appropriated from its use as a slur and employed intentionally as an umbrella term for les-bian, gay, bisexual, and trans subjects, who were trying to work together to improve sociopolitical reality. It was this grassroots activism outside of the academy that helped to spawn queer theory within.

Two texts by women, both published in 1990, kick-started queer theory as we know it: Eve Kosofsky Sedgwick's *Epistemology of the Closet* examines historical moments including the AIDS epidemic while considering literature, language use, and the closet in relation to queer visibility. Kosofsky Sedgwick's pursuit of non-dualism claims that binaries limit the understanding of sexuality; she coined the term "homosocial" for certain same-sex relationships that are neither romantic nor sexual.[23] Judith Butler's *Gender Trouble: Feminism and the Subversion of Identity* also challenges binaries to argue, via the employment of theorists such as Beauvoir and Michel Foucault, that gender is performative rather than inherent or natural.[24] Butler helped to spark a preference for research involving subjects with the most disruptive surface texts, regardless of the sexual acts they perform or the subjects of their desire, resulting in those who passed often being considered outdated, uninteresting, or anti-political. Indeed visual signifiers linked to gender "crossing" are frequently read as signs of a queer sexuality.

"Queer" is an umbrella term for a body of theory and a broad range of identities (LGBT+) and can be used in multiple ways, incorporating an ambiguity not present in terms such as lesbian or gay, while the verb "to queer" allows for what Kosofsky Sedgwick would call "the pleasures of reading against the visible grain" or inclusion of things or identities not traditionally considered LGBT.[25] The term queer evolved in part as a reaction to identity politics and some aspects of feminism; as "queer" became an increasingly important site for progressive art and thought, "feminism came to be viewed in a peculiarly totalizing way" and all feminists from before that period "tended to be lumped together and branded as prudes and anti-pornography partisans by queer theorists and third-generation feminists alike."[26] Lesbians must negotiate both queerness and feminism, while arguments among feminists, from radical to queer and across generations, continue, with the most vocal clash in both the USA and Germany today focusing on trans rights.[27] Despite both archives that figure in this essay, the LHA and Spinnboden, being staffed by people from a spectrum of ages, who self-define in a variety of ways, including lesbian and queer, and who follow different branches of feminism, each forms a community united in its creation of another form of archive.

This concept of community is not unproblematic, however. For a community to exist means some people must clearly belong and, because of this process, others are excluded. The archives aim to be inclusive, with queer material, staff, and visitors, but the presence of the term "lesbian" in the name of each poses a challenge to contemporary queer culture. While the vagueness and inclusivity of the term "queer" is often argued to be more favorable than "lesbian" in current academic and some activist discourses, both archives proudly announce a lesbian body of work. While this may be viewed as too restrictive and exclusionary, it demarcates a necessary space within patriarchy. The ambiguity of the term "queer," for example, can be problematic for the (cis) femme lesbian, who passes as straight: the word lesbian makes clear that her sexuality is unavailable to heterosexual men, the significance of which I will return to later. Making one identity visible at the cost of others is not without issue, and we must also remember that identity can be temporal and shifting, for instance, the archives contain work by people who formerly identified as butch lesbians, but are now straight trans men. The Lesbian Herstory Archives and Spinnboden are, therefore, inclusionary and open, with both welcoming volunteers, visitors and material across generations and identities.

The Lesbian Archive: Theoretical Interjections

The historian of power, knowledge, and sexuality Michel Foucault, who influenced the aforementioned queer theorists, pioneered the theoretical reading of the archive in 1969, which has led to a body of theory, by academics across several disciplines, that now constitutes an archive in itself.[28] Foucault's theory of the archive, removed from both the standard definition and physical space of the archive, focuses on power relations and the production of meaning, which serves to remind us that the storage, organization, and redistribution of information always informs and is informed by political and historical discourse. Jacques Derrida's archive, too, is theoretical, using the father of psychoanalysis, Sigmund Freud, as its starting point. I employ aspects of Derrida's theory in this essay, while acknowledging the perils of using heteropatriarchal texts to read queer and/or lesbian spaces. Derrida considers the challenge posed by psychoanalysis to the question of memory and both the production and preservation of an archive, employing the two Freudian tropes of the death drive and the pleasure principle.[29] Derrida considers the practicalities of the archive and, as with Foucault, the process of archivization, which "produces as much as it records the event" and, in turn, shapes our sociopolitical reality.[30]

Psychoanalytic discourse is bound up with sexual desire, meaning it is of significance to those of us exploring LGBTQ+ archives, as is the fact that, according to Valerie Vichy's work on the autobiographical graphic novel as queer archive, "queers are liable to an intense library cathexis. What sort of people, after all, must research who they are? Those whose difference is antifamilial, somatically unmarked, culturally veiled, and potentially shaming are drawn to lonely stacks and secret research, where the archive enables self-definition."[31] I explore the lesbian archive as a simultaneous site and sight of pleasure and pain, while acknowledging that this essay is a type of "mesearch," researching lesbian representation and remembrance because of my aforementioned identity.

While LHA co-founder Joan Nestle still continues to deliver talks about and publish on the archive to which she gave a home, there has been a recent burst of writing on lesbian-specific archives, particularly the LHA, by a young generation of scholars, who have been educated at a time when queer theory is much more prevalent within the academy than the older and previously prevalent subject areas of lesbian or women's studies. Recent writing on the archives includes Kate Davy's article, "Cultural Memory and the Lesbian Archive,"[32] which describes her LHA-based research on the WOW (Women's One World) Café Theatre in Manhattan, a venue co-founded by butch-femme performance artists Peggy Shaw and Lois Weaver.[33] Jen Jack Gieseking, who identifies as a woman and uses male pronouns, has published on his embodied experiences in the Lesbian Herstory archival space.[34] Madhu Narayan has written about the LHA's rhetorical strategies to preserve community and identity.[35] Cait McKinney has considered the digitization of images and sound in the LHA, and I shall return to the concept of the digital later.[36] Rachel F. Corbman, a member of the LHA collective, has written a genealogy of the LHA, for "there is still not much written about the Archives as an archive." Corbman focuses on the first five years of the LHA, and I push forward this research with my consideration of the LHA alongside Spinnboden, on which much less has been written; there is certainly a lack of English language scholarship.[37] Ann Cvetkovich's monograph *An Archive of Feelings: Trauma, Sexuality, and Lesbian Public Cultures* investigates emotional politics in relation to the construction and maintenance of North American lesbian archives.[38] For Cvetkovich, items which constitute an archive are not always housed together or curated alongside each other, and she dedicates part of her book to film as archive, which I examine later.[39]

Kate Eichhorn's book, *The Archival Turn in Feminism: Outrage in Order* briefly examines the LHA in her consideration of feminism, specifically the riot grrrl movement, which is generally considered to be part of the third wave. Eichhorn draws simultaneously on Pierre Bourdieu and Foucault to argue that "unlike either the gallery or art museum, which usually endows a literary or artistic work with value in the present, the archive's work is more often than not retroactive [. . .] the archive is first and foremost a temporal apparatus—at once committed to the endless accumulation of time," pointing to the queering of time, as documents are literally out of time and out of place in such a repository, with a temporal and spatial dislocation of both the archived material and the lives contained within, which simultaneously focuses on a form of survival and longevity beyond the documents' first life.[40]

Because key archival questions relate to temporality, memory, and generations, I turn to the queer theory of J. Jack Halberstam, as it foregrounds identities and locations considered to be out of time and place. Halberstam's 2005 book *In a Queer Time and Place: Transgender Bodies, Subcultural Lives* examines the archive of works and commentary surrounding murdered US trans man Brandon Teena and how "dyke subcultures" allow for the development of queer counterpublics and temporalities.[41] He argues that the archive has transformed from its literal meaning to a "floating signifier" extending beyond "a place to collect material or hold documents,"[42] before going on to claim that the transgender archive is "not simply a repository; it is also a theory of cultural relevance, a construction of collective memory, and a complex record of queer activity. In order for the archive to function, it requires users, interpreters, and cultural historians to wade through the material and piece together the jigsaw puzzle of queer history in the making."[43] In the aforementioned book, Halberstam argues that, "queer uses of time and space develop, at least in part, in opposition to the institutions of family, heterosexuality, and reproduction. They also develop according to other logics of location, movement, and identification."[44] He goes on to employ queer time as the antithesis of the middle-class logic of reproduction and the desirability of a long life and to claim that queerness has become compelling as a form of self-description because of its "potential to open up new life narratives and alternative relations to time and space."[45] Here, "queer" is being used beyond sexuality and/or gender, to describe non-normative lifestyles.

Halberstam's notion of a queer life "unscripted by the conventions of family, inheritance and child rearing," is one which rethinks the "adult/youth binary," for he argues that "queer subcultures produce alternative temporalities by allowing their participants to believe that their futures can be imagined according to logics that lie outside of those paradigmatic markers of life experience—namely, birth, marriage, reproduction, and death." This queer rethinking of time was radically influenced at the end of the twentieth century by the way gay communities were severely diminished and deeply touched by the AIDS epidemic. Young, untimely deaths and the fear of a death sentence via sexual acts result in a "constantly diminishing future," which "creates a new emphasis on the here, the present, the now."[46] Similarly to Halberstam, Lee Edelman's 2004 monograph *No Future: Queer Theory and the Death Drive* uses the queer relationship to AIDS and (non-)reproduction—that is, a link to premature death and lack of procreation leading to future generations—to argue that the homosexual future has been viewed as limited and to argue against heteronormativity's investment in, and sacrifices for, the child. In this essay, I discuss the queer temporality of the lesbian archive and the queer space it forms, physically and digitally, while arguing for a future created by queer kinship and matriarchal bonds, as the past is remembered and employed for the present and future.

Halberstam makes clear that not all LGBTQ+ lives are radically different from their straight and cis counterparts; this message must be contextualized, for Halberstam's work was published in 2005 and change has been rapid for same-sex couples obtaining legal rights relating to, for example, marriage and child rearing, before living rather straight suburban lives. As I finalize this chapter in 2017, gay marriage is legal in states across the USA and most of the UK—with the exception of Northern Ireland—and same-sex registered partnerships have been legal in Germany since 2001 with a majority vote in favor of same-sex marriage finally made on June 30, 2017 (although Chancellor Angela Merkel's own vote was a no) and forms of adoption are possible by gay people in each of these lands, we see a trend of normalizing same-sex desire in relation to family. However, while huge sections of LGBT communities and their straight cis allies have been consumed with the normalization of same-sex relationships, via marriage equality debates and related laws, which tend to benefit those who are otherwise privileged (middle-class+, white, cis), the existence of trans people, queers of color, and queers living in poverty—many of these intersect—remains under threat every day.[47]

Both the LHA and Spinnboden were founded when homosexuality was far removed from the more normalized status it has today in parts of the Western world. When the LHA's founder Joan Nestle speaks to younger generations, she has written, it is "very important for me to remind them that once I was a sexual criminal."[48] Recent trends of (white) nationalism and a regressive shunning of otherness such as is evident in the United States under Trump and in the UK context due to the Brexit vote have made clear that time and progress are not always linear and that rights can swiftly be revoked. Both archives make visible and accessible the private, sometimes invisible, and dangerous lesbian lives of the past, perhaps offering some hope for the future of identities most denigrated today.

Collectives and Collections: The Birth of LHA and Spinnboden

As a text by Nestle on the LHA website details, in April 1973 a group of mostly gay men and women, primarily staff and alumni from the City University of New York (CUNY), founded the Gay Academic Union (GAU), which was dedicated to the rights of lesbian and gay students and staff and the inclusion of homosexual material within courses.[49] Typical of the second-wave feminism of the 1970s and its fight against patriarchy from within the binary, many women from the organization decided to found a women-only space, resulting in consciousness-raising groups, in which out lesbians including LHA founders Joan Nestle, Julia Penelope Stanley, Pamela Oline, Sahli Cavallaro, and Deborah Edel (who still dedicates much of her life to working in the LHA over forty years later) discussed "the precariousness of lesbian culture" and took issue with how much lesbian culture from the past was seen through "patriarchal eyes" and came up with a new concept: grassroots lesbian archives.[50] These were conceived of more as community centers—social and safe spaces for items which might be lost or destroyed by homophobic or indifferent families—than as academic archives, which I argue intervenes into both Derrida's concept of the archive and Edelman's argument about queer time. This community-center approach somewhat queers patriarchal concepts of time, transmission, and space, for it favors a non-hierarchical and multi-generational exchange, while donors are requested to offer descriptions of objects and documents donated, as well as information about their lives, empowering them to "narrate the context around their own materials"; to be both subject and object of study, while being heard as an authoritative voice.[51]

The Lesbian Herstory Archives found a home in 1974 in Joan Nestle's apartment, which she shared with her then-partner, Deborah Edel, on 92nd Street in Manhattan's Upper West Side, welcoming into her private space thousands of visitors interested in lesbian history and culture, as well as numerous archival volunteers.[52] That same year, the five founders sent a news release to all US gay, lesbian, and/or feminist publications to see what the community response would be; it was resoundingly positive, and in 1975 the LHA published its first newsletter, which was and remains free.

Meanwhile, across the Atlantic in West Germany, the preparation for what would become Spinnboden lesbian archives was being made by Die Frauengruppe der Homosexuellen Aktion Westberlin (The Women's Group of Homosexual Action in West Berlin), a lesbian subsection of Homosexuelle Aktion Westberlin (Homosexual Action in West Berlin, HAW). The latter had formed on August 15, 1971, following a screening of Rosa von Praunheim's film, *Nicht der Homosexuelle ist pervers, sondern die Situation, in der er lebt* (It Is Not the Homosexual Who Is Perverse, But the Society in Which He Lives, 1971), and consisted solely of (around forty, predominantly student) men, with the primary aim of having Paragraph 175 abolished.[53] In spring of 1972, the Women's Group of HAW formed, reminiscent of the women of America's GAU wanting their own group, and began to collect documents such as meeting minutes, pamphlets, and newspaper articles on May 25, 1973. This group also created the Lesben-Frühlings-Treffen (Lesbian Springtime Meeting, LFT), which is still in existence and has become the largest and best known lesbian meet-up in Europe, with lesbians gathering over Whit weekend at a different German location each year, to socialize and discuss topical political issues. The first LFT event, in 1974, took place in West Berlin, posing the question as event headline: is feminism the theory and lesbianism the practice? This was often debated during the second wave women's movement, a time when some women who did not desire women opted to live lesbian lives as a feminist and political choice.

The Lesbisches Aktionzentrum (Lesbian Action Center), which would become Spinnboden, was established in 1973, using the documents collected by the women of the HAW.

In 1980, Gudrun Schwarz, a sociologist who was comfortably within the academy and has published on National Socialism and gender, took control of Spinnboden, locating new colleagues and organizing donations. Like LHA, Spinnboden created a newsletter; the first was circulated in 1982, and in October of that year, the archives opened with a collection of 800 books, 42 files of newspaper articles, as well as numerous newspapers, slides, and posters. It would also go on to publish work, not just house it. Beginning on August 8, 1983, the Spinnboden Archiv zur Entdeckung und Bewahrung von Frauenliebe (Spinnboden Archive for the Discovery and Preservation of Love between Women) became an official association with a contact and advice helpdesk, an archive, a reference library, and a research center.

Although there are academics among the LHA founders, their website foregrounds that "the Archives shall be housed within the community, not on an academic campus that is by definition closed to many women" and Nestle makes clear that "our archives, our family album, our library, was not primarily for academic scholars but for any lesbian woman who needed an image or a word to survive the day."[54] She underlines that no letter of introduction was ever needed to gain access, that proof of sexuality or other aspects of identity was never necessary, and that browsing was as important as research. In addition, Nestle makes clear the gravity of the archives' aims, "why we should be trusted with the photograph of a dead lover or diaries that spanned twenty years. [. . .] We had to be personal and public, political and confidential."[55] Spinnboden, too, takes seriously its aim of housing lesbian documentation, while ensuring accessibility and inclusion.

According to Nestle, "we realized that because the word 'archives' sounded formal and distancing to many of the women we wanted to reach, we would have to dedicate many years to spreading the word about this new undertaking. At first we carted samples of the archive holdings to homes, bars, churches, synagogues, anywhere we were asked to speak."[56] Their plan was to spend the first ten years building up the trust and support of the lesbian community, speaking wherever they received an affordable invitation, with venues ranging from people's homes to women's festivals, seminar rooms, bars, and religious institutions. The LHA collective also held frequent talks within the Archives themselves, such as the "At-Home-With-the-Archives" series, which still runs today, with the titular pun pointing to audience comfort with the archives and the collection's location.[57] And it is this concept of home which I explore in the next section of this chapter.

The Lesbian Home as Archive and
the Archive as Lesbian Home

Cvetkovich claims, "the history of any archive is a history of space" and that lesbian and gay archives have been significant in the transformation of space because their very existence "has been dependent on the possibility of making private spaces—such as rooms in people's homes—public."[58] Kate Davy recounts that the LHA "opened quite literally in [Nestle's] pantry," its materials stored in ten milk crates, and remembers "sitting on the end of Nestle's bed watching a videotape of a WOW weekly Variety Night performance on a screen only a couple of feet from my face."[59] This demonstrates the informal, and rather haphazard, style of these archives, while queering space and time, for daily lesbian reality existed alongside lesbian history from a range of cultures, queering the home and blurring public-private binaries as well as those traditionally tied to man and woman, for example, logic and nurturing, respectively.

This could be declared what I coin a home-osexuality, and could be considered alongside the more recent trend for normalization and bringing LGB subjects in line with conservative values, rather than queering society via the abolishment outdated structures such as marriage, which, as divorce statistics show, does not have a high rate of success beyond those societies in which women have few legal rights. The LHA, however, has queered the concept of home: queer lives are being welcomed into and housed in the home (that is the house containing the LHA), rather than the home housing same-sex lives that have been heteronormativized (marriage, mortgage, children, and straight temporality/time).

The concept of home is sometimes problematic for those who identify as LGBTQ, due to homophobic families and/or legal structures against same-sex marriage and forms of parenthood (adoption, access to artificial insemination etc). The LHA queers this while re-creating an affirmative sense of it. While a shared space of "home" is positive for lesbians, a minority group that has been both erased and discriminated against throughout history, it has the potential to be problematic for queer subjects who identify otherwise, for example, bisexual women or those who once identified as lesbian but now identify as men. Much like community, home depends on a binary of inside and out, of belonging and exclusion, but the LHA welcomes a spectrum of genders and sexualities, including heterosexual volunteers, researchers, and event attendees, who respect that the focus is on lesbian/queer lives and desire and wish to learn more about them from sources more authentic than representation in mainstream film and television, for instance.

Shortly before Nestle housed the Archives, they were taken by then-lovers Stanley and Cavallaro from New York to Tennessee with the aim of cataloguing the material while living as part of a lesbian separatist community during the second wave of feminism. Their breakup meant that the cataloguing was not completed; Stanley accepted an academic post at the University of Colorado, Cavallaro began a postgraduate degree, and Edel collected the material and drove it back to New York City.[60] According to Nestle, "this is when we learned never to let the Archives go travelling [. . .] We took it home."[61] Nestle offering a home to the archives positions her in a role that, viewed in traditional terms, is simultaneously feminine and masculine. Locating the archives, of which she was the guardian and authoritative voice, in the domestic sphere of her home, into which she invited the public, amounted to queering the public-private/masculine-feminine binaries.

In *Archive Fever*, Derrida examines the archive as house or domicile, using Sigmund Freud's house turned museum in London as an example, considering authority in relation to archives, while unpacking the etymology. Initially, "archive" meant:

> a house, a domicile, an address, the residence of the superior magistrates, the archons, those who commanded. The citizens who thus held and signified political power were considered to possess the right to make or to represent the law. On account of their publically recognized authority, it is at their home, in that *place* which is their house (private house, family house, or employee's house), that official documents are filed. The archons are first of all the documents' guardians.[62]

Nestle's home was an archival repository, the largest collection of lesbian documentation in the world, and the archive was her home as she nested among a spectrum of lesbianism, both representation (books, films, etc.) and sociopolitical reality (minutes from meetings, flyers etc.) Significant, too, is Derrida's use of the term "guardian," for woman is so frequently bound to the maternal. Indeed, Nestle has been referred to as a "matriarchal mentor,"[63] who claims that the "fullest record we can leave is the best legacy for the political and social survival of our lesbian *daughters* around the world."[64] This trans-generational and nurturing aspect, for the archive to which she gave a home acts as a shelter and refuge for both documents and people, creates a different kind of kinship; the Archives are described on the LHA website as "part library, part museum, part community gathering space." Nestle's role as a mother of these lesbian documents—keeping them safe, ensuring they have a future, wanting them to improve the world and much more, could apply to being the guardian of children, but here Nestle is the keeper of knowledge rather than flesh and bone.

In his work on the power of the archive and its limits, philosopher and political theorist Joseph Achille-Mbembe claims that archives are the product of a process of judgment, resulting in the granting of a privileged status to certain documents, while others are discarded. He concludes that the archive is "not a piece of data, but a status."[65] However, the first LHA newsletter, dated 1975, states:

> We will collect and preserve any materials that are relevant to the lives and experiences of Lesbians: books, magazines, journals, news clippings (from establishment, Feminist, or Lesbian media), bibliographies, photos, herstorical information, tapes, films, diaries, oral herstories, poetry and prose, biographies, autobiographies, notices of events, posters, graphics, and other memorabilia and obscure references to our lives.

Nestle interpreted the archives, offering knowledge about the lesbian past and how cultures can be remembered, while attempting to be as egalitarian as possible, via the inclusion of any items lesbians and their families wanted to donate. Like Spinnboden, which currently holds about 9,000 books, more than 1,000 magazines, as well as dissertations, posters, pictures, and audio files on the history of lesbians, LHA embraces all kinds of artifacts, from the highbrow to the banal, often not included in archives, including literature, film, letters and ephemera, such as a collection of T-shirts with political slogans, lesbian and feminist badges, a hard hat with a lambda sign, which was worn by a lesbian construction worker, posters from a range of events, both political and cultural,[66] to avoid institutional gatekeeping.

By the mid-1980s the collection had outgrown Nestle's apartment and a fundraising drive allowed the collective to purchase a new home for the archives in Park Slope, Brooklyn in 1990, where archivettes continue to work. The Park Slope location officially opened in June 1993 and is documented in the film *Not Just Passing Through* (Jean Carlomusto, 1994). The building was once a family home, and the floor plan of the archives makes clear that during renovation it was important to retain the "homeness" of it, for the cozy living room is also a library and reading room and the kitchen houses the photocopier (with no cost listed and copies to be paid for via donation only if one can afford to) thus subverting spaces typically in the private sphere, traditionally tied to woman as good wife and mother, and locating these alongside knowledge. A "principle" stated on the LHA website is that "the Archives will always have a caretaker living in it so that it will always be someone's home rather than an institution" and the top floor of the three-story brownstone Brooklyn townhouse, part of a long street of family homes and businesses, contains a bedroom, in which interns and archivists who work there may sleep. Returning to Derrida's theory of the archive, as outlined earlier in this chapter, and his work on the Freud house/museum, it is in "domiciliation" and "house arrest" that archives "take place." He declares that "the dwelling, this place where they dwell permanently, marks this institutional passage from the private to the public, which does not always mean from the secret to the nonsecret. (It is what is happening, right here, when a house, the Freuds' last house, becomes a museum: the passage from one institution to another.)"[67] The LHA, unlike Spinnboden, is simultaneously a home to humans—caretakers, and in the previous abode, Nestle—and to the archives.

In 1988, shortly before the fall of the Berlin Wall, Spinnboden got a space of its own, in Burgsdorfstraße, Wedding, West Berlin, a working-class area. Spinnboden made use of institutional funding unlike the LHA, which eschews all government funding as a matter of principle ("we take no money from the government, believing that such an action would be an exercise in neocolonialism, believing that the society that ruled us out of history should never be relied upon to make it possible for us to exist").[68] Spinnboden's funding included money from the German lottery, which was used alongside private donations, in the mid-1980s to fund a part-time post to run the archives. Then, between 1989 and 1995, the Senat für Jugend und Familie (the Senate for Youth and Family) subsidized both a three-quarter-time post and half of the building rental costs, which the Senat für Arbeit, berufliche Bildung und Frauen (Senate for Work, Vocational Education, and Women) took over in 1998.[69] Such official state sponsoring means collusion with authorities that according to Derrida and other scholars of the theoretical archive must affect Spinnboden's practice, but this was the lesser of two evils, because Spinnboden struggled financially and risked closure on at least one occasion.[70]

In 1995 the collection moved to the Weiberwirtschaft e.G., a cooperative for women established as part of a feminist business center in Anklamerstraße, where the then much more alternative quarter of Prenzlauer Berg meets Mitte, the center of reunified Berlin. Here, we can compare the fact that Spinnboden moved to a wealthier part of Berlin and the LHA moved from the hub of the city, the borough of Manhattan, to Brooklyn, at that point an even more alternative and certainly much more affordable space across the East River, with many more square feet for the price at that time than the island of Manhattan, which was being rapidly gentrified, even in the more traditionally artistic and bohemian areas. While the LHA has its own house, Spinnboden is on the second floor of an office block, which also contains a medical practice, an employment agency, and an osteopath among others, lending Berlin's lesbian archive a more institutional and business feel, for it is not immediately obvious to the first-time visitor that this is a women's business cooperative. With LHA and Spinnboden there is a queering of the home and a queering of the office/place of work, the private and the public, traditionally women's and men's domains, respectively, while the women's cooperative structure of both institutions attempts an alternative to hetero-patriarchal structures within capitalist society and queers the type of inheritance and transmission patriarchal society nudges us towards. Both archives not only render lesbian history visible via the information preserved and queer kinships formed inside each site, but also offer a sight, that is a visibility, to lesbianism within their respective cities by having lesbian institutions with lesbian names that occupy—and queer—space in each.

Within the lesbian archive context, I consider Halberstam's writing about how family, whether in hetero or homo contexts, most often "introduces normative understandings of time and transmission. [. . .]. An ideology of family pushes gays and lesbians toward marriage politics and erases other modes of kinship in the process."[71] Queerness is, traditionally, the opposite of hetero-domesticity, although the archives offer a different form of familial relation: community, rather than (blood) family, and the queering of the home via the Lesbian Herstory Archives and the femme's rejection of heterosexuality. According to Halberstam, family life and queer life are in opposition based on the "normative scheduling of daily life (early to bed, early to rise) that accompanies the practice of child rearing," and important here is a focus on the future, for generational time means "values, wealth, goods, and morals are passed through family ties from one generation to the next."[72] Unlike this normative time, the LHA and Spinnboden are queer spaces with queer time, both literally, for example the opening hours of LHA are irregular, but also figuratively for the past and present co-exist. Furthermore, there is transmission (of knowledge, community etc.) in multiple directions, which is not about inheritance and the family unit but the protection of a minority within society. Although the volunteers' arranging and tidying of the archive/home for free is gendered labor, which may recall the unpaid, and often thankless, work of the traditional housewife, the archivettes pass on a range of skills between generations, highlighting an intergenerational knowledge of use beyond the "home."[73]

Another theorist of queer temporality, Lee Edelman, considers time, discussing the "Child as the emblem of futurity's value" and problematizes heteronormativity's focus on the investment in, and sacrifices for, this future.[74] While the LHA and Spinnboden do not privilege the future, youth, or martyrdom, as child-rearing often does, the past and present do blend in each institution to promote a better future for lesbians of today through historical knowledge combined with activism and social opportunities. The past, present, and future intersect as a range of generations and identities work alongside each other, sharing knowledge alongside anecdotes, united in their queerness. Elizabeth Freeman has coined the term "temporal drag," which rethinks generational dynamics outside of traditional family frameworks: "the concept of generations linked by political work or even mass entertainment also acknowledges the ability of various technologies and culture industries to produce shared subjectivities that go beyond the family."[75]

Nestle describes the process of archival research as "erotic exchange," for there is "an erotic encounter that happens when someone comes and says 'do you have?' and I say 'yes' and 'you are welcome to it'. That is an incredible moment of an erotic exchange that is the desire to know and the desire to give."[76] Within the archive, there is a do-it-yourself mentality, ensuring no traditional hierarchy between archivist and researcher, as queerness cannot always be subsumed into a heteronormative prioritization of chronology and ranking. The LHA and Spinnboden do not neatly fit into a more traditional temporality, for although knowledge can be passed down to Nestle's aforementioned "lesbian daughters," it also transfers and loops from these daughters to their lesbian mothers and grandmothers at the archive in an exchange. The lesbian archive creates its own kind of queer futurity and queer family: these grandmothers, mothers, and daughters can enter into romantic and sexual relationships across generations, thus blending the maternal and the more literally erotic, rather than a martyr-like prioritization of the child and its future, as per Edelman's critique of a straight time, in a space that is both homosexual and homosocial. Temporal drag is the notion that even when the past feels, literally, like a bit of a drag, it can also be a site of hope and of political renewal. Nestle has been posited as maternal, thus creating a matriarchal space within a patriarchal society, while forming queer generational links. Although Spinnboden also forges such links, it has been presented more formally, perhaps due to its more academic and institutional approach.

The Personal Is Political: The Archive as Site of Research and Activism

My introduction to the archive was neither at LHA nor Spinnboden, and certainly did not bring me into contact with the concept of the archive as "home," but was instead at the storehouse of Berlin's Gay Museum and Archive, as I conducted research for my doctoral thesis on queer femininities in German literature, theater, and film. I sought documentation on the real-life tale of lesbian love between an Aryan and a Jew in National Socialism, which has been recounted in literary and filmic adaptations, thus a story and a (research) location in which history, memory, pleasure, trauma, as well as multiple layers of lesbianism and queerness converge.[77] My archival work was, in many ways, unlike those stories recounted to me by academic friends and colleagues over the years: tales of rooms overfilled with dusty files, requiring complex navigation, sometimes to find nothing of use; bureaucracy in order to gain access to the actual building and thus the specific documents within; and problems with regard to the use of documents (copying, copyright etc.), made worse by sometimes unhelpful archivists.

Although I encountered many dusty files while hunting for what I needed, and did not find any documents pivotal to my research, I perused them while stationed at a desk that had a large, wooden dildo and accompanying harness lying on it, further queering the already queer act of research—by a lesbian on lesbian history for a queer doctoral thesis—and initially offering some amusement when juxtaposed with the warnings I had received about boring archival work. Further research I undertook elsewhere later in that same research trip to Berlin, at Spinnboden, highlighted that an archival space can be multilayered and emotionally complex. I noted, then, that although the LGBTQ+ archive is significant in terms of preserving material and evidence of dominant culture's marginalized groups, it is not simply a space containing a history of LGBTQ+ subjects. As a social site it is also very much about the present and the future and not just in terms of coming into contact with forms of memory or sharing history in order to find solidarity or suchlike, but also in terms of space, as a place in which new encounters can lead to social and work connections and various forms of relationships. This means the archive can be a more personal space, whether for the hobbyist or researcher, than a traditional library, where evidence in the form of primary texts such as literature or film is readily available if access to the library is granted, unlike the digging needed to uncover items in archives; a digging that can, in this context, be tied to a search related to one's own identity, recalling the link between sexuality and psychoanalysis outlined earlier in this chapter. Gaining such access can be problematic in some state-owned or institutional archives, where visitors must show documents to prove a certain status or affiliation in order to enter the building and use the materials housed within, unlike the free archives of LHA and Spinnboden. Indeed, both LHA and Spinnboden are incredibly welcoming, with the former's statement of purpose from 1974 making clear: "1. All women must have access to the archives 2. The collection must never be bartered or sold 3. The collection must be housed in a lesbian community space and be staffed by lesbians."[78]

Before this research trip, it was my own identity—as a lesbian femme with a working-class background—that had led me to the writing of Nestle, which, in turn, piqued my interest in the LHA, years before I paid my first visit to this—or any—archive. Such hierarchy is absent from egalitarian archives like the LHA, where I went on to discover an inclusive and positive space so unlike the melancholia often associated with archives, from which poor and working-class people have often been excluded. In the LHA and Spinnboden, intersections of identities traditionally located on the second position of the binary, or on the queer spectrum, find a voice. The lesbian archives queer the canon, usually the home of straight, white, cis men, and queer history, by re-writing what is considered worthy of preserving and remembering. Furthermore, I had no archival training, but found that the LHA and Spinnboden are set up for everyone to be able to access the information they need, fostering inclusivity and accessibility.

In general terms, the archive is especially significant in the German cultural and sociopolitical context, particularly because of National Socialism's attempt to eradicate certain othered identities (including Jews, homosexuals, the disabled). Information contained in archives played a role in the identification, segregation, and subsequent murder of Jews, and by 1938, Jews were banned from using German archives, and many archives and collections were left abandoned when Jewish people fled. This highlights the link between archives and identity, both in terms of preserving the past and attempting to make future progress, although this progress certainly is not linear. Here, the importance of memory in relation to traumatic history is highlighted. Cvetkovich argues that queer archives throw into light the idea that we should "never forget," for the existence of gay and lesbian history has been a contested fact.[79] According to Nestle, the inspiration for the LHA was the Schomberg Center for Research in Black Culture, therefore another othered group, which makes pertinent Cvetkovich's insistence on remembering traumatic history, for the Schomberg Center started as one Black man's refusal to accept his teacher's edict that Black people have no history.[80]

Spinnboden hosts meetings for Black, trans, and disabled women who desire other women, thus promoting inclusivity, and its website expands its feminist focus beyond lesbianism, asking for donations to end female genital mutilation in Africa. In 1978, both Judith Schwartz, a grassroots lesbian historian, and activist Georgia Brooks joined the LHA collective. Schwartz shared her archival skills, while Brooks launched the first Black Lesbian Studies group at the Archives, thus striving to empower more minorities: women, lesbians, femmes, and Black people, and ensuring that the LHA is alive and pushing towards a future, rather than simply rescuing and recounting the past: lesbian archives are sites of politics and protest.

There has been much recent academic interest in archives, in the form of scholarly publications—some of which are outlined earlier in this chapter—and university course content, but precisely because it is a trend means that the pendulum may swing in the opposite direction, which would mean that archives would one day lose their scholarly appeal. Furthermore, to rely on a university or the government for the preservation of an archive is to hand over control to those with a different kind of—economic and political—interest to the grassroots founders of LHA. Their methods of funding and housing allowed Nestle, and an increasingly larger group of lesbians, to retain control, while her sole-authored overview on the multi-voiced website simultaneously locates her as historian and bearer of knowledge, albeit one who foregrounds inclusivity and collective work.

Having lesbians in control of a lesbian space, lesbian collections, and lesbian history is important with regard to the legal and political treatment of lesbians, whose rights and even existence have been denied. In the German context, during National Socialism lesbians were frequently detained in concentration camps as "Asozial" (antisocial) rather than explicitly for their sexuality, while their gay male counterparts were forced to don the pink triangle, a symbol of homosexuality. Women were expected to focus on "Kinder, Küche, Kirche" (children, kitchen, church) so for the woman who engaged in lesbian acts and/or relationships, her sexual transgression was foregrounded as a social one. Spinnboden offers a visible and safe space for the history that dominant cultures frequently tried to eradicate. For example, the entire contents of the library of Magnus Hirschfeld's Institute of Sexology, an academic foundation concerned with sexological research and homosexual rights, were removed and burned in Berlin's Bebelplatz on May 10, 1933. Non-normative sexualities were considered pollutants to be kept out of sight, although here the breaking of the public-private binary was a symbolic attack by Nazi officials meant to serve as a warning to others.[81]

Diana Fuss, professor of literature, who has published on sexuality, psychoanalysis, and the collection of items, argues that collections share the fundamental structure of memorials. Like Derrida, she considers Freud and describes the space of his London study, crowded with antiquities, in his house-turned-museum, "like all museums, this particular memorial site doubled as a mausoleum, showcasing the self-enshrinement of a collector buried among his funerary objects."[82] Both Freud and Nestle invited people into their respective homes so the visitors could find out more about themselves: for Freud, this was via him psychoanalyzing them in an analyst-analysand binary, while Nestle's visitors were granted free access to knowledge in the LHA's collection of books and other items. While analysands learned about themselves through Freud, visitors to Nestle's home learned about lesbians, past and present, through the knowledge and items she collected and accepted, rather than selected. This brings to mind the Valerie Vichy quotation I employed earlier, about queers being drawn to "lonely stacks and secret research," as both the LHA and Spinnboden allow people to conduct research to find out more about their/lesbian and queer identities, although this is within the safe space of each of the archives, so even if a visitor aims to pass, their presence in the simultaneously private and public repository can be kept secret from the outside world. There is no possibility of the contents from Nestle's home, which becamethe Lesbian Herstory Archives being left as some form of museum after her death (she currently lives in Melbourne, Australia), for the archive is a living space, despite it housing the past. Furthermore, even when Nestle resided in the first incarnation of the LHA, she did not allow this to become a place focusing solely on the past, for she ensured it was a living space—her home—and a safe space, full of visitors interested in researching lesbian history and improving the lesbian present and future. While Freud's museum contains his work, private obsessions, and blood-family history, Nestle's home was a public collection that helped to create a queer family, to queer the traditional man-public/woman-private binary, and to further queer the city in which she lived.

Queering the City: The Physicality of the Archive

Berlin and New York are cities of archives, museums, monuments, and memorials: spaces for us to confront and remember the past. Memorials in Berlin include Das Denkmal für die ermordeten Juden Europas (The Memorial to the Murdered Jews of Europe) and its gay counterpart, the Denkmal für die im Nationalsozialismus verfolgten Homosexuellen (Memorial to Homosexuals persecuted under Nazism). The latter, which makes use of film footage to remember lost lives, is easy to miss, unlike the large-scale Jewish memorial close by. As I worked in, and on, the archive (Spinnboden and the Gay Museum and Archive) in Berlin—not only a city of archives and memorials, but also a city of building sites, where the past is demolished to make space for the future—I was surrounded by the past in the present. When doing archival work in New York City in the summer of 2014, I lived in an apartment between the National Museum of the American Indian, One World Trade Centre, and the 9/11 memorial; located in front of my apartment building was the Statue of Liberty, a past sign of future hope and inclusivity in the present. While in Berlin conducting archival work in 2008 and again in 2013, my apartment was a short walk from a section of the Berlin Wall and several other memorials. Archives, too, serve as a ritual space within which cultural memory and history are preserved. Such sites are memory contained in objects, ensuring that we do not forget and that we acknowledge that memory is not simply individual and private but can also be public, collected, and collective. Collective memory is supposed to create a shared sense, including loss, but can also be somewhat institutionalized, unlike many of the personal and private memories collected in lesbian archives. Here, the person who donates chooses how things are stored. This lack of hierarchy is of significance as those events and people chosen to be remembered by governments (beyond atrocities such as the Holocaust and 9/11) usually focus on the lives and works of wealthy white people.[83]

Alongside memorials and archives, there are other physical signifiers of minority identities, such as LGBTQ+, in both New York and Berlin, the largest and most cosmopolitan cities in their respective countries; their significant LGBTQ+ populations can make use of bars, clubs, community centers (including those for LGBTQ+ elders and youths), and meet-up groups. Indeed the big city tends to attract LGBTQ+ people, who sometimes feel they can live more openly due to the increased anonymity and the access to queer communities, services, culture, and entertainment. Both archives further queer two already rather queer cities. What is significant here, however, is that they are not just queering—the ambiguous, umbrella term—the cities but they are rather lesbianizing them, for the term gay, and sometimes queer, often foregrounds and privileges cis gay men, regardless of intention.

New York nightlife for women who desire women includes the lesbian-focused bars Henrietta Hudson and Cubby Hole in Manhattan and Ginger's in Brooklyn, just blocks away from the LHA, as well as club nights such as Hot Rabbit, although gay—and specifically lesbian—bars have been closing at an alarming rate. As gay rights become increasingly conservative, focusing on family and finances, meaning less stigma and more integration, there is perhaps less apparent need for gay bars. Berlin no longer has a lesbian bar after the last of its kind, Serene, closed at the end of 2015, although it still has occasional lesbian club nights such as Mermaid Lesbenparty (Mermaid Lesbian Party). In New York City, closures in recent years include the short-lived The Dalloway (2013), while even San Francisco, long considered the gay mecca of the world, saw its last lesbian bar, The Lexington, shut its doors for the last time in 2014, and we are living in times when LGBTQ bookshops and other businesses are folding in quick succession. Reasons for this include the gentrification of cities and subsequent rent increases, although it must be noted that Berlin is significantly cheaper to live in and visit than either New York City or San Francisco. Furthermore, the so-called pink pound signifies the spending power of gay men, who tend to be more affluent than lesbians, just as straight men—due to the hugely unjust gender pay gap—are more likely to earn more than straight women.

For some time before the recent turn of normalization, gay bars were considered fashionable and/or fun beyond the target market, for example, for straight cis women who wanted to avoid sexual attention from men or celebrate a bachelorette party in a "camp" space, even when queers could not enter into civil partnership or marriage. This meant that gay people, who could not marry, were confronted with the trappings of impending heterosexual weddings in some of the only public spaces in society that were gay, and safe for gays. The LHA and Spinnboden, although frequently fun and social, do not attract such insensitive behavior and, as sites of knowledge, they offer one of the very few free lesbian public spaces. While heterosexuals derive pleasure—sometimes at LGBTQ+ expense—in gay bars,[84] and Gay Pride events have turned into parties for all sexualities rather than the protest they began as, both shame and pride are housed and remembered in lesbian archives.[85]

Both the LHA and Spinnboden are located in "wound cultures" of violence, trauma, and memorialization. In Halberstam's work on queer temporality, he discusses Brandon Teena in relation to the small town, the archive, and "wound culture," which Halberstam declares the US to be because of its level of violent (gun) crime and its "fascination with murder and mayhem."[86] I would certainly add other wounds from the US past, including colonization, slavery, and the aftermath to this. The notion of a "wound culture" has, however, most frequently been used to theorize Germany, a country inexplicably bound up with National Socialism, the Holocaust, and the subsequent division and re-unification. It is certainly significant that both of the archives discussed here are in countries so tightly linked to horrific patriarchal violence, traumatic wounds, and memorials. Indeed, archives are especially relevant in relation to countries linked to trauma, for trauma, psychoanalytically speaking, is also bound to memory or, more specifically, forgetting.

The LHA and Spinnboden do document positive moments from lesbian and queer history, such as information on the lesbian cafes and meet-up spots from the Weimar period, some of which continued to exist during National Socialism, demonstrating resilience and strength in the face of adversity. While both archives are used to uncover lesbian history, horrific, heroic, and heart-warming, Spinnboden operates as a lending library for books and DVDs, while offering multiple events and meet-ups. The lesbian past, always present via the collected memory of material, blends with the present to create a space for the future via cultural and social events. Spinnboden is not only open to the public, but ensures public spaces are open to lesbians—past (their history is temporarily revived) and present (those taking the tours)—through the monthly tours, relating to lesbian social and cultural history, taking place outdoors in the city of Berlin. Created and led by historian Katja Koblitz, these events are publicized on the Spinnboden mailing list and website. Examples of past tours include spots significant to lesbian and gay life in Weimar Berlin, which brings the past to life, thus enabling a group of women who desire women to connect their identity with what came before, while today re-queering public spaces such as supposedly straight buildings and parks via shared knowledge about the way these were used or appropriated by queers in the past. The tours not only make Berlin's rich lesbian past visible to lesbians, but also make lesbians, including those who usually pass, like the femme subject, visible to others in the city through the group dynamic, with tour group participants heard discussing lesbian topics in public, acting against the aforementioned silence often required to pass.

Furthermore, the tours allow lesbians to appropriate, en masse, otherwise straight public spaces, thus queering the city and going against the straight appropriation of gay spaces like bars and Gay Pride events. It is both the material contained within Spinnboden, used by Koblitz to curate the tours, and the reach of the archive in terms of creating a visible lesbian space and a place to discover cultural events, that make the outings possible, continuing to blur the distinction between public and private. Although LHA does not offer similar tours, the archivettes appropriate other parts of the city via their participation in the annual NYC Dyke March, among other events.

Queering the Screen: The Digital Lesbian Body

We move now from queering physical spaces to the digital archive, both film and the web, for it has been theorized that the archival turn in the arts and humanities happened when it did because of its relation to the digital turn, "a technological and epistemological shift that brought the concept and experience of archives into our everyday lives."[87] Such technology not only allows us to be passive consumers of culture, but also to create and disseminate cultural content and become part of the online archive, which is of significance with regard to those who have traditionally had less access to the arts more broadly, for instance, the poor. The internet, and more specifically website support platforms like WordPress (for blogs) and video-sharing sites like YouTube (for vlogs) have revolutionized who can both share and obtain information, somewhat equalizing the traditional active-passive binary, particularly for those who cannot visit the archives or even attend events in which they could network and circulate information, perhaps due to issues of finance (for those not living in New York City or Berlin, it may be prohibitively expensive to travel to the archives) or fear of appropriating certain spaces (despite good will, some people may feel uncomfortable for various reasons, including class and gender identity). Furthermore, the growth of the web, for work, leisure, and pleasure, means fewer people visit physical sites such as libraries or cinemas when literature and film is so easily accessible online. While the film industry is still dominated by white cis men with cultural, social, and economic capital, the rise of the internet has allowed the transmission of DIY productions for free, allowing for a level of agency—as foregrounded by the archives—that mainstream representation in literature, film, etc. does not always afford.[88] YouTube's success is partly based on the idea of egalitarianism (but it is owned by Google and certainly has its own place within the capitalist economy) and does allow anyone with internet access to record their lives without dependence on publishers or other institutions, for mainstream historical accounts tend to be on the side of wealthy, straight, white, cis men, but we cannot forget that those who are privileged and economically comfortable have both the time and self-confidence to deliver creative output.[89]

Lesbians having some control of how lesbians are represented is hugely important. Film and television is often our first contact with other lesbians. It also helps to form straight people's opinions about lesbians while at the same time making lesbians feel visible. There are, however, three dominant categories of lesbian representation onscreen, and all of them are problematic: first, the lesbian as invisible or erased, for example when a lesbian character or storyline is removed when a novel is adapted for the screen or, more frequently, when a gay character is killed off as punishment for supposed sexual and social transgression. The second is the lesbian as monstrous, which is often tied to female masculinity and a supposed gender transgression (although this can be quite literal, e.g., the lesbian vampire is the second most frequent filmic representation of the feminine woman who desires other women). The third is the antithesis of the monstrous butch, but sometimes overlaps with the vampire motif: "lesbian chic." This is the representation of the glamorous, eroticized, feminine lesbian, the femme, who is considered palatable, even titillating, to a mainstream heterosexual audience. The feminine "lesbian" is most frequently found, filmically, in pornography aimed at heterosexuals: two women have sex in front of a male actor, for his and the viewer's pleasure, before he physically interrupts the scene and penetrates both actresses to reinstate his power, heteropatriarchy, and the binary system. When he takes over, lesbian identity is erased, which ties into the first trend outlined here as well as the outdated notion that lesbianism is nothing more than a phase, especially for the femme subject. In addition to these three dominant types, I have identified a new trend in lesbian representation onscreen: normalization, which ties into the normalization of lesbians in parts of the Western world as evidenced by marriage equality and adoption and financial rights.

While the lesbian archive, physical and digital, simultaneously normalizes same-sex desire and queers time and place, both the physical (the city) and the digital (the web), it also acts against lesbian erasure as a space dedicated to the preservation of lesbian lives—butch, femme, and everything in between—and is not primarily intended to entertain, repulse, or arouse heterosexual men as the screened "lesbian" sometimes is. Both LHA and Spinnboden include moments of lesbian history that have been consumed by the mainstream, as well as mainstream literature and film that have been read against the grain to queer them, particularly in the past when being gay held greater repercussions in the Western world than today.[90] This reinforces that lesbian preservation and representation by lesbians is significant, for it allows for the kind of agency that aforementioned (filmic) trends do not grant.

It is not only narrative film intended for public consumption that documents moments in queer history, as LGBTQ people have made and appeared in home movies about themselves, and about queer events and organizations. Film scholar and critic B. Ruby Rich coined New Queer Cinema, which comprised films by and for queer people from the start of the 1990s and, although there are disputes about when it ended, the piggybacking on the momentum created by this movement by *Brokeback Mountain*, which was directed by a heterosexual cis man, Ang Lee, and which enjoyed huge commercial and critical success, is often acknowledged as the death knoll in 2005. New Queer Cinema, which started in North America, but arguably includes some German films—notably the work of queer lesbian feminist filmmaker, Monika Treut[91]—arose out of a certain sociopolitical situation, "the conjunction of four things: Reagan, AIDS, the invention of camcorders [. . .] and cheap rent."[92] Because LGBTQ+ people have consistently been pushed to the margins, or even erased from mainstream cinema and television, much representation of LGBTQ+ subjects is found in independent and amateur works and both these and the aforementioned New Queer Cinema help to portray a range of identities, rather than relying on tired stereotypes, therefore helping to counteract dominant trends. Lynne Kirste, a film archivist who has written articles on her archival practice, laments that independent and amateur films often remain in "filmmakers' closets and basements [and] will eventually deteriorate, suffer damage, or be discarded or lost. [. . .] To make these images viewable now and in the future, archival outreach is essential."[93] Although some of these works are available in the brick-and-mortar archives, including LHA and Spinnboden, where archivists and volunteers are working incredibly hard to digitize them, lesbian and queer internet archives are essential and anyone with access to a computer with an internet connection can curate a channel of videos, private or public, and those who do not have the ability (for reasons of health, finances, fear of being outed etc) to travel to the physical buildings of LHA and Spinnboden can access them online.

The year 2001 saw the introduction of Spinnboden's own website, making its holdings more accessible, although back in 1997 Spinnboden began working with FAUST, an online compiler, to facilitate the sharing of information with other women's projects in Berlin via databanks. On May 30, 2008, the archive celebrated its 35th birthday, marking it with the rolling out of an online catalogue of documents, allowing interested parties to search from a distance, which is significant for research accessibility and for those who want to browse anonymously, before, or indeed without ever, visiting the physical lesbian repository.[94] Such online presence also offers a space for those who are still in the closet to continue to pass and to queers who cannot, for various reasons, visit the building, allowing people to explore (homo)sexuality in privacy. This is, of course, also true for YouTube and online film streaming devices such as Netflix, which allow LGBTQ+ content to be screened in private. That both archives, which had previously mailed printed newsletters, can now send them online ensures a greater reach at no (or low) cost.

The internet has become a queer archive, with sites such as spinn-boden.de and lesbianherstoryarchives.org offering a curated collection of queer material amidst a swamp of information. Technologizing the queer archive is important on multiple levels and scholars of the queer archive have noted how a variety of media are needed to (re)construct queer experiences.[95] While online LGBTQ+ presence has significant advantages, lesbian dating sites (the older German-language LilaLust and English-language Gay.Com and GaydarGirls, as well as newer and increasingly international ones like Her), mainstream dating site options for women to meet women, the increase of connectivity in general, via Facebook, Tinder, Twitter etc. has meant that there are more opportunities than ever to meet fellow LGBTQ+ people. As a consequence, offline meeting spots are suffering, recalling the death of the lesbian bar outlined above.

Boundaries between film and the archive are sometimes porous. Film often becomes meta, and, like archives, it can preserve other forms of media. As Ann Cvetkovich notes, "[o]ne of the ways that documentary film and video expands the archive is by documenting the archive itself."[96] Cvetkovich highlights that the first-ever feature film by a Black lesbian, Cheryl Dunye's *The Watermelon Woman* (1996), part of New Queer Cinema, parodies the LHA, thus elevating its status.[97] Within the narrative, the character Cheryl, played by Dunye, is fascinated by the eponymous Watermelon Woman, an African-American actress, whose Hollywood parts were always the stereotypical roles for Black women, for instance the maid. Cheryl journeys from Philadelphia to New York to visit the Center for Lesbian Information and Technology (CLIT), which stands in for the LHA. Here, she is told by novelist and Jewish lesbian activist Sarah Schulman, in the role of an archivist, that the mountains of material are not filed or indexed (recalling Davy's account of hunting for material on WOW at the LHA) because CLIT is a volunteer-run collective, and that items cannot be reproduced without the consensus-based approval of the collective, which meets only every other month. But Cheryl uses her video camera to document the items regardless.

Jean Carlomusto's documentary film *Not Just Passing Through* (1994) opens with the inauguration of the LHA's Park Slope space, before going on to document the significance and challenges of preserving and communicating lesbian history; a history which, as Nestle states in the film, has been located from within "piles of garbage." Highlighting the intersectional and inclusive focus of the LHA, one of the four subsections of *Not Just Passing Through* focuses on the Asian Lesbians of the East Coast, while another pays homage to Mabel Hampton, an African-American lesbian who served as a matriarchal mentor to Nestle with regard to the preservation of history across generations, much like Nestle as the mother to lesbian "daughters."

More recently, Megan Rossman has been making work both in and about the archives, such as the documentary short *Lesbian Herstory Archives: A Brief Herstory* (2017), available at no cost online via a link from the LHA homepage. Indeed, Rossman was filming a new documentary feature film on the archive and archivettes, as I attended an At Home with the Archives event and also while I worked in and on the lesbian archive, both conducting research and also filming a documentary, *Femmes on Film* in the summer of 2017. My documentary features both archives and archivists, while recounting the significance of femme reality and representation. This use of film as part of the archive, and archives as part of film (for background research or onscreen) demonstrates intersections between archives and the arts; while film and literature are housed within the archives, the archives are also actively being used and represented to produce more lesbian artistic output. This also highlights the invaluable generosity among archivists, artists, authors, and academics, via a continued reciprocity and a queer circularity, with the proliferation of work aiding preservation.

Queer Circles: Concluding Notes

It cannot be denied that both the brick-and-mortar lesbian archives discussed here, which function as social and historical sites, and the websites and academic papers housed in the massive archive of the web made the writing of this chapter significantly easier. This connectivity between both lived reality and representation has allowed me to write about lesbian archives as simultaneously queer and homely spaces that create their own kind of futurity and family, while this chapter will be donated to archives such as LHA, Spinnboden, and Glasgow Women's Library, which holds the largest collection of lesbian material in the UK. This inclusion of my written work in archival spaces, as well as the fact that I have organized and hosted an event as part of the Scottish Queer International Film Festival at GWL, where I screened a series of films on the femme, including Melissa Levin's 2002 short *Cherries in the Snow: An Ode to Joan Nestle*, ensures that I can share my academic LGBTQ+ research with the general public. Furthermore, Catherine Gund, who co-produced and co-directed *Not Just Passing Through*, which is detailed in this essay, not only showed a series of her films at the 2017 Scottish Queer International Film Festival, but also hosted a documentary filmmaking workshop as part of the Festival. This further helps demonstrate the organic circularity of academic research and public events, as well as the intersection of lived reality and the significance of the archive. As with LHA and Spinnboden, I intend to work on, rather than just in, the GWL archives in future, coming full circle.

Circularity, temporality, dialogue, and reciprocity among those who are, or have been, othered is hugely significant in the current political climate. While I was in New York City working in the LHA in the summer of 2017, President Trump tweeted that he would ban trans people from the military, and while this piece was being written a White Supremacist rally, replete with Nazi salutes and chants, was held in Charlottesville, Virginia.[98] The latter incident came to international prominence when a counterdemonstrator was killed. Earlier in the summer, across the Atlantic, equality for minorities was under the spotlight as German Chancellor Angela Merkel voted no on same-sex marriage, even though there was a majority in favor, so that Germany became the world's twenty-third country to make it legal.[99] As our consideration of temporality shows, the progression of time does not always equal political progress, and fear exists that the Trump administration in the US will remove equal rights, positioning all LGBT subjects as non-normative in a negative way (read: abnormal) once again. In times of racism, Islamophobia, and blatant misogyny, the LHA's foregrounding of the presence of both queer subjects and people of color (POC) in US history is pivotal. This, too, is the case for Spinnboden in relation to Turks, Jews, and refugees in the German context. Memorials to victims of the Holocaust, from monuments to film, serve as haunting reminders of what can happen when the government decides to other, expel, or worse, and it is here that archives can be of further use. The LHA and Spinnboden, for example, not only archive the history of previously demonized minorities, but also provide a social site, both physical and digital, to form community and foster protest, including organization of women's marches against Trump. They employ the queer space and make use of a queer temporality to mobilize against oppressors, highlighting how we need to preserve the lesbian and queer past in order to make use of it in the present for the sake of a queer and lesbian future.

Notes

Epigraphs: Joan Nestle, "The Will to Remember: The Lesbian Herstory Archives of New York," *Feminist Review* 34 (1990): 86–94; here 87; Jacques Derrida, *Archive Fever: A Freudian Impression; Religion and Postmodernism* (Chicago: University of Chicago Press, 1996), 4.

[1] German examples are as varied as: the Deutsches Film Archiv (German Film Archive); the Historisches Archiv der Stadt Köln (Historical Archive of the City of Cologne); the Bundesarchiv (Federal Archives); and the Deutsches Literatur Archiv Marbach (German Literature Archive Marbach). Similarly, the United States of America maintains archives such as: the Academy Film Archive

(Hollywood); the National African American Archives and Museum (Mobile, Alabama); the New York City Municipal Archives; the Smithsonian Institution Archives (Washington DC).

[2] We must also remember that much LGBTQ+ history "is housed in straight archives and circulated in straight collections, requiring that we queer the archive" and foreground hidden LGBTQ elements. Charles E. Morris, "Archival Queer," *Rhetoric and Public Affairs* 9, no. 1 (2006): 145–51; here 147.

[3] Laura Doan and Sarah Waters, "Making Up Lost Time: Contemporary Lesbian Writing and the Invention of History," in *Territories of Desire in Queer Culture: Refiguring Contemporary Boundaries*, ed. David Alderson and Linda Anderson (Manchester: Manchester University Press, 2000), 12–28; here 12.

[4] Heather Love, *Feeling Backward: Loss and the Politics of Queer History* (Cambridge, MA: Harvard University Press, 2007), 1.

[5] I am making use of LGBTQ+ here as it most closely ties in to the research I undertake. Although this acronym changes and is sometimes contested, more recently, LGBTQIA+ has been used to accommodate both intersex and asexual.

[6] Spinnboden.de.

[7] The term "cisgender," or "cis," is used to describe those whose sex and gender are aligned, while "trans" is used for people whose sex and gender are not aligned and also includes non-binary people, who self-define as trans because they do not belong to one side of the traditional gender binary.

[8] "Fish" is still used today in queer culture, however, as both gay men and drag queens sometimes use it to refer to women in general, rather than the lesbian femme.

[9] Today, the term femme is used more broadly to include a range of genders and sexualities including, but not limited to: feminine gay men; trans and trans non-binary people; straight women who want to express a femininity beyond the confines of heteropatriarchy.

[10] Cvetkovich, *An Archive of Feelings*, 242.

[11] This is linked to the idea of passing, although not always with intention, and even when with intention, not always with success.

[12] Michelle Cliff, "Passing" in *The Land of the Look Behind* (Ithaca, NY: Firebrand Books, 1985), 22.

[13] "Archivettes" is the name the LHA gives to their volunteers and committee members.

[14] Simone de Beauvoir, *The Second Sex*, trans. H. M Parshley (London: Vintage, 1997).

[15] Terry Castle, *The Apparitional Lesbian: Female Homosexuality and Modern Culture* (New York: Columbia University Press, 1993), 15.

[16] Some lesbians throughout history have employed the pronouns he and him and the possessive adjective his, which are still in use today in the LGBTQ+ context, alongside the rise of the usually plural pronoun "they/them" for the singular non-binary subject. There are also more recently coined pronouns, such as "hir" and "herm."

[17] S. E. Case, "Toward a Butch-Femme Aesthetic," in *The Lesbian and Gay Studies Reader,* ed. H. Abelove, M. A. Barale, and D. M. Halperin (New York: Routledge, 1993), 294–306; here 296.

[18] Nestle, "The Will to Remember," 225–35.

[19] For more on recordings, as well as digitization practices, see the work of Cait McKinney.

[20] Nestle, "The Will to Remember," 93.

[21] Nestle, "The Will to Remember," 228.

[22] Verena Stefan, *Häutungen: Autobiografische Aufzeichnungen; Gedichte, Träume, Analysen* (Munich: Verlag Frauenoffensive, 1975).

[23] Eve Kosofsky Sedgwick, *The Epistemology of the Closet* (Berkeley: University of California Press, 1990).

[24] Judith Butler, *Gender Trouble: Feminism and the Subversion of Identity* (London: Routledge, 1990).

[25] Kosofsy Sedgwick, *Epistemology of the Closet*, 55.

[26] Kate Davy, "Cultural Memory and the Lesbian Archive," in *Beyond the Archives: Research as a Lived Process,* ed. Gesa E. Kirsch and Liz Rohan (Carbondale, IL: Southern Illinois University Press, 2008), 132.

[27] According to Kate Eichhorn, in her work on feminism and the archive, throughout the 1990s, differing temporal identifications and orientations would also surface as a major source of tension within the feminist movement. The "generational debates" that reached their peak around the turn of the new millennium were often rooted in accusations: older feminists dismissed younger feminists as politically naïve and thereby either unaware of their need for long-term institutional change or oblivious to *their* histories of struggle; younger feminists complained that the so-called "second-wavers" were simply "behind the times." Kate Eichhorn, *The Archival Turn in Feminism: Outrage in Order* (Philadelphia, PA: Temple University Press, 2013), viii–ix.

[28] Michel Foucault, *Archaeology of Knowledge* (Paris: Editions Gallimard, 1969).

[29] Derrida considers the challenge posed by psychoanalysis to the question of memory and both the production and preservation of an archive, employing two Freudian tropes: the death drive and the pleasure principle to argue that the archive is where the former, the primal urge for archive destruction, and the latter, the desire to conserve, which is tied to the pleasure principle, are mediated.

[30] Foucault, *Archaeology of Knowledge,* 17.

[31] *The Well of Loneliness* (Radclyffe Hall, 1928) is a lesbian novel that was the subject of legal battles because of its homosexual subject matter, which increased the awareness of lesbianism, particularly in British and North American culture. Valerie Rohy states, "In Radclyffe Hall's *The Well of Loneliness,* Stephen Gordon is drawn to the locked bookcase in her father's study: 'She opened the battered old book, then she looked more closely, for there on its margins were notes in her father's small, scholarly hand and she saw that her own name appeared in those notes—She began to read . . . she read on and on in the dusk.' [. . .] But while there is nothing essentially queer about archive fever, there is something distinctly queer about

accepting its negativity." Valerie Rohy, "In the Queer Archive: Fun Home," *GLQ: A Journal of Lesbian and Gay Studies* 16, no. 3 (2010): 341–61; here 355–58. This citation was taken from an article on the graphic novel *Fun Home* by Alison Bechdel (2006), which both embodies and interrogates what Ann Cvetkovich terms the queer archive, as it examines the life of lesbian Alison and her closeted father, who is in a straight marriage and runs a funeral home, before he dies in a suspected suicide. Bechdel's graphic novel has since been turned into an award-winning Broadway musical. The difficult issues of suicide and of lesbian representation, which is often exploited in the arts, can be read alongside another graphic novel: *Maus* (Art Spiegelman, 1991). Although I do not wish to draw a parallel between the Holocaust, lesbianism, and suicide, it should be noted that the use of a graphic novel allows for a greater freedom in representation. Mice, for example, are used to depict Spiegelman interviewing his father, a Polish Jew, about his experience during the Holocaust, which he survived. Graphic novel, *Blue Is the Warmest Colour* (Julie Maroh, 2010), which examines the life and death of a lesbian, also allows for a greater freedom when dealing with difficult subject matters such as lesbian sex than the 2013 film adaptation by Abdellatif Kechiche, which has been widely criticized for its graphic sex scenes. The medium of the graphic novel can offer a space for topics that should not be exploited for any kind of pleasure to be depicted.

32 Davy, "Cultural Memory and the Lesbian Archive," 128.

33 In my forthcoming documentary, *Femmes on Film*, I interview performance artist Lois Weaver in relation to femme representation and sociopolitical reality.

34 Jen Jack Gieseking, "Useful Instability: The Queer Social Order and Spatial Production of the Lesbian Herstory Archives," in "Queering Archives: Intimate Tracings," special issue, *Radical History Review* 122 (May 2015): 25–37.

35 Madhu Narayan, "At Home with the Lesbian Herstory Archives," in *Enculturation* (East Lansing: Michigan State University Press, 2013). Accessed online.

36 Cait McKinney, "Body, Sex, Interface Reckoning with Images at the Lesbian Herstory Archives," *Radical History Review* 122 (May 2015): 115–29.

37 Rachel F. Corbman, "A Genealogy of the Lesbian Herstory Archives, 1974–2014," *Journal of Contemporary Archival Studies* 1 (2014): 1–16, here 2.

38 Ann Cvetkovich, *An Archive of Feelings: Trauma, Sexuality, and Lesbian Public Cultures* (Durham, NC: Duke University Press, 2003).

39 I explore film as archive in a forthcoming book chapter on femme performance artist Bird La Bird and femme performer Rosie Lugosi in relation to queer time and the internet as archive.

40 Eichhorn, *The Archival Turn in Feminism: Outrage in Order*, 89–90.

41 I explore the representation of Brandon Teena in my article, "Passing and Policing: Controlling Compassion, Bodies and Boundaries in *Boys Don't Cry* and *Unveiled/Fremde Haut*," in "Queer European Cinema: Queering Cinematic Time and Space," ed. Leanne Dawson, special issue, *Studies in European Cinema* 12, no. 3 (2015): 205–28.

42 Judith Halberstam, *In a Queer Time and Place: Transgender Bodies, Subcultural Lives* (New York: New York University Press, 2005), 169.

43 Halberstam, *In a Queer Time and* Place, 249.

44 Halberstam, *In a Queer Time and Place,* 1.

45 Halberstam, *In a Queer Time and Place,* 4–5.

46 Halberstam, *In a Queer Time and Place,* 2.

47 See the introduction to this book for more information on same-sex adoption, and other laws affecting LGBTQ+ people in the German-speaking lands.

48 Nestle, "The Will to Remember," 228.

49 The GAU focused on making academia better for those who identified as LGB. Alongside Nestle, members included Andrea Dworkin, who later argued against Nestle's viewpoints in the Sex Wars.

50 lesbianherstoryarchives.org.

51 Madhu Narayan, "At Home with the Lesbian Herstory Archives," in *Enculturation,* here 7.

52 Later, Ann Allen Shockley, associate librarian of Fisk University, would begin to advise the LHA on best practices for preservation.

53 The origins of Spinnboden and the LHA were conceived of around the same time, but I have been unable to locate any communication in the archives from between the two archives during this period. Furthermore, when we conversed about the matter, LHA co-founder Edel could not recall direct contact with Spinnboden during this time. This conversation took place while I was filming *Femmes on Film,* July 28, 2017.

54 Lesbianherstoryarchives.org.

55 Nestle, "The Will to Remember," 228.

56 Nestle, "The Will to Remember," 87.

57 On July 27, 2017, I attended an At Home with the Archives event on Native photographs, where a member of the LHA collective, Colette Montoya, discussed, among other things, her personal and family history.

58 Cvetkovich, *An Archive of Feelings,* 245.

59 Davy, "Cultural Memory and the Lesbian Archive," 134.

60 There is fascinating correspondence between the co-founders about the founding and early years of the LHA, which is still accessible in the LHA today.

61 Joan Nestle quoted in Mary A. Caldera, "Women, Gays and Libraries: And the Case of the Lesbian Herstory Archives," Master's Thesis, Graduate School of the Texas Woman's University, 1990, 210.

62 Jacques Derrida, *Archive Fever,* 9.

63 Cvetkovich, *An Archive of Feelings,* 115.

64 Nestle, "The Will to Remember," 93.

65 Achille Mbembe, "The Power of the Archive and its Limits," in *Refiguring the Archive,* ed. Carolyn Hamilton, Verne Harris, and Graeme Reid (Cape Town: David Philip Publishers, 2002), 19–26; here 20.

66 There is much information about groups including the AIDS Coalition to Unleash Power (ACT UP) and Lesbian Avengers (minutes from meetings, publicity fliers, badges, stickers, and financial records).

67 Derrida, *Archive Fever,* 9–10.

[68] The LHA does, however, accept small municipal grants, including state-sponsored digitization grants.

[69] Spinnboden.de.

[70] Documents about this were also housed in the LHA, demonstrating transatlantic communication between both lesbian archives as time progressed.

[71] Judith Halberstam, *The Queer Art of Failure* (Durham, NC: Duke University Press, 2011), 71.

[72] Halberstam, *In a Queer Time and Place* (New York: New York University Press, 2005), 5.

[73] The LHA website contains detailed information about the current collective and is much fuller that the Spinnboden website in this respect.

[74] Lee Edelman, *No Future: Queer Theory and the Death Drive* (Durham, NC: Duke University Press, 2004), 4 and 29.

[75] Elizabeth Freeman, *Time Binds: Queer Temporalities, Queer Histories* (Durham NC, Duke University Press, 2010), 64–65.

[76] Joan Nestle quoted in Madhu Narayan, "At Home with the Lesbian Herstory Archives," 5.

[77] The texts I was writing about, based on the real life lesbian relationship I was researching, were Erika Fischer's book, *Aimée und Jaguar: Eine Liebesgeschichte, Berlin 1943* (1994)/*Aimee & Jaguar: A Love Story. Berlin 1943* and Max Färberböck's film, *Aimée & Jaguar: eine Liebe grösser als der Tod* (1999)/*Aimee & Jaguar: A Love Larger than Death*. For an analysis of both the book and the film see Leanne Dawson, "Aimée, Jaguar and Gender Melancholia," *Studies in European Cinema* 9 (2012): 35–52.

[78] Joan Nestle, "The Will to Remember," 232–33.

[79] Cvetkovich, *An Archive of Feelings,* 242.

[80] Nestle, "The Will to Remember," 232.

[81] According to Nestle's writing on the LHA website, "the archives should share the political and cultural world of its people and not be located in an isolated building that continues to exist while the community dies. If necessary the archives will go underground with its people to be cherished in hidden places until the community is safe." (lesbianherstoryarchives.org). This consideration of communities in danger is not just relevant with regard to queers, but also other marginalized groups, both throughout history and today.

[82] Diana Fuss, *The Sense of an Interior: Four Writers and the Rooms That Shaped Them* (New York: Routledge, 2004), 79.

[83] Here, "collected memory," is different to collective memory, for the former marks memory's inherently fragmented, collected, and individual character, thus allowing multiple voices to be heard, some of them conflicting. For further information see James Young, *The Texture of Memory: Holocaust Memorials and Meaning* (New Haven, CT: Yale University Press, 1993).

[84] Camp men and glamorous femmes are often considered fun—read femininity as non-threatening—while butch lesbians are often viewed as an aberration.

[85] Furthermore, in opposition to the commercialization and mainstreaming of Gay Pride, there has been a Gay Shame movement within some queer

communities, with Gay Shame parades and/or events taking place in cities such as New York, where the movement started, San Francisco, and London. These Gay Shame events focus on activism and highlighting political issues.

[86] Halberstam, *In a Queer Time and Place*, 22.

[87] Kate Eichhorn, "Archival Genres: Gathering Texts and Reading Spaces," *Invisible Culture* 12 (2008): 2–12; here 12.

[88] Pierre Bourdieu, "The Forms of Capital," in *Handbook of Theory and Research for the Sociology of Education*, ed. J. Richardson (New York: Greenwood, 1986), 241–58.

[89] Jonathan Alexander and Elizabeth Losh detail how mini-archives or collections of such videos document the coming-out experience in their article "A YouTube of One's Own: Coming Out as Rhetorical Action," in *LGBT Identity and New Online Media*, ed. Christopher Pullen and Margaret Cooper (New York: Routledge: 2010): 37–50.

[90] Germany in particular has a long-standing tradition of anti-normative gender and sexual representation. For further detail see the introduction to this volume.

[91] For more information on Treut's filmmaking career, see Leanne Dawson and Monika Treut, "Same, Same but Different: Filmmakers Are Hikers on the Globe and Create Globalisation from Below," in "The Other: Gender, Sexuality and Ethnicity in European Cinema and Beyond," ed. Leanne Dawson, special issue, *Studies in European Cinema* 11, no. 3 (2014): 155–69.

[92] B. Ruby Rich, *New Queer Cinema: The Director's Cut* (Durham, NC: Duke University Press, 2013).

[93] Lynne Kirste, "Collective Effort: Archiving LGBT Moving Images," *Cinema Journal* 46, no. 3 (2007): 134–40; here 134.

[94] Such room for exploration is important, as increasingly more women are openly identifying as bisexual, bi-curious, or sexually fluid.

[95] Vito Russo, in both the book (New York: Harper Collins, 1981) and then the film version (Rob Epstein and Jeffrey Friedman, 1996) of *The Celluloid Closet*, traces the movement and development of lesbian and gay representations in a hundred years of mass-market film. José Esteban Muñoz, in *Disidentifications: Queers of Color and the Performance of Politics* (Minneapolis: University of Minnesota Press, 1999) focuses more specifically on Latinx experiences, drawing on a variety of media, from photographs to film to performance pieces.

[96] Cvetkovich, *An Archive of Feelings*, 251.

[97] Cvetkovich, *An Archive of Feelings*, 251.

[98] See the introduction to this volume for further information.

[99] It is certainly problematic when those located in the first position of the binary, for example, white, straight cis subjects, deny equal rights, such as marriage, to those in the second and less powerful position. This is quite unlike LGBTQ+ people taking issue with the conservativism of, and energy spent on campaigning for, same-sex marriage, when there are much more pressing issues to deal with such as the huge homicide rate of trans women of color and the great percentage of homeless youths identifying as LGBTQ+.

"Die zarte Haut einer schönen Frau": Fashioning Femininities in Weimar Germany's Lesbian Periodicals

Cyd Sturgess, University of Sheffield

Introduction

IN THE YEARS FOLLOWING the end of the First World War, Berlin developed a reputation as a site of unfettered sexual liberalism. Spurred on by an increasingly hedonistic climate and the waning of punitive Wilhelmine moral codes and conventions, the cosmopolitan cityscape was lined with private clubs for local "deviants" and European sex tourists, and the modern German metropolis fundamentally shaped the postwar erotic imaginary. It was the well-established homosexual scene in the southern district of Schöneberg, however, that firmly cemented the city's position in central Europe as the "Hauptstadt des Vergnügens" (Capital of Pleasure).[1] In conjunction with Berlin's ever-expanding gay nightlife, the relaxing of censorship laws after the foundation of the Weimar Republic also enabled publishers to cater to the needs and desires of a queer readership in print. Although many of these early magazines were intended predominantly for male readers, *Die Freundin* (The Girlfriend) and *Frauenliebe* (Women's Love) were the most recognized and widely distributed journals for women who desired women in the interwar era. Acknowledged by historian Florence Tamagne as the "definitive reference point for lesbians of the 1920s," these publications addressed exclusively the concerns and interests of non-heterosexual women and were available to purchase from newspaper kiosks throughout Berlin and across Germany and Europe via subscription.[2] The emergence of regular periodicals for queer citizens enabled alternative grassroots discourses to reach a broader audience and provided a platform for positive and self-affirming models of same-sex desire. Yet, although the emancipatory aims of these publications arguably engendered a culture of open debate and political activism among their readers, the conflicting agendas of the organizations to which the magazines were affiliated sparked enduring ruptures within queer social and political circuits.

Focusing on the representation of feminine women in Weimar lesbian print media, a subject that has garnered little attention in previous studies of queer interwar publications, this chapter will explore the conflicting cultural and sexological theories to which *Die Freundin* and *Frauenliebe* subscribed and the approaches of their writers and readers to the subject of queer femininity. Combining textual analysis with historical survey, I will suggest that the assimilationist tactics employed by the Bund für Menschenrecht (League for Human Rights, BfM) appears to create what Lisa Duggan has termed a culture of "homonormativity" in the publication *Die Freundin*.[3] The editorial team behind *Frauenliebe*, the Deutscher Freundschaftsverband (The German Friendship Association, DFV), however, acknowledged and celebrated the existence of modern, queer femininities, yet simultaneously reinforced and promoted traditional ideals of female experience through its advertorials and promotions. Employing Deleuze and Guattari's concept of the "rhizome" as a way of exploring the tension between sexual modernity and moralistic traditionalism that is perceptible in the periodicals, I will examine the extent to which constructions of femininity in the magazines can be interpreted as an intention to map alternative queer identities, and in what ways these representations departed from the dualistic regimes of the time.

As Sarah Cefai has noted, a sustained academic interest in the expression of female masculinities has led to a historical focus on the nineteenth-century congenital female "invert," and the subject of femininity in contemporary publications such as *Die Freundin* and *Frauenliebe* has, with a few notable exceptions, remained a relatively unexplored terrain.[4] Although I certainly do not suggest that lesbian masculinities are no longer a subject worthy of exploration, this chapter will contend, in an echo of Shane Phelan's earlier writings, that historical same-sex desire must be depicted in its "irreducible plurality" and that historians must break away from narratives that serve only to reinforce sexual and gender identities that are masculine centered.[5] Using this chapter as a way to rethink the historical relationships between femininity, agency, and lesbian desire, I will begin with a close reading of the sexological constructions that informed the aims and objectives of the two homosexual movements in question and their respective publications. Following this, and looking more closely at the structure and content of *Die Freundin* and *Frauenliebe*, I will explore the multiple, and at times conflicting, ways in which queer feminine identities are fashioned through their scientific frameworks, literary supplements, and advertisements. As both journals included *Sonderteile* (special sections) for the primarily male-to-female "transvestite" community, this chapter will also include an examination of the relationship of "the marker femininity" to sartorial, somatic, and sexual signs in each of the magazines, a particularly pertinent discussion point given the recent debates around transwomen, their femininities, and their place within lesbian and feminist communities.

Historicizing Queer Feminine Desire

On 30 May 1864, German neurologist and psychiatrist Carl Otto Westphal became acquainted with a patient at the Charité hospital in Berlin who would shape scientific discourses on female same-sex desire long into the twentieth century. Thirty-five-year-old Fräulein N., described in the opening of Westphal's article *Die conträre Sexualempfindung* (The Contrary Sexual Feeling, 1869), was admitted to the Charité's psychiatric ward and placed under Westphal's care after a prolonged series of manic episodes. In the study, Westphal explains to his reader that Fräulein N.'s yearning to "love and kiss" other women had driven her to obsessive onanism in her teenage years and repeated behavioral disturbances throughout her adult life.[6] Informed by the developing fields of criminology and psychiatry, Wesphal's article on *amor lesbicus* was also greatly indebted to the work of lawyer and classicist Karl Heinrich Ulrichs. Considered the forefather of the first modern homosexual movement, Ulrichs's series of pamphlets *Forschungen über das Räthsel der mannmännlichen Liebe* (Research on the Riddle of Man-Manly Love, 1864–79) put forth the first comprehensive and affirmative framework of same-sex desire. Deemed highly controversial at the time of publication, Ulrichs's pamphlets suggested that homosexual desires could be considered congenital and occurred in men as the result of a female "spirit" (*anima*) in a male body.[7] Although the nuances of female sexuality were paid little attention in Ulrichs's study, his proposal that same-sex desire was caused by an inversion of gender traits provided the framework for Westphal's conclusions on his subject's desires. Although the psychiatrist ultimately determined that his patient's physiognomy had "nichts vom weiblichen Typus Abweichendes" (nothing that deviated from the female type), Fräulein N.'s declaration that she felt "überhaupt als Mann und möchte gern ein Mann sein" (entirely as a man and wanted to be a man) confirmed for Westphal that her desires were indeed congenital and linked to an innate masculine sensibility.[8] The anchoring of queer female desire to masculinity in Westphal's study reflects the contemporary social dichotomy in which masculinity was the only legitimate lens through which to conceive of active sexual feelings. While more recent studies of Ulrichs's framework have noted that his theory of inversion arguably creates space for the existence of feminine desire through the figure of the homosexual male, it was not until the end of the nineteenth century that feminine women with queer tendencies became subjects of scientific attention in their own right.[9] Returning to Deleuze and Guattari's concept of the rhizome, mentioned briefly in the introduction to this chapter, the attempts of Ulrichs and his contemporaries to trace the origins of female homosexual desire back to an innate masculine sensibility employs what Deleuze and Guattari term "arboric systems of knowledge."[10] Stating that arboric knowledge systems are those that refer to a single origin from which related concepts emerge, Deleuze and Guattari liken binary knowledge systems to a tree and its constituent parts; roots, branches, and leaves. The rhizome, on the other hand, is a "subterranean stem" that "sends out both roots and shoots" and contains "no top or bottom, no beginning or end."[11] The "root" in these "arboric" systems of sexual deviance, then, is located in the psychic and somatic inversion of an individual's gender; the fixedness of these desires is key to establishing their authenticity.[12] Yet, within this dyadic system of gender complementarity there appears little conceptual space for authentic queer feminine desire.

British sexologist Havelock Ellis's seminal study *Sexual Inversion* (1897) also endeavored to tackle the issues of feminine same-sex desire. Although "authentic" queer desire was still linked to a congenital masculine drive in Ellis's work, he believed that the feminine woman who desired women also warranted the attention of sexologists and experts. Describing such women as neither "robust" nor "well developed physically," Ellis suggested that the feminine homosexual was "the pick of the women whom the average man would pass by."[13] Implying with this observation that it was possible to distinguish between the heterosexual and feminine homosexual woman based on the latter's "lesser" form of femininity, Ellis's argument served to safeguard the cultural ideal of "true" femininity as a property of the "normal," heterosexual woman. Furthermore, unlike the fixed and immutable disposition of the masculine female invert, Ellis suggested that the desires of feminine women for the same sex were often temporal and transient. That the sexual aspect was claimed by many sexologists and social commentators to transcend all other elements of female experience led Ellis, and sex researchers such as Iwan Bloch and Auguste Forel, to conclude that many feminine women possessed a "genetic predisposition for responsiveness to the advances of other women."[14] The temporality of these feelings, however, meant that there was a distinct possibility that feminine women could be cured of their non-normative desires. If they could be redirected to a more suitable partner through marriage, for example, feminine women could still fulfill their pre-destined roles as reproductive members of society. In comparison to the virile female invert, the desires of feminine women were a situational and temporal phenomenon; through the practice of a healthy heterosexual partnership, normal instincts were likely to return and flourish. Yet, as Clare Hemmings has observed, the ultimate conclusion this deduction led to was not entirely unproblematic. If the feminine (heterosexual) woman was attracted to the masculine element, the logical corollary was that *all* feminine women had the potential to be temporarily seduced by the masculinity of a congenital female invert.[15]

The temporal and passive nature that characterizes the "pseudo-homosexual" in Ellis's study has other significant implications, too. Vibeke Rützou Petersen writes that because explicit and active sexual expression at the fin de siècle was considered to be a "vulgar and working class characteristic" it was "absent in decent, middle-class women."[16] As Marti Lybeck has noted further, therefore, the passivity of Ellis's feminine homosexual was key "to class identity and differentiation" and effectively separated her from the wanton working-class woman.[17] In order to present a counterpoint to the romantic friendships between women of the upper- and middle-classes, sexologists often positioned the working-class woman in terms of her voracious sexual appetite. Appearing in a category comparable to the pseudohomosexual prostitute, who would engage in sexual acts with women because they repulsed by their male clients or simply "oversexed," women with homosexual tendencies from the lower classes were said to have exhausted their desire for men and turned temporarily to women to satisfy their excessive lusts. Occupying a lower social position, as Kathleen Rowe has suggested, meant that the working-class woman was often conflated with the "unruly order of bodily functions," which precluded her from embodying true and ideal femininity.[18] Thus, while Ellis's bourgeois homosexual woman appeared less feminine than her heterosexual counterpart due to her failure to meet male standards of beauty, it was the association of the working classes more generally with activities that were vulgar and base that led to the conclusion that they were less feminine than "normal," here meaning middle-class, heterosexual women.

In sexological studies that made homosexual identities contingent upon gender inversion, there existed a vested interest in maintaining traditional femininity as the preserve of bourgeois heterosexual women. The suggestion that the feminine lesbian woman could never be *as* feminine as her heterosexual counterpart meant that queer desire remained rooted in a degree of gender nonconformity. Distinguishing a physical difference between queer and heterosexual feminine women served, therefore, not only to allay fears that any feminine woman could be seduced into deviant acts, but it simultaneously reinforced the cultural codes that moored heterosexuality and traditional femininity to the bourgeois female body. Ellis, like Ulrichs and Westphal before him, locate the origins of female homosexual desire in an innate masculine sensibility, ultimately tracing the heterosexual paradigm of gender complementarity onto queer individuals. Their "arboric" systems of knowledge employ the paradigm of gender inversion to account for a broad spectrum of sex-gender discrepancies and, in a cultural climate in which feminine desire was muted and taboo, dismiss the sexual attraction of feminine women for their own sex as an inauthentic and excessive expression of degenerate lust. Yet, among the advocates of theories of inversion, there were also more progressive sexologists who were moving away from strict binary categories in their attempts to map what I will term "rhizomatic" theories of gender and sexual preference and present increasingly innovative sexual topographies that questioned the existence of "true" forms of gendered and sexual expression.

In Magnus Hirschfeld's study *Die Homosexualität des Mannes und des Weibes* (The Homosexuality of Men and Women, 1914), he identifies two "entirely analogous" groups of female homosexuals. Bearing resemblance to the studies discussed above, the Berlin-based sexologist and founder of the Institut für Sexualwissenschaft initially outlines the traits of the virile homosexual woman but nonetheless contends that there exists a group of women of equal size who "in ihren Gefühls-, Geschmacks- und Gedankenäußerungen so durchaus weiblich, daß sie niemand für homosexuell halten würde" (are so thoroughly feminine in their expression of feeling, taste, and thought, that no one would consider them homosexual).[19] Hirschfeld's pioneering point of departure deviates decidedly from the conclusions of his contemporaries, particularly in the suggestion that feminine women could be homosexual "in genau so fixierter Weise wie ihre virilen Schicksalsgenossinnen" (in exactly the same fixed manner as their virile sisters).[20] Although Hirschfeld's theory remains within a framework that posits fixedness as the ultimate marker of "authentic" homosexual desire and, therefore, as Jonathan Kemp suggests, "oscillates between the lines established by the arboric systems," his broader framework suggests the existence of a spectrum of sexual and gendered experiences that is perpetually "becoming."[21] In a manner similar to Deleuze and Guattari's rhizome, then, unlike studies that relied on gender complementarity to posit an inversion of gender traits as the origin of homosexual desire, Hirschfeld's research offers a "map and not a tracing."[22] Thus while Hirschfeld's studies present a homosexual subject with fixed preferences, an assertion that initially appears anathema to the concept of the rhizome, his theory of "sexuelle Zwischenstufen" (intermediate sexual states) dismisses the existence of true forms of femininity and masculinity as "constructed abstractions" and ultimately resists arboric structures.[23] The tension between Hirschfeld's more fluid approach to sexuality and Ellis's traditional binary conclusions, presented in this chapter in terms of "arboric" and "rhizomatic" systems of knowledge, was characteristic of Weimar sexological thought. Focusing on two of the largest emancipation movements for homosexual citizens in Germany, the Bund für Menschenrecht (League for Human Rights, BfM) and the Deutscher Freundschaftsverband (German Friendship Association, DFV), the following section will explore the ways in which Magnus Hirschfeld's work on "intermediate sexual states," as discussed above, formed the fundamental ideological difference that divided the two movements.

Discursive Divisions: The Bund für Menschenrecht and the Deutscher Freundschaftsverband

Founded in Berlin in 1919, the Deutscher Freundschaftsverband (DFV) was the first national organization to work with affiliated groups across Germany to undertake combined actions for civil rights reforms for homosexual citizens.[24] Although the organization was successful in disseminating educative materials on the subject of homosexuality throughout Germany, a series of disagreements among the directors of the DFV led to a leadership challenge in the early 1920s. Friedrich Radszuweit, chairperson of the Berlin-based Vereinigung der Freunde und Freundinnen eventually assumed control of the DFV in 1923 and renamed it the Bund für Menschenrecht (BfM). With Radszuweit in control, the organization distanced itself from the previous publications of the DFV and established several new periodicals for homosexual people, which were printed by Radszuweit's own private publishing company. Already in 1925, however, several key members of the newly formed BfM had become unhappy with the way that Radszuweit was running his "personal empire" and decided to secede and resume the activities of the former DFV.[25] Under the auspices of the Bergmann Verlag, the DFV soon began to publish its own periodicals for queer readers, which ran in direct competition with those of the BfM.

Central to the ideological rift that divided the DFV and BfM was Magnus Hirschfeld's work on "intermediate sexual forms," as discussed in the previous section. While Radszuweit and the BfM forcefully rejected the "elitist scientific attitudes" of Hirschfeld and his acolytes, the DFV were keen to use Hirschfeld's theories to further their cause. At the core of the BfM's criticism of Hirschfeld was their claim that the sexologist had "cast a shadow" over the campaign for homosexual emancipation by perpetuating an image of the male homosexual as a psychologically impaired *Zwitter* (intersexual).[26] Instead, Radszuweit and the BfM were advocating for the rights of masculine and *anständig* (respectable) male homosexuals. Although this position appears to align Radszuweit and his movement with "antifeminist, antimedical, antimodernist" masculinists of the time, such as Adolf Brand and Benedict Friedlaender, the latter's "nostalgia for nationalism" and celebration of a pederastic *Eros* had very little to do with Radszuweit's desire to create a sense of "homonormativity" within the BfM.[27] Radszuweit made clear that the mission of the BfM was to weave morally respectable homosexuals "discreetly into the social fabric." Inherent within this notion of middle-class morality was a rejection of both gender nonconformity and the Hellenic pederastic ideal.[28] Significantly, however, although Radszuweit and the BfM scorned the effeminacy of male homosexuals and male prostitutes, their glorification of the masculine element meant that the organization took little issue with the "inverted" masculinity of female homosexuals. Their celebration of masculine culture also had some practical implications for the content of their women's magazine. Towards the end of the Weimar era, many of the main articles in *Die Freundin* focused increasingly on the actions of the male homosexual movement and the abolition of Paragraph 175 of the German Penal Code of 1871, the law that criminalized "widernatürliche Unzucht zwischen Männer" (unnatural sexual relations between men), and when the magazine returned after being blacklisted in 1928 the editorial team was replaced exclusively by male members of the BfM.[29] From this point forward, fewer articles were published by female contributors, and many of the literary supplements were replaced by additional scientific articles on homosexuality that were often copied directly from Radszuweit's leading publications for male homosexuals.

Launched on 8 August 1924 by the BfM, *Die Freundin* was the first magazine to be published for queer women in Germany. Initially appearing as a monthly publication, the periodical was later issued in twice monthly editions until 1926 when it was printed sporadically as part of the magazine *Das Freundschaftsblatt*. In 1928, the magazine was placed on the blacklist for Schund- und Schmutzschriften and was not published during that year but returned in 1929 until it was banned in 1933.[30] As the official organ for female members of the BfM, the publication had a broad and loyal readership.[31] Two years after the first edition of *Die Freundin* appeared, however, a rival publication was established by the newly reconciled DFV. Printed as a weekly periodical, *Frauenliebe* was the mouthpiece for women involved with the organization. Although there are no exact dates on the covers of the DFV's publication, which makes it impossible to give an exact outline of the history of its publication, the periodical was also affected by the law against Schund- und Schmutzschriften in 1930, and was forced thereafter to appear rebranded as *Garçonne*, which remained in print until 1932.[32] The opposing agendas of the two organizations responsible for the publication of *Die Freundin* and *Frauenliebe* were shaped not only by their diverging approaches to achieving social emancipation but also by the wider debates taking place in the field of sexual science, as outlined above. The conflicting ideologies dividing the two organizations are fundamental, as the following section will argue, to understanding the decisions behind the content of the respective periodicals and, ultimately, their approaches to the construction of queer femininity and desire.

The BfM's crusade against femininity, and particularly effeminacy, relied on what Carroll Smith-Rosenberg has termed the "ancient polarity of woman/body-man/mind."[33] Suggesting that the feminine element is sensuous and irrational in nature, the masculine element is positioned as the logical counterpart that is capable of a love that is pure and, above all, *anständig*. Radszuweit and the BfM's understanding of homosexuality as a complementary dyad mirrors the root-like system of thought underpinning sexological works on sexual inversion and fundamentally informed *Die Freundin*'s approach to lesbian femininity. It was the DFV's close connection with Hirschfeld and his Wissenschaftlich-Humanitäres Komitee, however, that shaped the direction of *Frauenliebe*. The growing influence of the *Lebensreformbewegung* (life reform movement) in Berlin, an undertaking that promoted nudism, sexual liberation, and a simpler "back-to-nature" lifestyle, also inspired *Frauenliebe*'s more liberal approach to the conceptualization of gender and sexuality in its publications and activities. With regular recommendations to pamphlets with titles such as *Die freie Liebe* (Free Love) and *Der schöne Körper* (The Beautiful Body), Frauenliebe embraced many of the ideals of the *Lebensreformbewegung*. The promotion of lectures such as "How do I keep myself young and beautiful?" ("Wie erhalte ich mich jung und schön?") and "Rejuvenation of Appearance through Cosmetic Treatment" ("Verjüngung des Äußeren durch kosmetische Selbstbehandlung") in the magazine, however, highlights the disconnect between the magazine's promotion of consumerist ideals of modern beauty and its attempts to maintain the "contempt for materialism and bourgeois values" that was characteristic of Berlin's body culture.[34] Hirschfeld's unwavering support for the Viennese endocrinologist and surgeon Eugen Steinach and his works on rejuvenation also appears to have influenced the DFV's emphasis on cosmetic enhancement and beauty, which will be discussed in more detail in the following section.[35] While *Frauenliebe*'s seemingly frivolous focus on rejuvenation and beauty stands in stark contrast to *Die Freundin*'s scientific studies on the etiology of homosexuality and political emancipation, it is the former's support of the potential of the *Körperkultur* as a way of liberating the individual "from traditional bourgeois restrictions and taboos" that highlights its greatest departure from the mentality of middle-class morality that permeates the publications of the BfM.[36] The two periodicals had remarkably different ideological underpinnings, which means that the audiences of *Die Freundin* and *Frauenliebe* came from largely separate social spheres. As a sign of how strict the separation of these queer spaces was, *Frauenliebe* denounced its former private clubhouse Violetta for its "treachery" after it opened its doors to male and female members of the BfM during the Great Depression: "Alles Schöne ist vergänglich. [. . .] Nun muß *Violetta* sterben. Die letzte Zuflucht ist der vollständige Verrat an der Frauenbewegung: Anschluß an den B.f.M., an die Bewegung der Männer!" (All beauty is fleeting. [. . .] Now *Violetta* must die. Their last refuge is the complete betrayal of the women's movement: an affiliation with the BfM, the men's movement!).[37] The BfM's reputation as a "men's movement" that promoted bourgeois moral standards puts them in clear opposition to the DFV's promotion of beauty and body culture and Hirschfeld's more liberal, and rhizomatic, approach to sexuality and gender. Looking more closely at the structure and content of their respective publications, I will now examine the extent to which these ideological differences influenced their depiction of and approaches to non-heterosexual femininities in their publications.

"Maps" and "Traces":
Representing Queer Feminine Desire

Fashioning queer femininities in *Die Freundin* and *Frauenliebe* appears to have been an incredibly complex process; one that was mired in inconsistencies and contradictions. While at times femininity appears in each of the publications as an identity that is protean and transmutable, and one that transgresses the strict stratification between rationality and emotion and between activity and passivity, at others the agency of feminine women is reduced to an innate and vacuous drive to fulfill a "duty to beauty" in which they are presented as untrustworthy lovers of loyal, masculine partners. Both *Die Freundin* and *Frauenliebe* offered a range of scientific, literary, and political articles to their readers, who were often invited to comment on the intricate interplay of discourses at their disposal. In an issue from 1927, for example, readers were invited to respond to the theme "Zusammenleben oder nicht?" (To Live Together or Not?). The call sparked an animated discussion between readers and editors that continued in the following five issues. Yet, as Margaret Beetham notes in her work on desire in the Victorian woman's magazine, there is a powerful and hierarchical relationship inherent in the exchange between readers, writers, editors, publishers, and proprietors, which should not be overlooked in a content analysis. While contributors of serial fictions may construct a narrative of their choosing—so long as it recursively bears the characteristics of the periodical to which it belongs—readers are also at liberty to construct their own narrative from the contents of the periodical: "we do not read a magazine straight through from front to back as we do a novel. The form invites us to flip through, read in any order, omit some sections altogether and read others carefully."[38] The reader/writer binary in *Die Freundin* and *Frauenliebe*, however, was not always easy to discern; readers were invited to become writers through letters to the editors and the submission of short stories and poems, which enabled readers to exert influence over the discourses presented about queer femininities in both periodicals.[39]

The basic divergences between the *Die Freundin* and *Frauenliebe*, as discussed in the previous section, appear initially to position the periodicals in dialectical opposition. *Die Freundin* attempted to create a sense of normativity through a strict adherence to middle-class morality while *Frauenliebe* renounced the bourgeois restrictions of the middle classes to promote the ideals of *Körperkultur*, suggesting more innovative approaches to sex and sexuality. To conceive of the two publications as being at opposing ends of a spectrum would, however, in terms of Deleuze and Guattari's concept of the rhizome, be to position them in "a simple dualism [. . .] as good and bad sides."[40] Yet, the approaches and aims of the two publications are not mutually exclusive. Indeed, as Deleuze and Guattari suggestively propose: "is it not the essence of the map to be traceable? Is it not the essence of the rhizome to intersect roots and sometimes merge with them?"[41] Although *Die Freundin* appears to have been structured around more arboric and root-like systems of sexological knowledge, and *Frauenliebe* favors Hirschfeld's rhizomatic spectrum of sexuality, there are intermittent interruptions to traditional modes of thinking about gender and sexuality in both periodicals, with each magazine adopting a different method to explore the desires of queer feminine women. Indeed, this analysis corresponds to much of Beetham's research on the periodical form, which draws on psychoanalysis to distinguish between "open" and "closed" forms of the periodical: "'Closed' or 'masculine' forms are seen as those which assert the dominant structures of meaning by closing off alternative options and offering the reader or viewer only one way of making sense of the text and [. . .] the self. By contrast the 'open' form, the form which refuses the closed ending and allows for the possibility of alternative meanings, is associated with the potentially disruptive, the creative, the 'feminine.'"[42] In terms of Beetham's framework, then, *Die Freundin* would appear to be a closed form, which asserts the dominant discourse of congenital homosexual desire onto its content, while *Frauenliebe* appears as an open form that disrupts contemporary understandings of what it meant to be a feminine woman who desired women. As I will now discuss, however, these forms are not entirely without similarities. Neither are the periodicals simply conduits to disseminate the movement's diverging approaches to sexological thought; readers of the magazines were also active agents in the construction of the periodical content and, in turn, helped to shape their discursive positions.

As mentioned earlier in this chapter, many of the scientific articles published in *Die Freundin* were copied directly from Radszuweit's publications for male homosexuals and were written primarily by men. Indeed, the elements of sexological thought that structured explicitly scientific contributions are perceptible in most elements of the magazine, including the social commentaries and news items written by female contributors. In the inaugural issue of *Die Freundin*, for example, editor Aenne Weber invokes the theory of inversion and gender complementarity in her article "The Homosexual Woman" as she outlines for her readers the two primary categories of female homosexuality: "Es gibt zwei Arten von homosexuellen Frauen. Die virile—d.i. männliche—und die feminine—d.i. weibliche—Frau. Die Virile zeichnet sich vor allen Dingen durch ihre Selbständigkeit [. . .] Die feminine Frau ist ganz das Gegenteil [. . .] Sie ist durch und durch Frau, von zartem Wesen und anschmiegendem Charakter" (There are two types of homosexual women. The virile—that is, masculine—and the feminine—that is, the womanly—woman. The virile woman is characterized first and foremost by her independence [. . .] The feminine woman is completely the opposite[. . . .] She is through and through a woman of delicate nature and compliant character).[43] Characterizing the masculine woman in terms of the framework of psychic and somatic inversion, Weber distinguishes the virile homosexual of the BfM from the mannish "woman without morals," described by conservative sexologists as being predisposed to "unbridled sensuality," "alcoholism," and "pathological gambling."[44] By employing dualistic sexological systems to new effect, Weber positions the virile invert in "the role of a protector," which serves to reinforce the BfM's bourgeois ideal. In accordance with *Die Freundin*'s codes of moral behavior, then, the feminine "Mädel" in Weber's article is restricted to a passive role. Feminine homosexual desires are nonetheless given a degree of authenticity by Weber, especially in her claim that, the queer feminine woman, just like the virile invert, was unsuitable for marriage.[45] Yet, although Weber's article appears to provide conceptual space for imagining authentic queer feminine desires, the image of the sexually voracious pseudohomosexual characterized many of the discussions of the feminine homosexual in the BfM's periodical. In a letter that raised concerns about the propriety of certain lesbian locales, for example, one reader claimed that many of the feminine women in queer bars are "not at all homosexual" but simply "curious."[46] In an echo of the sexological descriptions, the reader claims that the feminine woman's "uncontrolled passion" and her innate desire "to experience something by any means,'" is what lies at heart of her longing to sexually experiment with other women.[47]

Despite Weber's claim in the first issue of *Die Freundin* that there existed two distinct types of homosexual woman in the community, Xela Eckats's article "Freundschaftsehen" (marriages of friendship) makes recourse to the sexological stereotype of the feminine homosexual as a fickle figure, whose desires are defined by their temporality. Eckats claims that the masculine partner is invariably loyal but, in times of difficulty, the feminine homosexual cannot be relied upon:

> Es ist für den maskulinen Teil in überwiegendem Maße eine Selbstverständlichkeit, in Zeiten der Not der Freundin ganz besonders beizustehen; denn gerade dann haben wir ja Gelegenheit, unsere Liebe zu beweisen! Warum versagen in solchen Fällen fast immer die femininen Partnerinnen? [. . .] Wäre es nicht an der Zeit, darauf hinzuwirken, dass bei den "femininen" Frauen solche Gesinnungslosigkeit endlich einmal aufhört?[48]

[In the majority of cases, it is for the masculine part a matter of course to stand by the girlfriend, particularly in times of need; because it is just at that moment that we have the opportunity to prove our love! Why do feminine partners almost always fail in such instances? [. . .] Is it not time to ensure that such a lack of principles in feminine women ceases once and for all?]

In perhaps the ultimate example of the BfM's attempts to create a sense of homonormativity in their publications, Eckats also argues that queer couples should strive to achieve monogamous and long-lasting *Freundschaftsehen*. The betrayal of the loyal nature of the masculine woman by the temporal and pathological desires of the feminine homosexual woman caused a threat to the BfM's broader aim to assimilate homosexuals into heterosexual institutions. Faithful "Freundschaftsehen," Eckats's article suggests, would enable the homosexual community to prove themselves worthy of respect: "Menschen, die in allen Lebenslagen fest und true zusammenhalten, wird auch die normale Welt respektieren" (People who hold firmly and faithfully together through thick and thin, will also be respected by the normal world).[49]

In comparison to its rival, *Frauenliebe* published far fewer scientific articles, instead dedicating space in the magazine to serial stories, news items about the activities of the DFV, and event reviews. Yet, although the magazine had less of a focus on sexological developments than *Die Freundin*, some of Hirschfeld's sexological works were reprinted in the magazine, and editors also appeared keen to contribute their own original discussions on the scientific and social study of female same-sex desire. The article "The Position of the Homoeroten in Society" by Hanna Blumenthal, for example, and the reader debate "Is Homosexuality a Sickness or Predisposition?" suggests a continued commitment from the contributors to communicate contemporary sexological and social discourses to their readers. It is because of this shift in focus from the sexological invert to more open categories of desire, as discussed earlier, that the magazine appears to have provided a greater platform for the discussion of queer femininity. In an article from 1926, for example, editor Herta Laser discusses the difficulties that face the feminine woman within the homosexual community. Unlike *Die Freundin*'s position that feminine homosexuals were only "curious" and whimsical, Laser claims that the "current fashion trend" had little to do with a feminine woman's queer desire, and, in fact, most feminine women in the homosexual community were "real Homoeroten" with very specific struggles:

Hat es nicht die weibliche Frau unserer Kreise viel schwerer als eine heterogene Frau? [. . .] Eine heterogene Frau wird in den meisten Fällen, lebt sie mit einem Manne zuzusammen, nicht mehr ihrem

Beruf nachgehen [. . .] Leben aber zwei Frauen zusammen, so gehen beide ihrem Beruf nach [. . .] Der weibliche Teil muß nun nach Schluß den Dienststunden sich mit Hausarbeiten beschäftigen, soll eine gemütliche Wohnung herrichten, ein freundliche Lächeln zeigen, und soll der Freundin eine geistige Gefährtin sein.

[Does the feminine woman in our circles not have it much harder than a heterosexual woman? [. . .] If she lives with a man, a heterosexual woman will, in most cases, no longer pursue her profession [. . .] But, if two women are living together, both go out to work [. . .] At the end of the working day, the feminine partner must deal with the housework, arrange a cozy apartment, show a friendly smile, and be a spiritual companion to the girlfriend.][50]

While this quote suggests perhaps more explicitly that the readers and contributors to *Frauenliebe* are of a certain class than it does about their attitudes towards the feminine homosexual woman, there is doubtless a departure from *Die Freundin*'s notion that queer feminine desire is a temporal curiosity. Although the framework Laser employs to discuss queer female relationships remains inherently dyadic and, as such, appears to conform to more arboric knowledge systems, the creation of a space in which to discuss the issues faced by queer feminine women in a culture that dismissed the existence of feminine desire remains nevertheless an innovative point of departure.

Whereas the influence of the BfM meant that scientific and sexological discourses were given a primary place in *Die Freundin*, the promotion of beauty and body culture in *Frauenliebe* gives rise to a specific form of "pseudoscientific" approach. The cover story "The Personal Perfume," for example, which was aimed at the "office clerks," "stenographers," and "housewives," exploits the contemporary trend towards taxonomification to give authority to a specific type of feminine ideal. The author depicts an intricate equation to deduce which perfume is best suited to which feminine temperament:

zarter Veilchenduft oder diskretes Irisparfüm entspricht der Bescheidenheit, und darum passen diese beiden vornehmlich zu der äußerlich bescheiden und zurückhaltenden Frau. Die Frau zwischen 20 und 30 Jahren kann zwischen Flieder, Jasmin, Ylang-Ylang, Heliotrop und Peau d'Espagne wählen.

[the soft scent of violet or a discreet iris perfume corresponds to modesty and they would both especially suit the outwardly modest and reserved woman. The woman between twenty and thirty years of age can choose between lilac, jasmine, ylang-ylang, heliotrope, and Peau d'Espagne.][51]

Likely inspired by Steinach's and Hirschfeld's studies on rejuvenation, and the models of healthy living promoted by the *Körperkultur* movement, the contributors to *Frauenliebe* consistently constructed femininity around notions of youth and beauty, and the pseudoscientific framing of their articles and advertisements lent legitimacy to this ideology. In *Frauenliebe*'s supplement *Femina*, for example, which appeared as a regular feature of the magazine after 1928, a recurring advertisement promoted beauty supplies, which were supposedly produced in the publication's very own "cosmetic laboratory." "Harlem Drops," the advert suggests, were to be purchased for the "eines belebten feurigen Blickes" (a lively fiery gaze) while "Nerana-Crème" should be used daily to maintain "die zarte Haut einer schönen Frau" (the delicate skin of a beautiful woman).[52] The engagement of *Frauenliebe*'s readers with the periodical's beauty columns and adverts suggests, however, that they were not simply passive consumers. At times readers challenged the publication's suggestions and recommendations in the "Upon Request" section of the supplement. One reader complained curtly "alle von Ihnen genannten Cremes sind wirkungslos. Wenn sie schon nicht schaden, so helfen sie doch wenigstens auch nichts" (all the crèmes you have mentioned are useless. Even if they do not hurt, they do not help either), while another young woman gives her own simple suggestion to her fellow readers: "Use Eau de Cologne."[53] The discussion between the readers of *Femina*, and their appraisal of the supplement's products, indicates that women engaged critically with *Frauenliebe*'s consumer culture and were active participants in the fashioning of their femininities.

While *Frauenliebe* engaged with feminine women directly as consumers, *Die Freundin* did not include these kinds of beauty supplements. Fashion and beauty were discussed, but contributors often appeared far more critical of modern standards of beauty, discussing contemporary trends most often in terms of the functionality of fashion. In the article "Which Skirt is most Suitable?," for example, the readers of *Die Freundin* are presented with a broad range of suggestions for the most practical skirts to wear to work based on the results of a scientific study: "Am raschtesten ermüdeten die Damen in Röcken aus Leinen, Samt und anderen schweren Stoffen, während sie in Röcken aus Seide und Gabardine die geringsten Ermüdungserscheinungen aufwiesen" (The ladies in skirts of linen, velvet, and other heavy materials tired the most quickly, while those in skirts made of silk and gabardine showed the slightest signs of fatigue).[54] That contributors and readers often resorted to scientific discourses in articles about fashion can also be seen in the debate "For or Against the Bubikopf," which ran over several issues. In the series, readers drew on the model of inversion to discuss the appropriateness of the modern and androgynous bobbed haircut for homosexual women, claiming that shorter hair was "appropriate" for an invert. Other readers deployed arguments rooted in physiognomic ideas to dispute the afore-mentioned claim: The shape of a woman's head, as one reader argues, "ist ganz anders als die eines Mannes, folglich bedingt sie eine ganz andere Haartracht" (is entirely different to that of a man, consequently it requires a very different type of haircut).[55] Science and sexology are deployed in *Die Freundin*, therefore, not simply as a way of promoting the periodical's specific ideology but also as a way of engaging with popu-lar trends and social debates. *Frauenliebe*'s adoption of a pseudoscientific framework appears more calculated in its attempt to give legitimacy to its promotion of health and beauty products. Yet, the ideological underpin-nings of Hirschfeld's theory of intermediate sexual states also serves to broaden the parameters of what could be described as "natural" sexual behavior in the magazine, giving space to feminine desires.

Social trends in fashion and beauty were also discussed at great length in the regular "transvestite" (*Transvestiten*) supplements that appeared in both *Die Freundin* and *Frauenliebe*.[56] Focusing primarily on the expe-riences of male-to-female cross-dressers, these supplements provide an invaluable source for the examination of the ways in which femininities were fashioned in queer magazines by individuals who were not biologi-cally female. Much like the content and layout of the principal publica-tion, *Die Freundin*'s transvestite supplement *Die Welt der Transvestiten* (The World of Transvestites) and *Frauenliebe*'s *Der Transvestit* (The Transvestite), included a diverse range of articles on scientific, cultural, and social issues as well as reader letters and serial stories. In general, the approach of these articles deviated little from the ideologies and positions adopted by the main magazines to which they were affiliated. *Die Welt der Transvestiten*, as both Katie Sutton and Marti Lybeck have noted, takes great pains to maintain a sense of authentic transvestite femininity, which is carefully distinguished from the "effeminacy" of male homosexuals and male prostitutes.[57] In a bid to differentiate his behavior from the effemi-nacy of the *Zwitter*, for example, one contributor argues that his feelings of womanliness surpass even those of biologically born women: "Es ist mir unmöglich, mich irgendwie weibisch zu benehmen, wie es leider so viele glauben tun zu müssen. Aber trotzdem, oder gerade deshalb, glaube ich in vieler Hinsicht weiblicher zu empfinden wie manche wirkliche Frau" (It is impossible for me to behave in an effeminate way, as unfor-tunately so many believe they have to. But despite this, or perhaps pre-cisely for this reason, I believe in many respects to feel more womanly than some real women).[58] While transvestites who felt themselves to have been born in the wrong bodies sought to prove the authenticity of their femininities in *Die Freundin*'s supplement by comparing themselves to biologically born women, those who practiced discrete periods of cross-dressing conversely asserted their masculinity and heterosexuality in order to differentiate themselves from male homosexuals. In countless reader letters and personal ads, "part-time" transvestites discuss the difficulties of finding understanding wives and female partners, and many of the literary contributions offer the protagonist a "Happy End" by presenting him with a sympathetic wife. *Die Freundin*'s *Die Welt der Transvestiten* even published an article written by the wife of a temporary transvestite, who attempts to encourage more women to attempt to be what she describes as "transsensibel" (transsensitive).[59] By foregrounding the heterosexuality of the temporary transvestite, *Die Freundin* succeeded in making sure, as Sutton has suggested, that "notions of hegemonic masculinity continued to define hierarchies of value" in its transvestite supplement.[60]

In a similar manner to the supplement of its rival, *Der Transvestit* strays very little from the ideological interests of its chief publication, *Frauenliebe*. Like the content of the main magazine, *Der Transvestit* favors literary submissions over scientific articles and has a strong focus on fashion and beauty. Articles such as "The Essence of Transvestism" by Maria Weiß and the series "Clothing and Transvestism," however, highlight the blend of scientific and social discourses in the supplement. Unlike the subject of transvestism in *Die Freundin*, topics concerning cross-dressing are not only confined to the supplement *Der Transvestit*, but are covered much more broadly in the magazine. On the front cover of a 1930 issue of the publication, for example, *Frauenliebe* gives the topic of transvestism a central position in the article "Transvestism and Society." The classified section of *Frauenliebe*—used for sales, personal ads, and promotions—also targeted the transvestite community. Announcing a miracle cure against beard growth, one sales pitch claims: "Transvestiten! Nach jahrelangen Experimenten fand ich endlich ein Radikalmittel gegen Bartstoppeln und andere Körperhaare mit Wurzeln!" (Transvestites! After years of experiments, I finally found a radical solution to beard stubble and other body hair with roots!).[61] These kinds of advertisements highlight an awareness of the more routine issues faced by transvestites, such as the notice that provided details of a sympathetic seamstress offering a space in which transvestites could safely and discretely complete their "Umwandlung" (conversion). In the schedule of lectures and tutorials compiled by *Frauenliebe*, there are also courses in how to apply cosmetics "with practical demonstrations" offered by the Vereinigung D'Eon, the suborganization for transvestites in the DFV. With a primary focus on fashion and "passing," the emphasis of *Frauenliebe*'s transvestite supplement was on traditional ideals of beauty which are bound to somatic and sartorial simulations of the female form. For "part-time" transvestites in *Die Freundin*'s supplement, however, femininity appears to be a more spiritual notion that is closely associated with morality and respectability and that could be embodied, albeit temporarily, even by heterosexual men.

The processes of "becoming," "undoing," and "redoing" that are visible in *Die Freundin*'s understanding of temporal transvestism are also perceptible in other elements of the magazine. Looking at its literary contributions, *Die Freundin* not only produced original queer stories but also reproduced excerpts from larger collections and popular poems by famous authors. Heinrich Heine's poem "Mädchen mit dem roten Mündchen" ("Girl with the little Red Mouth") from his collection *Buch der Lieder* (*The Book of Songs*, 1827), for example, was printed in *Die Freundin* in early 1928. While reproducing relics of high culture served to bolster attempts to promote a sense of bourgeois mentality in the BfM's publications, Heine's poem also acquires a subversive Sapphic subtext when situated in the context of a queer magazine. Although the feminine protagonist remains the passive object of a presumably "masculine" female gaze, the assumed heterosexuality of the subject is unavoidably brought into question. Traditional markers of bourgeois femininity, such as the protagonist's "little red mouth" and "white hand" are thus resignified as potentially queer, challenging the meaning of dominant cultural motifs of heterosexual femininity. As Clare Rogan observes of the images used in *Die Freundin* and *Frauenliebe*, it is possible to suggest that by removing Heine's poem from its original setting and placing it within a new queer context, *Die Freundin* engages in a form of "bricolage," the French term for a creation formed from a diverse range of items.[62] Postcolonial and literary theorist Gayatri Spivak uses the term "bricolage" to denote a process of "re-constellation" that is achieved by removing culturally rooted items from their assigned function and conferring upon them new meanings that subvert or disrupt their original intended purpose.[63] Poems such as Heine's, then, can be seen as part of what Spivak terms "a radical proto-deconstructive cultural practice."[64] By placing culturally significant poems in the context of a queer magazine, *Die Freundin* revises and destabilizes traditional notions of femininity, putting them in a perpetual process of becoming.

Although *Die Freundin*'s resignification of high cultural artefacts suggests a deviation from the arboric systems of knowledge that appear to structure the rest of the magazine, in its original literary contributions, as Heike Schader has previously suggested, authors "repeatedly constructed an image of the masculine lesbian."[65] Despite the frequency of the image of the masculine invert in *Die Freundin*'s original stories, however, not all stories and poems were narrated from a masculine perspective. In some instances, *Die Freundin*'s literary submissions subvert the masculine-subject/feminine-object position and present the perspectives of feminine protagonists. In the serial story "The Girlfriend of Olga Diers," for example, the "dearest" stagehand Gudrun Garell is a passive and shy character who develops a romantic longing for the masculine actress, Olga Diers. As Olga and Gudrun grow closer, Olga confesses her love for Gudrun in an emotional speech. The surprising revelation of the masculine woman's softer side is followed by Gudrun actively controlling their first sexual encounter: "Den Abend gab Gudrun die Freundin, wonach diese seit Tagen, seit ihrem ersten Kennenlernen lechzte." (That evening Gudrun gave the girlfriend that which the latter had been craving for days, indeed, since their first meeting).[66] Gudrun is not seduced by Olga's aggressive lust; instead it is she who pursues the actress bringing into question the inherent passivity of feminine desire. Despite the reversal of the traditional active/passive binary, however, Gudrun is shown to be a figure of conflict and she bears many of the negative associations with queer femininity described by sexologists. In a dramatic turn of events that also serves to confirm Xela Eckats's earlier accusations in her article "Freundschaftsehen," Gudrun is revealed to be a devious and cunning woman who engages in affairs with both men and women and ultimately breaks Olga's heart.

In her guidebook *Berlins lesbische Frauen* (Berlin's Lesbian Women, 1930), Ruth Margarethe Roellig claimed that the "literary standard" of the contributions to *Die Freundin* and *Frauenliebe* were "pretty much below zero."[67] Yet many of the short stories and poems appear to have been crafted by authors as poignant social critiques and some were used to explore new approaches to gender and sexuality. Unlike *Die Freundin*, *Frauenliebe* rarely recycled or borrowed literary material from other sources, and much of the fiction published in the periodical was written either by *Frauenliebe*'s own authors, famous queer writers on the lesbian circuit, or readers who submitted their amateur poems and prose. In comparison to its rival, the stories in *Frauenliebe* are often more playful and critical of gender roles; feminine women are more frequently positioned as protagonists, and there are also more stories narrated from the male perspective. The cover story "The Gender [Geschlecht] of Tomorrow," that follows a conversation between Georgia and her boyfriend Werner, is one example of *Frauenliebe*'s light-hearted but critical approach to the socially constructed roles of men and women:

> Werner gähnte gelangweilt und griff mit seiner gepflegten Hand in die Konfektschachtel. Plötzlich hüstelte er etwas gezwungen. "Georgia," sagte er, "ich glaube Du rauchst schon wieder einen anderen Tabak, Du weißt, daß ich bei solch kratzigem Zeug, wie es der heutige ist, stets Halsaffektionen bekomme." Sie legte erschrocken die Pfeife aus der Hand und strich ihm übers Haar. "Verzeih,"—wagte sie dann nur noch zu sagen. "Uebrigens," fuhr er fort, und ließ dabei wieder eine Süßigkeit den Weg der anderen gehen, "finde ich, daß Du Dich in der letzten Woche fast gar nicht um mich bekümmert hast. [. . .] Du weißt, wie ich dann immer seelisch leide.

[Werner yawned languidly and reached with his well-groomed hand into the confectionary box. Suddenly he coughed somewhat restrainedly "Georgia," he said "I believe you are smoking another tobacco again, you know that I always get such a sore throat with scratchy stuff such as today's." Startled, [Georgia] laid down the pipe and stroked his hair. "Forgive me,"—she ventured to say. "By the way," he continued, allowing another chocolate to follow the way of the first, "I find that you have scarcely troubled yourself about me over the past week [. . .] you know how I then always suffer emotionally"][68]

In its criticism of gender *Frauenliebe* does not remain silent on the negative associations with the feminine woman. The first-person narrator in "Those Who Live from Love," for example, tells the story of her encounter with a feminine girl. After feeling an immediate connection with her, the protagonist offers to take the young feminine shop assistant for lunch. There, she buys her food and wine and as they walk home the protagonist kisses the young woman. The girl promises to meet the protagonist the following day but fails to show up. Weeks later, and suffering from a broken heart, the protagonist catches the girl with another woman and realizes that she has been duped: "So eine also war sie—mit dem lachenden Leichtsinn im Blut würde sie morgen mit einer Anderen wieder hier sitzen—würde wieder mit derselben sorglosen Freude Wein trinken—wieder mit derselben harmlosen Verliebtheit ihr Gegenüber küssen" (so, she was one of those—with the laughing frivolity in her blood she would sit here again tomorrow with another person—with the same careless joy she would drink wine again—and, with the same harmless infatuation, she would kiss the person opposite her).[69]

Although, like *Die Freundin*, *Frauenliebe* configures many of the relationships in its narratives around binary constellations, authors in the magazine are more willing to trouble gender categories, using male protagonists to explore queer desires and, at times, turning gender roles entirely on their head. Engaging with various forms of narrative to map out new boundaries of gender and sexuality, *Frauenliebe* provided a unique platform for the discussion of queer feminine desires. The periodical's promotion of the feminine woman's "duty to beauty," however, shows the inconsistencies and contradictions tied up in this position. In comparison, the root-like framework of congenital inversion visible in the articles and stories in *Die Freundin* does little to challenge the image of the degenerate queer femme fatale, yet the magazine's engagement with a subversive form of *bricolage* gives new meanings to existing arboric paradigms by resignifying traditional heterosexual codes of femininity.

Conclusions

As this study of *Die Freundin* and *Frauenliebe* has suggested, representations of women who desired women in Weimar periodicals were often more colorful in their gendered expressions and desires than has previously been suggested. Although masculinity was the most obvious cipher for female homosexual desire during the interwar era, representations of queer feminine women in the two periodicals highlight the complex negotiation of feminine desire in a culture structured by complementary sex-gender behaviors. Looking at the content of the two periodicals, at times it appears that representations of feminine homosexual women were used to destabilize assumptions that feminine partners are passive objects of active masculine desires. In other instances, however, the feminine woman was used simply to shore up the gender binary and to reinforce the notion that authentic lesbian identities are masculine centered. The "polyvocal collaborative form"[70] of the periodical and the complex relationship between the reader/writer means that articulations of gender and sexual preference were made and re-made in every issue; femininity remains, therefore, in a constant state of "becoming." The role that the reader played in the act of becoming certainly demands more attention in future studies of queer Weimar magazines, particularly given the reduced role of the reader in the content produced by *Die Freundin* after 1928.

By exploring the tension between the ideological underpinnings of the two periodicals it becomes possible to understand more fully the motives behind their diverging representations of queer femininity. Magnus Hirschfeld's mapping of increasingly innovative sexual topographies, for example, can be seen to have influenced *Frauenliebe*'s discussion of the desires of feminine homosexual women, broadening the parameters of what can be conceived of as authentic homosexual desire in that publication. The magazine's celebration of the "back-to-nature" lifestyle of the *Körperkultur* and its promotion of the feminine woman's "duty to beauty," however, highlights the conflict between traditional femininity and modern consumer ideals that appeared throughout its existence. Friedrich Radszuweit and the BfM's rejection of Hirschfeld's theory of inversion created a strict gender orthodoxy in *Die Freundin* that left little space for morally acceptable queer feminine desire within its celebration of masculine culture. The "moments of becoming" offered by temporary transvestite femininities in *Die Freundin*'s supplement, however, which contain bound up within them a complex negotiation between hegemonic bourgeois masculinity and traditional respectable femininity, highlight perhaps most explicitly the plurality of queer feminine experience that I have attempted to explore in this chapter. The diverse images of feminine identities that are visible in *Die Freundin* and

Frauenliebe suggest an ongoing critical engagement by writers and readers with the sexological discourses that structured debates on femininity and homosexuality. While challenging dominant medico-social discourses clearly wasn't the sole purpose of such periodicals and, just as Beetham observes of British periodicals, the desire of readers "to be confirmed in the generally accepted or dominant discourse may [have been] more powerful than the dream of a different future or the fantasy of alternative," the periodicals are nonetheless informed by sexological discourses prevalent in the societies they were a part of, just as much as they themselves informed the debate on gender and sexuality at the time. Both *Die Freundin* and *Frauenliebe* oscillate between the lines established by contemporary dyadic structures. However, their intermittent interruptions to these arboric knowledge systems ultimately emphasize the fragility of dualistic paradigms within historical queer communities.

Notes

I would like to thank the Wolfson Foundation for the generous funding that made this research possible. I would also like to extend my thanks to the peer reviewers and editors for their insightful comments and feedback. Unless stated, all translations are my own.

[1] Heike Schader, *Virile, Vamps und wilde Veilchen: Sexualität, Begehren und Erotik in den Zeitschriften homosexueller Frauen im Berlin der 1920er Jahre* (Königstein/Taunus: Ulrike Helmer Verlag, 2004), 7.

[2] Florence Tamagne, *The History of Homosexuality: Berlin, London, Paris Volume I & II* (New York: Algora Publishing, 2006), 78.

[3] In her article "The New Homonormativity," Lisa Duggan defines homonormativity as "a politics that does not contest dominant heteronormative assumptions and institutions, but upholds and sustains them, while promising the possibility of a demobilized gay constituency and a privatized, depoliticized gay culture anchored in domesticity and consumption." Lisa Duggan, "The New Homonormativity: The Sexual Politics of Neoliberalism," in *Materializing Democracy: Toward a Revitalized Cultural Politics* ed. R. Castronovo and D. Nelson (Durham, NC: Duke University Press, 2002), 179.

[4] Sarah Cefai, "Navigating Silences, Disavowing Femininity and the Construction of Lesbian Identities," in *Geography and Gender Reconsidered*, ed. Women and Geography Study Group (2004): 108–17.

[5] Shane Phelan, *Getting Specific: Postmodern Lesbian Politics* (Minneapolis: Minnesota University Press, 1994), 96.

[6] Carl Westphal, "Die conträre Sexualempfindung," *Archiv für Psychiatrie und Nervenkrankeiten* 2 (1870): 77.

[7] Ulrichs first suggested that male homosexual desire was the result of a "passive animal magnetism," although he later dismissed this notion in favor of his theory of the existence of a "third sex" (*drittes Geschlecht*). For a more comprehensive

outline of the development of Ulrichs's theory, see Hubert Kennedy, *Ulrichs: The Life and Works of Karl Heinrich Ulrichs, Pioneer of the Modern Gay Movement* (Boston: Alyson, 1988).

[8] Westphal, "Die conträre Sexualempfindung," 77.

[9] See, for example, Robert Deam Tobin, *Peripheral Desires: The German Discovery of Sex* (Philadelphia: Pennsylvania University Press, 2015).

[10] See Gilles Deleuze and Félix Guattari, *A Thousand Plateaus*, trans. Brian Massumi (London: Continuum, 2004).

[11] Ibid.

[12] Chrysanthi Nigianni and Merl Storr, *Deleuze and Queer Theory* (Edinburgh: Edinburgh University Press, 2009), 161.

[13] Havelock Ellis, "Sexual Inversion in Women," *Alienist and Neurologist* XVI (1895): 147–48.

[14] Leila J. Rupp, *Sapphistries: A Global History of Love between Women* (New York: New York University Press, 2009), 147.

[15] Clare Hemmings, "Out of Sight, Out of Mind? Theorizing Femme Narrative," *Sexualities* 2 (1999): 451–64.

[16] Vibeke Rützou Petersen, *Women and Modernity in Weimar Germany: Reality and Its Representation in Popular Fiction* (New York: Berghahn Books, 2001), 75.

[17] Marti Lybeck, *Desiring Emancipation: New Woman and Homosexuality in Germany, 1890–1933* (Albany: State University of New York Press, 2014), 20.

[18] Kathleen Rowe, *The Unruly Woman: Gender and the Genres of Laughter* (Austin: University of Texas Press, 2011), 64.

[19] Here "niemand" presumably means no *heterosexual* individual. Magnus Hirschfeld, *Die Homosexualität des Mannes und des Weibes* (Berlin: Louis Marcus, 1914), 272.

[20] Ibid.

[21] Jonathan Kemp, *The Penetrated Male* (Brooklyn, NY: Punctum Books, 2013), 188.

[22] Gilles Deleuze and Félix Guattari, *A Thousand Plateaus*, trans. Brian Massumi (London: Continuum, 2004), 25.

[23] Given the nature of Hirschfeld's theory, the feminine female invert would not be able to assume the same position on the spectrum as the feminine heterosexual woman and, as such, the theory is still contingent on some level of gender nonconformity, meaning that the overarching thesis of Hirschfeld's "intermediate sexual forms" remains problematic. For more information on Hirschfeld's life and his theories see: Ralf Dose, *Magnus Hirschfeld: Origins of the Gay Liberation Movement* (New York: NY Monthly Review Press, 2014); Charlotte Wolff, *Magnus Hirschfeld: A Portrait of a Pioneer in Sexology* (London: Quartet Books, 1987); Elena Mancini, *Magnus Hirschfeld and the Quest for Sexual Freedom: A History of the First International Sexual Freedom Movement* (New York: Palgrave Macmillan, 2010).

[24] Tamagne, *The History of Homosexuality*, 32.

[25] Lybeck, *Desiring Emancipation*, 161.

[26] Tamagne, *The History of Homosexuality*, 155.

[27] Tobin, *Peripheral Desires*, 79; Jason Crouthamel, *An Intimate History of the Front: Masculinity, Sexuality, and German Soldiers in the First World War* (New York: Palgrave Macmillan, 2014), 112.

[28] *Die Freundin*, February 17, 1932.

[29] § 175 reads as follows: "Die widernatürliche Unzucht, welche zwischen Personen männlichen Geschlechts oder von Menschen mit Thieren begangen wird, ist mit Gefängnis zu bestrafen; auch kann auf Verlust der bürgerlichen Ehrenrecht erkannt werden" (unnatural fornication, whether between persons of the male sex or humans with beasts, is punishable by imprisonment and can result in further loss of civil rights). After the magazine returned in 1929, the author, poet, and longstanding member of the BfM, Bruno Balz, was made editor. From 1930, Martin Butzkow-Radszuweit, the adopted son and rumoured lover of Friedrich Radszuweit, managed the editorial functions of *Die Freundin* as well as the publications for queer men *Die Insel* (The Island) and the *Blätter für Menschenrecht* (Journal for Human Rights). See Micheler, "Zeitschriften, Verbände und Lokale."

[30] Schader, *Virile*, 44.

[31] There are no circulation figures for *Die Freundin*, or, in fact, any of the publications by the Radszuweit Verlag. The magazine's association with the Bund für Menschenrecht (BfM), however, means that it can be assumed that circulation figures were reasonably high. While several sources cite the membership figures of the BfM at 48,000 members by 1929, it is doubtful that the organization achieved such great success. Its rival Frauenliebe, produced by the Deutscher Freundschaftsverband (DFV) reported sales figures of around 10,000 copies in 1928. For further information on the divisions between the BfM and the DFV and the popularity of Weimar lesbian periodicals, see, for example: Stefan Micheler, "Zeitschriften, Verbände und Lokale: gleichgeschlechtlich begehrender Menschen in der Weimarer Republik," in *Invertito—Jahrbuch für die Geschichte der Homosexualitäten* 10 (2008): 2–72; Schader, *Virile*; Angeles Espinaco-Virseda, "'I feel that I belong to you': Subculture, die Freundin and Weimar Lesbian Identities," in *Spaces of Identity: Tradition, Cultural Boundaries and Identity Formation in Central Europe* 4 (2004): 83–100; Amy D. Young, "'Club of Friends': Lesbian Periodicals in the Weimar Republic," in *Tribades, Tommies and Transgressives: Histories of Sexualities, Volume I*, ed. Mary McAuliffe and Sonja Tiernan (Newcastle: Cambridge Scholars Press, 2008).

[32] Schader, *Virile*, 51–53.

[33] Carroll Smith-Rosenberg, *Disorderly Conduct: Visions of Gender in Victorian America* (New York: Oxford University Press, 1985), 278.

[34] Editors, "The Cult of the Body: *Lebensreform*, Sport, and Dance" in *The Weimar Republic Sourcebook*, ed. Anton Kaes, Martin Jay, and Edward Dimendberg (Berkeley: University of California Press, 1995), 673.

[35] Steinach believed that the process of sterilization, which became known the Steinach Operation, had rejuvenating effects on the body. Steinach also proposed

that replacing the testicles of a homosexual man with those of a heterosexual man would help the patient be redirected to a normal sex drive. See P. Södersten et al., "Eugen Steinach: The First Neuroendocrinologist," *Endocrinology* 3 (2014): 688–95; Thomas Schlich, *The Origins of Organ Transplantation: Surgery and Laboratory Science, 1880–1930* (Rochester, NY: University of Rochester Press, 2014).

[36] "The Cult of the Body" in *The Weimar Republic Sourcebook*, 673.

[37] N.N., "Der Verrat des mann-männlichen Damenklub 'Violetta,'" *Ariadne: Heft 29* (Kassel: Archiv der deutschen Frauenbewegung, 1996), 36.

[38] Margaret Beetham, *A Magazine of Her Own?: Domesticity and Desire in the Woman's Magazine 1800–1914* (London: Routledge, 1996), 12.

[39] In the first two issues of *Die Freundin* readers were invited to submit poems and short stories to the magazine. Following this initial encouragement, no further attempts appear to have been made to reach out to the readers for poems which suggests that there was no lack of submissions. For the discussion section of the magazine, suggested topics and themes were given to readers which often continued to structure the discussion across several issues. When a topic was considered closed, a new subject for discussion was presented.

[40] Deleuze and Guattari, *A Thousand Plateaus*, 13.

[41] Ibid.

[42] Margaret Beetham, "Open and Closed: The Periodical as a Publishing Genre," *Victorian Periodicals Review* 22, no. 3 (1989): 98.

[43] *Die Freundin*, August 8, 1924.

[44] Ibid.

[45] Ibid.

[46] *Die Freundin*, February 20, 1928.

[47] Ibid.

[48] *Die Freundin*, April 30, 1928.

[49] Ibid.

[50] Herta Laser, "Aus der Bewegung," *Frauenliebe*, Number 28, 1927.

[51] Adele, "Das persönliche Parfum," *Frauenliebe*, Number 42, 1931.

[52] "Schönheit und Jugend der Freundin," *Frauenliebe*, Number 36, 1927.

[53] Ibid.

[54] "Im welchen Rock geht es sich am besten?," *Die Freundin*, April 16, 1928.

[55] Paulowna, "Für oder gegen den Bubikopf," *Die Freundin*, April 16, 1928.

[56] Given that experiments in gender reassignment surgery were not being practiced until the early 1930s, the term "transvestite" in the magazines is used to encompass a diverse range of experiences. The term was used both to describe individuals who engaged in discrete periods of cross-dressing and those whose gender identity did not align with their birth sex. However, as it is difficult to distinguish in the supplements between cross-dressers and historical subjects who would now be considered transgender, I will continue to deploy the term "transvestite"

throughout this discussion as the term that was most often employed by the individuals themselves, unless they described themselves otherwise.

[57] Katie Sutton, "'We Too Deserve a Place in the Sun': The Politics of Transvestite Identity in Weimar Germany," *German Studies Review* 2 (2012): 335–54; Lybeck, *Desiring Emancipation.*

[58] "Die Welt der Transvestiten," *Die Freundin*, August 8, 1924.

[59] Here, the wife talks specifically to other women about being sensitive to the issues of transvestite men. Interestingly, although perhaps not surprisingly, the suggestion that a relationship between a male-to-female transvestite with fixed gender preference as female and a biological woman could be interpreted as a lesbian configuration is not considered in either periodical.

[60] Sutton, "We Too Deserve a Place in the Sun," 345.

[61] "Kleine Anzeigen," *Frauenliebe*, Number 32 1927.

[62] Clare Rogan, "'Good Nude Photographs': Images for Desire in Weimar Germany's Lesbian Journals," in *Tribades, Tommies and Transgressives: Histories of Sexualities, Volume I*, ed. Mary McAuliffe and Sonja Tiernan (Newcastle: Cambridge Scholars, 2008), 146.

[63] Gayatri Chakravorty Spivak, *In Other Worlds: Essays in Cultural Politics* (New York: Methuen, 1987), 170.

[64] Ibid.

[65] Rogan, "'Good Nude Photographs'," 154.

[66] N. Lermann, "Die Freundin der Olga Diers," *Die Freundin*, August 8, 1924.

[67] For a reprint of Roellig, Adele Meyer, *Lila Nächte: Die Damenklubs der Zwanziger Jahre* (Cologne: Zitronenpresse, 1981), 38.

[68] "Geschlecht von Morgen," *Frauenliebe*, Number 13, 1930.

[69] Inge, "Die von der Liebe leben . . .," *Frauenliebe*, Number 35, 1927.

[70] Fionnuala Dillane, "Forms of Affect, Relationality and Periodical Encounters or 'Pine-apple for the Million'," *European Society for Periodical Research* 1, no. 1 (2016), 6.

Based on a True Story: Tracking What Is Queer about German Queer Documentary

Kyle Frackman, University of British Columbia

THE 2012 DOCUMENTARY *Unter Männern—Schwul in der DDR* (Among Men: Gay in the GDR, 2012, dir. Ringo Rösener and Markus Stein) begins with a kind of cinematic overture.[1] This overture introduces the viewer to three of the film's interviewees whose comments set the stage for the biographical and documentary nature of what follows as well as the themes that will surface in the subjects' narratives: the gay experiences of a bygone time and place and under a now-extinct social system. The first man, Jürgen (b. 1932), calls himself old and is amused that his life now involves working in the garden; Christian (b. 1934), the second man, reveals that he long debated whether to participate in the film and to out himself, since he says that part of his life is over; the third, Frank (b. 1959), also reflects on his current situation and ponders the fantastical thought of waking up and no longer being gay.

At this point, the film's first act begins. Accompanied by music with an electronic feel, the film cuts to establishing shots of Berlin, a tracking shot of a young man on a bicycle (who we come to find out is one of the directors, Ringo Rösener) and a cut to this same man's entrance into a gay club replete with flashing disco lights and go-go boys. The tracking shot both quotes and foreshadows the use of footage from the landmark film *Coming Out*, the only East German feature film to focus on homosexuality. A voice-over narration by Rösener addresses the viewer, introducing us to his on- and off-screen presence, informing us that he was born in rural East Germany, not long before the fall of the Berlin Wall and Reunification, and dared to be openly gay only after fleeing this more remote part of the country. This first act, in which Rösener positions the film in the present but consciously in juxtaposition to an historical past, gives us a reason for this film: a contemporary German gay man expresses his surprise at what he does and does not know about the German Democratic Republic (GDR, East Germany), the land in which he was born, and also at how his life would be different if the Berlin Wall had not come down and the GDR had survived. This self-conscious engagement with the topic and the structuring of the film are important to understand since it points to the film's straddling of time and place in its effort to present the past, almost as a secondary source, but also to represent a component of the past's ongoing development, as a primary source. In an examination of German queer documentary, I will discuss this film and situate it in the broader context of this genre of nonfiction or documentary cinematic productions. The fate of this film is also a desideratum in its queerness, for, as we will see, it has found different audiences and opportunities in its national and international availability from, for example, a kind of fraternal twin production released the following year, which I discuss in less detail: *Out in Ost-Berlin—Lesben und Schwule in der DDR* (Out in East Berlin: Lesbians and Gays in the GDR, 2013, dir. Jochen Hick and Andreas Strohfeldt). As we will see, these films engage with—and partly aim to tell—history while also becoming artifacts themselves. In this essay, I will analyze the use of and play with cinematic grammar and describe how the documentary *Unter Männern* relates to and departs from other examples of documentary and ideas from film theory.

I find the film that I discuss here, *Unter Männern*, to be queer, indeed, almost overdetermined in its queerness, but not necessarily in ways that one might expect. In subject matter, it focuses on gay men who lived in East Germany, which ventures beyond the heteronormative in the obvious way in that the individuals evince same-sex affections that positioned them as outsiders in Europe more generally but definitely within the GDR. Less obvious, however, is the degree to which an examination of East Germany, and non-heteronormative affections and behaviors in addition, ventures into the realm of the strange and extraordinary. Studying the GDR requires a sort of time travel to a country that is stuck in time perhaps like few others. Remnants, markers, and reminders of the nation exist, but the GDR remains a remarkable turn of German history—an experiment in socialism, surveillance, and extensive bureaucratic control that has curiously inspired nostalgia and diverse popular and scholarly debates over its legacy.[2] It will become clear that *Unter Männern* is an apt example of what Elizabeth Freeman describes, interpreting Derrida, as she engages with historiography and history itself: one is bound to what was "impossible in a given historical moment" and "to the other who . . . has priority and thus splits our selfhood, detours our forward-moving agency."[3] The unintelligibility and near impossibility of queer GDR moments become clear in the film and appear in my discussion below. Not to be forgotten, aesthetic decisions made in the film have their own oddities that render the work queer, including with respect to the genre or subgenre into which the film might be placed for classification.

Unter Männern weaves together three threads of, first, historically relevant memory recited by its chosen protagonists; second, some personal history on the part of the primary filmmaker (i.e., director Ringo Rösener); and, third, between and among them, filmic artifacts or evidence of life in the GDR. This documentary presents the aforementioned interviews, but it is intriguing not for this inclusion, but rather for the mobilization of self-reflexivity, autobiography, and self-presentation on the part of the filmmaker as a means of processing and presenting what the interviewees relate.[4] *Unter Männern* offers a compelling examination of gay individuals who lived in the GDR and who recount and relive diverse experiences with the apparatus of the GDR state. This film is one that does not do purely or customary documentarian work in a way that one might expect of an expository historical narrative. Instead the film points toward discontinuities that mark distinct eras of gay experience and possibility: pre- and post-Wall in the GDR and post-GDR. Before engaging with the film in more detail, I will work through some contextual considerations of genre and subgenre, as we also explore how *Unter Männern*, its topic, and its style display and play with their queerness.

Queerness and Queer Cinema

Engaging in such an inquiry—on "things queer"—has customarily required that one assert one's definition or the scope of one's understanding of "queer" itself. Generally, the idea of queerness encompasses abrasion and a (usually) sexual quality of exceeding boundaries of identity and behavior, especially with respect to transcending conventional limitations of heteronormative classification. This excessive attribute often accompanies an audacious playfulness, sometimes evoking camp aesthetics, which can irritate the status quo. In an East German context, a notoriously prudish nation in which the expectation for non-heterosexual, unconventional sexuality and gender was *inconspicuousness*, "queer" becomes even more inclusive. Standards of gender and sexuality in East Germany depended at certain points on the widely shared understanding of a "socialist personality," which itself relied on supposedly "moral" and "proper" behavior.[5] Here, then, queerness antagonizes what is allegedly "natural" in unadventurous, reproductive, monogamous heterosexuality.

Given the fertile ground of queer and feminist studies, I will be building on a rich foundation of other scholars' work in relating my understanding of queerness to cinematic production. Advancing from the understanding of queerness, then, we can comprehend queer film to embody not exclusively the presentation, thematization, or display of sexualities that do not fit in with normative heterosexuality. Cinematic queerness can come in the form of "an authorial voice, a character, a mode of textual production, and/or various types of reception practice."[6] Similarly, queer cinema can indicate "alternative cinematic aesthetics organized around non-normative desires."[7] In *The Queer German*

Cinema, Alice Kuzniar, developing ideas coming out of B. Ruby Rich's conceptualization of New Queer Cinema, posits that, if we operate on the assumption that sexuality can be expressed or "determined" visually, whether through "word or image," "the role played by art or experimental cinema is crucial for fantasizing and promoting alternative representations."[8] The rich cinematic tradition and potential which we certainly see in queer (German) film attests to Kuzniar's idea that "queer cinema is one of baroque display and theatricality that paradoxically hides as much as it reveals."[9] This evocative description of what one can potentially find when peering toward, through, or behind queer cinematic images is germane to the examination of *Unter Männern*; we will see that the film can be simultaneously excessive and miserly with its forms, objectives, and presentation of these as it interacts with our expectations for what will appear on screen.

German-language cinema has a long history of associations with queerness. With just a few selected examples here, this spans the wide range from the earliest cinematic engagements with gayness in *Anders als die Andern* (Different from the Others, 1919, dir. Richard Oswald), gender-bending and cross-dressing (*Viktor und Viktoria*, Viktor and Viktoria, 1933, dir. Reinhold Schünzel), to Rainer Werner Fassbinder's complicated treatments of transsexuality (*In einem Jahr mit 13 Monden*, In a Year with 13 Moons, 1978) or gay sexuality (*Faustrecht der Freiheit*, Fox and His Friends, 1975; *Querelle*, 1982), from Monika Treut's exploration of gender identity (*Gendernauts*, 1999) and Pierre Sanoussi-Bliss's thematization of race and HIV/AIDS (*Zurück auf los*, Return to Go, 2000) to Sabine Bernardi's take on transsexuality in *Romeos* (2011). Despite this long and varied tradition, in a 1998 essay on German film from 1970 to 1994, a period in which there were several prominent queer films of note, Les Wright laments a paucity of scholarship on queer German film, a vexation that was soon to be addressed by Kuzniar's study in 2000.[10] Wright's essay itself, as well as much of the other related scholarship on "queer" (variously defined) film, devotes the majority of its energy to analyzing feature films, especially mainstays of gay and lesbian criticism by Rainer Werner Fassbinder, Ulrike Ottinger, and Monika Treut, as examples.

There have been few scholarly treatments of the queer side of German documentary filmmaking. Kuzniar points out that the genre is underrepresented in scholarship on film.[11] Terri Ginsberg and Andrea Mensch's survey of German film, *A Companion to German Cinema* (2012), includes essays on depictions of cross-dressing and the (documentary) work of Jochen Hick.[12] Only one essay in a more recent collection on a related nonfiction subgenre (autobiographical film) treats a queer topic.[13] Robert M. Gillett, too, has noted the glaring absence of material on the subspecialty of queer German documentary film.[14] Indeed, he writes that, given the presence of notable filmmakers in and adjacent to this genre—like the arguably most prominent Rosa von Praunheim as well as Monika Treut, Elfi Mikesch, Jürgen Brüning, Jörg Fockele, Claudia Schillinger, and Jochen Hick—"The sheer number and weight of these names, and the contexts in which they occur, suggest that something important has been marginalized."[15] In his examination of Jochen Hick's work, Gillett has instructively surveyed German docu-cinematic tendencies and found links to queer German films, a project that I will not duplicate here.[16] Even analyses of filmmakers whose work is usually included in the queer cinematic canon, like Ulrike Ottinger, have avoided direct engagement with the "queerness" of the work.[17] In an essay on biopic documentaries, Rich notes that many of these, affected as they have been by both the tradition of Holocaust testimonials, coming out narratives, and the HIV/AIDS epidemic, can strike elegiac tones.[18] Though many related films have appeared since Rich wrote that essay, one can still find a pervasive or latent melancholy in many queer cinematic works, including those that I discuss below.

Documentary Style

British filmmaker John Grierson (1898–1972), whose work in the 1930s contributed to the understanding of what "documentary" is, gave it an excellent definition, calling it "the creative treatment of actuality."[19] Taking a more definitive perspective, Erik Barnouw grants that documentary filmmakers can play a wide range of roles, from "explorer" to "advocate" to "observer," among others—roles that can and do overlap depending on historical and social context.[20] Perhaps most influential, judging by the number of other scholars citing it, is Bill Nichols's *Representing Reality* and his follow-up study *Blurred Boundaries*, which also create a documentary taxonomy of "expository," "observational," "interactive," "reflexive," and, later, "performative" modes.[21] Much of the definitional theorization is based on the acceptance or rejection of the assumption that nonfiction film, of which documentary is sometimes called a subgenre, has a mandate of objectivity and what Nichols calls "sobriety," or that nonfiction film ought to be assessed, again at least in part, by the degree to which it remains "authentic" or "true to reality."[22] That is an assumption that *Unter Männern* and films like it challenge. Given what we know about queer cinema and its tendency and drive toward the theatrical or inexplicable, one can perceive that there may very well be a contradiction brewing here under the surface. Indeed, this may be one of the reasons for the reticence many scholars have had in trying to understand what queer documentary might be, German or not, particularly since the filmmakers are likely to weave threads of their own sensibility and biography into the fabric of the nonfiction works, which adds yet another complicated layer of what can be critically analyzed.

In *New Documentary*, Stella Bruzzi criticizes exclusive understandings of what this genre may achieve or how filmmakers are or are not supposed to avail themselves of various stylistic and formal methods in their work. Most important among these are editing and narration, but also other uses of sound, lighting, and mise-en-scène. In other words, the sobriety and objectivity about which so many, including Nichols, have written are naturally challenged by the very medium in which filmmakers employ them, especially as these films are increasingly made in the context of steady self-broadcasting in venues on social media and online video distribution services like YouTube.[23] In Bruzzi's words, "what else is a documentary but a dialogue between a filmmaker, a crew and a situation that, although in existence prior to their arrival, has irrevocably been changed by that arrival?"[24] Bruzzi writes from the perspective that "documentaries are inevitably the result of the intrusion of the filmmaker onto the situation being filmed, that they are performative because they acknowledge the construction and artificiality of even the non-fiction film and propose . . . the truth that emerges through the encounter between filmmakers, subjects and spectators."[25] By means of devices like the narration the viewer hears in a film, the "conscious structuring" of the film's story becomes even more perceptible.[26] These considerations should not be surprising to consumers of documentary films, or even photography, since these debates have persisted for many decades. Indeed, as Elizabeth Cowie notes, "the documentary film nevertheless involves more disreputable features of cinema usually associated with entertainment film, namely, the pleasures and fascination of film as spectacle."[27] Thus, we can see one of the ongoing debates among film scholars with respect to the authenticity, objectivity, and the *nonfiction* quality itself of the documentary film. Cowie's observation also gives us a glimpse of the special queer potential that documentary can and does have as it perversely and equitably satisfies varying desires. Although I will not argue for or against any genre categorization of *Unter Männern*, the question of its nonfictional nature and the filmmaker's "intrusion" into, or presence in, it is a crucial one for my interpretation.

An interaction between the two sides of the camera, like we see in *Unter Männern* (I described one example above), is not a new phenomenon, neither for nonfiction film in general nor for documentary film that focuses on lesbian and gay subjects. Nonetheless, scholarship on the subject multiplied in the first decade of the 2000s; one could argue that the increasing availability of digital methods in filmic production has fostered burgeoning possibilities for experimentation in form, style, and genre.[28] Alisa Lebow, in her study of Jewish autobiographical documentary, identifies two primary features of what she calls first-person documentary: "subjectivity and relationality." The former, as I discussed above, had been supposedly eschewed—or at least critically debated—in documentary film; the latter will usually require the involvement of others (e.g., crew, acquaintances, interviewees) in order to "construct[ ]the self on screen."[29] Robin Curtis and Angelica Fenner and the contributors to their anthology on the subject have observed that the trend toward autobiography has expanded or made its way to German-language film if sometimes in ways that deviate from the styles of other geographic and national areas.[30] Frequently appearing in films that Curtis and Fenner mention are the drive toward intergenerational exchange and topics that have hints of *Vergangenheitsbewältigung* (coming to terms with the past), if not explicitly with the German national past—particularly the Holocaust—then with the filmmaker's own personal past, including one's place within a changing ("transnational") Germany and Europe. *Unter Männern* is an example of this broader trend, combining as it does the autobiographical and biographical with a retrospective examination of East German history and the development, however stunted, of LGBTQ rights and public consciousness. This is another of the ways in which the film is both a primary and secondary source of historical assessment.

A willingness to experiment with media and genre is also present, often leading to difficulties with straightforward categorization and analysis of the work in question.[31] It must be noted that the majority of the scholarship either ignores or only cursorily treats the subject of queer documentary. Indeed, it is striking how infrequently the subject of documentary (and nonfiction film more broadly) appears in research on queer cinema and queer German cinema, especially since there is no shortage of relevant works to analyze. A possible explanation is that these works may either purposely aim to subvert the categorization or blend genres in a way that resists customary classification—often one of the first steps of critical analysis. Another practical consideration, and one that affects *Unter Männern* itself as we will see below, is that of distribution; these films often have difficulty finding viewers when it can be a tremendous challenge for them to locate companies or infrastructure for distribution, especially internationally. One could also deem this a paradoxical problem in an age in which there have never been so many opportunities and venues for online, digital publication.

One of these characteristics of categorization, an awareness of the filmmakers' presence (or interjection) in the subject matter their works are addressing, will be crucial for understanding the interpretation I offer. As I noted above, *Unter Männern* is enacting and becoming a part of the history it is also reporting. Appropriately, theories of performative documentary will be useful for this discussion. Performative documentary, as theorized by Nichols (in *Blurred Boundaries*) and Bruzzi, offers approaches and filmic styles that were either unavailable to many earlier filmmakers—newly possible with different equipment and editing software, for example—or were undesirable as inappropriate for the documentary form. According to Nichols, performative documentary can "suspend[ ] realist representation" and "put[ ] the referential aspect of the message in brackets, under suspension. . . . These films make the proposition that it is possible to know difference differently."[32] Bruzzi argues that these documentaries "use[ ] performance within a non-fiction context to draw attention to the impossibilities of authentic documentary representation," more in the sense of Judith Butler's mobilization of J. L. Austin.[33]

Unlike examples of the New Queer Cinema as theorized by B. Ruby Rich, the queer works I mention here are less technically or thematically exuberant in their abrasion as well as sometimes more conventional in their form.[34] Nonetheless, these films, especially *Unter Männern*, create different frames for the narratives they deliver and make use of unexpected on-screen visual techniques that mark the works with non-realistic or stylized features. Although documentary, as Stella Bruzzi has argued, is often seen as a purely "cerebral, intellectual genre . . .; quite often it is virtually the opposite: emotion-driven, sensual and . . . primal in its appeal."[35] There is definitely an overlap between these approaches (intellectual and emotional); indeed, as Michael Renov writes, fiction and documentary "inhabit one another."[36] This overlap, or even a creative tension, is visible especially in *Unter Männern*. We can see that the film at least hints at the multitude of routes toward queer experience. The film illustrates a diversity of queer experience during and after East Germany's existence, which is another of its goals.

Documentary within LGBTQ Cinema

A crucial question involves the parameters of an examination of "queer documentary." Several of the filmmakers discussed in this essay have moved into and out of the generic field of "documentary," often forcing the viewer and critic to ponder where to place the work in relation to the artist's oeuvre or even in relation to other filmic texts. To provide a fuller view of *Unter Männern*, it can be useful to understand how it does or does not fit into trends in queer (German) documentary filmmaking.[37] The film features primarily interviewees' own individual, first-person accounts of topics that are often included in gay and lesbian documentary and personal history. The various interviewees recount experiences related to childhood, growing up, the realization of gayness, searching for other gay contacts, cruising, coming out, and fear of discovery. In many respects, these accounts resemble what one finds in other documentaries on related topics, like *Portrait of Jason* (1967, dir. Shirley Clarke), *Word Is Out* (1977, dir. Mariposa Film Group), *Gay USA* (1977, dir. Arthur J. Bressan, Jr.), *Before Stonewall* (1984, dir. Greta Schiller and Robert Rosenberg), *The Times of Harvey Milk* (1984, dir. Rob Epstein),

Tongues Untied (1989, dir. Marlon Riggs), *The Celluloid Closet* (1995, dir. Rob Epstein), and *Paragraph 175* (1999, dir. Rob Epstein and Jeffrey Friedman).[38] Like *Paragraph 175*, which presents experiences of men persecuted under the Nazis, and, indeed, like these other American "gay films," *Unter Männern* is doing important *documentarian* work, in that it is cataloguing the fading memories of people who lived under now-extinct social systems. It thus creates what Bruzzi has called "film as record," which also becomes archaeological in Foucault's sense.[39] The inclusion of autobiographical elements is not uncommon to queer documentary film, as Harry M. Benshoff and Sean Griffin have observed; these films often complement conventional autobiographical details with additions like "fictional vignettes, found footage, and activist video."[40] The emergence and surge of the HIV/AIDS epidemic inevitably colored much of the cinematic work of this period, producing a preponderance of narratives reflecting grief, loss, and mourning.[41] A recent and popular example is *How to Survive a Plague* (2012, dir. David France), a compilation of interviews juxtaposed with contemporarily collected footage in the founding and active years of ACT UP, the activist organization formed to advocate and fight for HIV/AIDS funding and education in the most devastating times of the epidemic in the United States.

One can observe that the roles played by, and the presentation or composition of, lesbian and gay film, documentary film, and documentary impulses shifted in the post-Stonewall era and again in the 1980s in the face of HIV/AIDS. Films from these eras presented—though not strictly sequentially—tales of the outcast queer or the vampiric lesbian or the "sexual intermediate" in the German tradition, eventually followed by histories, coming out narratives, activist campaigns, and sometimes elegiac confrontation with the realities of HIV/AIDS.[42] Dealing specifically with lesbian and gay film, Richard Dyer defined the "affirmation film" (e.g., *Word Is Out* and *Gay USA*, both 1977), which contributed to consciousness-raising efforts and utilized typical narrative devices like stories of coming out, first gay experiences of sex and community, and early pride parades.[43] The goals of the films were often twofold: first, the affirmational aim of giving LGBTQ individuals a forum in which to write their own history and hear others' stories, and second, to do "outreach" of a sort to the (heterosexual) community beyond. They usually failed in the latter as their audiences consisted mostly of gay viewers.[44] In the (West) German case, without doubt films with this topic mostly follow the decriminalization of male homosexual acts in the late 1960s and subsequent social visibility; they include the work of filmmakers like Rosa von Praunheim, Monika Treut, and Frank Ripploh, for example, often with the effect of making LGBTQ narratives more visible if not more palatable, while transcending the earlier drive toward advocacy and activism that had characterized much of LGBT (and later queer) cinema.[45] The work of Jochen Hick, one of the directors of *Out in Ost-Berlin*, a film related to *Unter Männern*, ought also to be mentioned. Hick's films usually go in a more audacious direction than *Out in Ost-Berlin* does, seemingly being directed toward a broader public and possibly with a television viewership in mind.[46] The directors of *Unter Männern* faced decisions about how to present supposed reality by using an aesthetic and stylized method, again in a genre in which the viewer often expects, rightly or wrongly, the objective absence of any *auteur*.[47]

Unter Männern

Responding to my interview question of why he and Stein wanted to create a film on this subject, Rösener, born in Mecklenburg-West Pomerania in 1983, illustrates the central dilemma or structuring issue for this genre and this film in particular:

> Der Antrieb für mich war herauszufinden, wie man als Schwuler in der DDR leben musste. Da ich noch in der DDR geboren bin, habe ich mich irgendwann gefragt, wie es denn wäre, wenn es die Mauer noch geben würde. . . . Was wir letztlich . . . zeigen wollten, war, wie die Schwulen sich selbst verstanden haben.

> [The impetus for me was to find out how one had to live as a gay man in the GDR. Since I was actually born in the GDR, I asked myself at one point what it would be like if the Wall still existed. . . . In the end what we wanted to show was how gay men understood themselves.][48]

Rösener's present experience (at the time of the film production) as a 29-year-old gay man living in what used to be East Germany, presented autobiographically albeit selectively, thus becomes the connective tissue that draws the other disparate experiences of the film's interview subjects together. He is placed literally in the footsteps and positions of other protagonists. Within this framework, then, the filmmakers' goal in presenting these men's self-understanding was to reach contemporary young people in a different historical and social context. This educational, quasi-activist, and historical impetus aimed to create a history-telling text that would illustrate how these East German men lived out their gayness often in secret, meeting in public toilets or using surreptitious means to find sexual, erotic, or social contact. Discussions of sex in *Klappen* (public toilets), for example, mark a difference between the narrator (Rösener) and the protagonists, one that is both generational and contextual. It is one marker of the post-1980s developments in gay culture on both sides of the Wall and *Wende*. While this covert behavior also occurred in the West, these men in the GDR lived in a state that, while at times legally and sometimes superficially more liberal or leftist, embodied myriad contra-dictions—a daily world that will seem far removed from most (western European and North American) younger viewers today. This was a con-text in which primarily male same-sex sexual activity, while legal in the GDR after 1968, was the target of massive state surveillance and manipu-lation, a consequence that could not be rivaled by anything in the West.[49]

To present and interact with this context one can say that *Unter Männern* has two main parallel tracks which interweave in its narrative arc: the first one, which is primarily biographical and consists mostly of interviews, and the second and smaller one, which is autobiographical, more stylized, and in a different sense historical. The film begins and ends with its focus on the six interviewees, its so-called protagonists.[50] It does not construct a revelatory narrative path; with these protagonists we know what their sexuality is—or we can claim to know it or at least why they are in the film, although their experiences with sexuality were not always directly linear. For my examination of this film I focus on two aspects of the film's two tracks: first, sequences that relate directly to Rösener's experience and the construction of the interactive quality of the film, and second, subjects' interviews which testify to the strange nature of East German gay experiences. I have chosen these interviewees from the film on the one hand for the uniqueness of their experience among the other protagonists and the insights they provide into East German gay history, and on the other hand for the filmic and narrative devices that become apparent in their segments.

Above I described what I called the film's first act, which followed the introductory overture of three interviewees' appearances. After direc-tor Rösener's self-placement within the narration, a cut takes us to a sta-tionary medium shot of Rösener in front of a TV and VCR into which he inserts a cassette with a clip from Heiner Carow's 1989 East German film, *Coming Out*. The narrator reveals a degree of surprise: "Das gab es wirklich: einen Film über Schwule in der DDR" (There was such a thing: a film about gays in the GDR). Largely because of the complicated and thorny discourses surrounding same-sex sexuality in East Germany, one has relatively few filmic artifacts to which we can refer, especially if we contrast this legacy with that of West Germany. The final years of the GDR's life, indeed the day the Berlin Wall fell (November 9, 1989), saw the release of *Coming Out*, a bold and intriguing film from one of East Germany's most popular and celebrated directors. Unlike in West Germany, the GDR's gay movement, as Bert Thinius writes, got its cin-ematic debut at the end of its existence.[51] *Unter Männern* absorbs this historic film and uses it as a means with which to engage the viewer and to provide an initial conduit to connect to East German gay history.

The method, used multiple times in the film, allows whatever sequence might be playing on the VCR to transition from being framed by our screen to occupying our screen itself. We then partake of what Thomas Waugh calls an "interactive realism" in which the viewer is introduced to the informants, in this case also generically, without their names appearing on screen.[52] Waugh has summarized the conventional approach as a "formulaic mix of interviews and archival footage joined by a mortar of observational vérité and musical interludes."[53] The narrator's persona is not the common documentarian "voice of God," nameless and faceless while providing contextual information or interpretation with apparent generic and omniscient authority; instead, we hear Rösener himself, a gay man taking a kind of ownership of history and identity: he is professing to be a "verhinderter Ossi" (stunted Easterner), a man born late into the GDR (in 1983) but lacking a knowledge of the social and cultural history of his community of gay men within that country.

Further, through the re-enactment of certain scenes or actions, the film draws repeated links between Rösener and Philipp, the main protagonist in *Coming Out* (played by Matthias Freihof) and the other informants. Quoting the 1989 film, shots of Rösener on a bicycle mimic those of Philipp in the earlier film, as mentioned above: long and medium tracking shots show the cyclists and what lies behind them, as usually the camera is moving in front of the bicycles. Rösener indicated to me that the filmmakers aimed to make the narrator more naïve than Rösener himself—thus providing a means by which the film could again enact the performative history it hopes to present. This doubling of Rösener and Philipp gives the former, our guide through the interviews and stories of the film, any necessary credentials to participate in this historical quest for comprehension. Not anonymous yet uninitiated in the topic as a generic narrator could be, Rösener instead assumes the position of a simultaneously naïve and knowing fellow traveler, who aims to stand in for viewers who are otherwise ignorant of any related background and context. This stepping back and forth between the worlds of *Unter Männern* and *Coming Out* thus serves these two purposes: to link the narrator with Philipp and to allow for the viewer's empathetic identification with the narrator.

Unter Männern demonstrates its playful self-awareness as a documentary bridging eras with another unexpected tactic. A visual effect that imitates graffiti or a highlighter pen appears at numerous points in the film to mark (or "out") the locations and individuals on which it alights. We first see it as the director-narrator Rösener cycles past Dmitri Vrubel's Berlin Wall painting *My God! Help Me to Survive This Deadly Love* (Господи! Помоги мне выжить среди этой смертной любви) at Berlin's East Side Gallery. The most recognizable of the 1990-era Wall art, Vrubel's painting inspired confusion and surprise among many who viewed it, the artist's attempt to render what he saw in the original inspirational photo from 1979, "a repulsive, revolting thing that almost made me throw up."[54] That photo illustrates part of the 1979 meeting in which Soviet Union General Secretary Leonid Brezhnev and East German General Secretary Erich Honecker kiss during the former's visit to the GDR, a visit partly to commemorate the thirtieth anniversary of the GDR's founding and also to seal an economic deal between the two countries.[55] After Rösener has exited the frame to the right, the palimpsestic highlighting colors in Honecker pink in his brotherly kiss with Brezhnev. This stylized effect emphasizes the artificial nature of the medium, as well as the film's understanding of itself as a creative exponent of the documentary genre, while also communicating or giving a clue to the viewer that the graffiti will focus on same-sex intimacies, erotic or not. Moreover, this first and trendsetting use of the onscreen intervention throws into relief the contradictory and occasionally grotesque quality of East German gender and sexual discourse.

At another point in the film, archival footage of a gathering of the Freie Deutsche Jugend (Free German Youth) freezes, and two young men who had glanced back toward the camera are colored in. This latter example—and there are more in the film—also illustrates one of the main critical concerns about where the boundaries at the edge of the documentary genre might lie. Either of the examples I have discussed could be potentially problematic or odd, given the possibilities for interpretation. In Bruzzi's critique, she notes that the acknowledged presence of the filmmaker has customarily been seen as a problem for this genre, since it would call into question the authentic nature of what is supposed to be nonfiction.[56] For some, the former example could push the film out of the purely documentary genre into the realm of autobiographical or, more likely, essay films; the latter provides a stylistic alienation that creates a different kind of playful artwork, though one with the implication that locations and individuals thus marked are, for the viewers, proof of the existence of gay people in the GDR and, for the East Germans in the pre-1989 reality discussed in the film, potentially vulnerable targets. Further, this film's occasional use of archival material, like the FDJ footage, in its bare format recalls other documentaries (including *Out in Ost-Berlin*), but *Unter Männern* instead edits, develops, or tweaks the material in a mode that is differently historical.[57]

On the heels of this example of its own kind of deviation, I will proceed to examine the kind of documentary approach that *Unter Männern* takes in its portrayal of gay men's lives in the GDR. The experiences of one of the film's subjects, Eduard "Eddy" Stapel (1953–2017), an important figure in the East German gay movement, illustrate the wide historical and contextual gap between contemporary German gayness and the East German gayness of the 1970s and 1980s. Although he provides insider information about gay life in the GDR, as he does when he leads Rösener into an abandoned underground public bathroom in Leipzig, the so-called "Bürgermeister" (mayor) *pissoir* (named for its proximity to the city hall), Stapel's function in the film primarily relates to his status as an activist and organizer working toward gay liberation and equal rights. Stapel had been active in his church community and planned to become a pastor before eventually being denied his ordination because of his sexuality. Ironically, it was under the auspices of the Protestant Church that Stapel, along with a few other interested men and women, brought together interested individuals in a discussion group and later working groups in Leipzig in the early months of 1982.[58] This initiative spread, partly through Stapel's efforts, to a number of other cities and towns like Berlin, Magdeburg, Aschersleben, Karl-Marx-Stadt (now Chemnitz), Halle, Dresden, and others.[59] Groups involved included at different times the Arbeitskreis Homosexualität (Homosexuality Working Group), Homosexuelle Selbsthilfe (Homosexual Self-Help), and later the twin groups Schwule in der Kirche (Gays in the Church) and Lesben in der Kirche (Lesbians in the Church). During one interview segment with Stapel filmed in a train compartment, the film cuts to an animated map of East Germany. The aforementioned graffiti or highlighting appears again, this time to mark the names of cities and towns that Stapel mentions and others where there were organized meetings of gay and lesbian groups.

The Stasi took notice of Stapel because of his active involvement with these consciousness-raising groups, an undertaking that required him to travel around the GDR to encourage lesbians and gay men to organize and work toward achieving equal rights—what Stapel calls a "schwule Volkshochschule" (gay college). One of the film's uses of private and public archival material is the inclusion of photos of these educational gatherings which document Stapel's and others' efforts to raise awareness of issues affecting gay men and lesbians in the GDR. These occasional glimpses at photos and some of the precious few publicity materials that still exist in various collections are relatively rare in examinations of this movement, for, as Stapel himself has noted, the participants in such gatherings and in the movement more broadly tried to produce as little written material as was necessary and to discuss much only verbally.[60] The challenges that organizers faced are exemplified in a later sequence when another of the film's interviewees, Helwin (b. 1934), remarks that he had had no idea these "gay college" gatherings were taking place. Thus, the film illustrates quite well the variability and degree to which personal contact as well as geographic location could determine one's ability to connect to the nascent gay rights movement.

We see the result of the state surveillance of Stapel when he leads Rösener into a room in his home, handheld camera following them, and shows the young filmmaker, our guide, the many volumes of his Stasi files that line the shelves of multiple bookcases. Through his files, Stapel confirmed what he had suspected: that the Stasi, in what was officially called

"Operativer Vorgang Aftershave" (Operation After Shave), had pursued one of its detailed surveillance plans to investigate him fully. This included the use of four operatives (called "Romeos") to initiate sexual relationships with him in order to put him under even more, and more revealing, scrutiny; other operatives tried to sow discord with his actual boyfriends. This moment in the film is another in which the differing contextual codes and historical discourses become apparent, as Stapel laughingly says in response to Rösener's question about why the Stasi went to such trouble, "Wir waren Staatsfeinde. Das könnt ihr euch heute nicht mehr vorstellen!" (We were enemies of the state. Today you can't really imagine it!). The state's efforts to surveil Stapel and other homosexuals are rendered in their absurdity. The lengths to which the Stasi—an astonishingly bureaucratic and far-reaching agency with hundreds of thousands of unofficial collaborators among the East German citizenry—went to observe these individuals remain perplexing and disconcerting, to say the least.[61] The Stasi's preposterous and sometimes farcical techniques would be laughable if they had not also had serious consequences. *Unter Männern* in no way trivializes surveillance or the threat of surveillance, but it interestingly renders it queerly, prompting the viewer to consider the contemporary intelligibility of GDR experiences in their relative strangeness.

Contextually far removed from Stapel's activism and organization, and geographically distant from the "headquarters" of the eventually nascent gay movement in Berlin and Leipzig, were the experiences of the gay men and women who lived in rural communities, small towns, and farming villages scattered around East Germany. These individuals surely embodied some of the strangeness, deviation, and difference of queer GDR experience in their social, cultural, and communal isolation.[62] The film engages with these experiences in one of its more compelling interviews, with John (b. 1968) from Lauscha, a Thuringian town today of approximately 3,500 inhabitants long known for its glassblowing industry. In his interview segments John, whose narrative becomes conclusive for the film as I will discuss below, tells of growing up gay, his intense feelings of horror at the potential discovery by his parents, falling in love with a straight friend, an aborted attempt to flee East Germany, and his eventual coming out and acceptance in his local community. Following a long shot of John walking through the woods, we also see him in medium close-up in the forest explaining his plan to escape to the West, pointing out his route through the woods and his view of the border. The film follows this with a sequence of Rösener along the same path through the woods, placing himself in John's footsteps, with plentiful sylvan sounds accompanying his walk. Indeed, as Rösener's narration early in the film would indicate, this kind of rural, provincial experience evokes the director's own, though for him in the different context and time of northeastern Germany (Mecklenburg-West Pomerania), the *former* GDR, in the mid- to late 1990s.

Unter Männern resides simultaneously in the related subfields of documentary, gay/queer documentary, and autobiographical or first-person documentary. Some of these films, like *Hollywood to Dollywood* (2011, dir. John Lavin), *Der Kreis* (The Circle, 2014, dir. Stefan Haupt), and *Re:Orientations* (2016, dir. Richard Fung)—and *Unter Männern* can be counted among them—increasingly raise genre questions or make categorization difficult, which is a trend in contemporary filmmaking, as it depends less on, for example, studio backing.[63] This becomes relevant especially when one attempts to chart the trends in a particular field or topic—in this case, the small area of queer German documentary or nonfiction film. John's story certainly stands out among available materials in this subject area. Time after time, the majority of narratives delivered in documentarian texts, both literary and filmic, describe lesbians' and gay men's searches for and usually discoveries of urban networks of likeminded individuals and groups as well as the limited success in locating bars, cafés, and dancing venues in which their social contacts and displays of affection might be welcome (or even ignored).[64] Instead, in these glimpses of John's life we see a small-town gay man, a talented glassblower who also uses his skill to make risqué creations, in a picturesque village; these sequences vividly convey an impression of another queer reality, one faced by countless unnamed individuals and one that could be translated *mutatis mutandis* to other national and cultural contexts.

A further way in which *Unter Männern*'s extraordinariness comes to light is in its availability, or lack thereof, especially if we consider the fate of its twin, the following year's *Out in Ost-Berlin*. Both films had premieres at the Berlinale International Film Festival in the Panorama section.[65] Both films have also had screenings at other international film festivals and have been broadcast on German television. The latter film had the good fortune of finding a North American distributor, an event that can play a key role in determining a film's wider success. *Unter Männern*'s experimentation with the documentary genre and its presentation of the subject matter are arguably queerer in comparison to *Out in Ost-Berlin*, of the two the more conventional film made by a much more experienced filmmaking team. Issues with copyright and distribution have also left the former more difficult to view outside of Europe.

In an annotated filmography, Lynda McAfee observed in 1997 that the realities of distribution, a large aspect of the economics of global cinema, "exclude[] many historical queer documentaries that have fallen out of distribution, international documentaries that do not have a US distributor, and documentaries and home movies that were never picked up for distribution. These harder-to-find documentaries may be found at libraries, archives, public and private film collections, community and art house screenings, and film and video festivals."[66] The volume in which McAfee's contribution appears—one of the few scholarly treatments of queer documentary—focuses on American films and obviously appeared at a very different time for global film distribution (and production) than the present. The internet and easier shareability of digital media have removed some obstacles to the wider viewing of filmic works.[67] Gillett has observed that Hick has repeatedly had difficulty obtaining sufficient funding for his projects, so it is in a way ironic that *Out in Ost-Berlin* is the more conventional in appearance (likely, in part, due to available resources and filmmaker experience) and has, as is clear, been the one of the two I have discussed here to find wider acknowledgment, screening, and distribution.[68]

Conclusion

By the end of *Unter Männern* we have received a set of different reflections on gay GDR history. The protagonists illustrate the truism of the variability of LGBTQ (or any group's) experience. The film shows that this is also the case under a totalitarian system, in various ways repressive and restrictive of its citizens' behavior. These men come from different beginnings and levels of comfort with what they may or may not have seen as a distinguishing part of themselves, namely their sexuality, because of which they were targets of prohibitive power, whether individually or collectively.

Stapel, one of the crucial figures in the history of the East German gay movement, has been reduced from his earlier importance in light of the difficulties and outright prohibition he faced in trying to pursue his chosen vocation as a pastor. Although one can see him occasionally in various media today to give interviews on this subject, including around the twenty-fifth anniversary of the fall of the Berlin Wall, our final view of him in the film is his exit from a church—one of his interview locations in the film—and the closing door.

Although Christian's interviews—including those in which he appears with his friend and fellow interviewee Helwin—and old photos of his illustrate that Christian, who appears in the film's opening overture and whom I mentioned above, the most reticent of the interviewees, was not a loner, he concludes with regret that he was "zu feige" (too cowardly) unable to assert himself more publicly. Christian's interviews, the most uncomfortable in the film for their long silences and his taciturnity, illustrate his struggles with his own tolerance, not to speak of acceptance, of his sexuality. He remained closeted for most of his life, maintained a limited social circle in connection to gayness (including visits to the *Klappen*), and went so far as seeing a psychologist to try to treat and "cure" his homosexuality. For his part, Helwin has a different recollection of the gay experience in the GDR—or perhaps a conflicted or contradictory one. Born in Chile, he has narrated personal history including intense homophobia from his parents (to whom he never came out), a relationship with a teacher, and a certain perceived tolerance on the part of other coworkers and acquaintances. It is not stated clearly when Helwin became friends with Christian, but they have a rapport on camera that makes their pair-interviews entertaining. In one of these, Christian chides Helwin for describing gay life in the GDR as if it were a paradise. Up to then Helwin had stood out among the interviewees in the film for his intriguing refutation of the common assertion that gay life under socialism and totalitarianism was overly difficult.

Artist Jürgen (b. 1932) and hairstylist Frank (b. 1959), both of whom appear in the film's overture mentioned at the start of my essay, also provide insight into different facets of a gay GDR memory. Although Christian was born only two years later, Jürgen is unique for his mentioning the Nazis and the Hitler Youth. He also recounts how he was able to gain a degree of erotic satisfaction by persuading straight male acquaintances to pose nude for him. Frank's experience is unique among the interviewees because of his success in leaving East Germany for Munich, even though he had not originally planned on fleeing the country by staying in the West.

The viewer can gather that John, the interviewee with whom the film ends, has achieved a striking degree of personal acceptance and social integration in his small Thuringian community. He describes the "bunte Truppe" (motley crew) of friends, including other gays, who eventually coalesced after John's coming out. John did come out to his father, who responded that it did not matter to him, if he was a good worker—a perfect, if stereotypical, East German response. The final sequence we see in the film shows John in drag in long shot, in the attire of a *Glasprinzessin*, the annually crowned "glass princess" of the Christmas season, walking through Lauscha waving to passersby, while Puccini's "O mio babbino caro" is heard non-diegetically. As mentioned above, his interview stands out for its highlighting of the rural and urban divide within East German society, especially in the lives of gay individuals. It is also clearly distinct among the men's interviews here for the kind of unabashed integration of the protagonist into his surrounding environment. John is unique among the other interviewees in that he planned to flee the GDR and turned back, unlike another interviewee, hairstylist Frank (b. 1959), who was allowed to travel to the West for a short trip and never returned. John, on the other hand, glimpsed the border crossing but returned, later to come out and find his own measure of success in his rural milieu.

While the film began by using the director's personal biography to connect the interviews to each other and to engage the viewer with the coming recollections of the interviewees, Rösener's role has changed by the end of *Unter Männern*. In one of the final sequences, we see him determinedly bicycling, as before, mimicking *Coming Out*'s Philipp, as the former rides by the Kino International cinema where the film premiered in 1989. This is followed by clips from the premiere of Carow's film as well as short excerpts that seem to point to the communal feeling among many gay East Germans where there were enough to congregate, like in Berlin. Rösener's own story has lost prominence and faded into the background by the end of the film, which, as described above, leaves the viewer with another individual, one who managed to find his way to personal fulfillment—at least as shown by the film—through an integration into what had been earlier a hostile or at least less tolerant environment. In that the film does not make the purely contemporary (i.e., post-GDR) biography the lasting impression of the film, the interviewees' biographical-historical narratives are given a relevance that links them to Germany's present and the situation of gay rights today. Further, the change in emphasis by the end of the film stresses the diversity of experience in this group of interview subjects, creating its own "bunte Truppe," and allowing for the insertion of the viewer's individuality and strangeness in the reception of the film. This does not supersede or overshadow the narrative we have received in the film; on the contrary, it becomes adjunct, like a foreign-language dictionary or glossary, which the reader can use to compare the interviewees' stories and historically contextual and visual display.

The interviews in *Unter Männern* further connect us to the world that *Coming Out* inhabited. As with other similar documentaries—that is, in which interviews comprise the primary material—the diversity or rather the uniqueness of the informants' experiences is one of the structuring unities of the film. History in this case comprises diachronic conceptualizations of coming out, hiding, public and private sex, joy and fear, and often eventual blending in. These mark especially the post-1980s developments in Western gay culture that illustrate generational and geographic differences. In these segments we do see how these men understood and understand themselves, an offering-up of biographical history that provides a complementary counterpoint to the receptive historical discovery of the narrator's persona. *Unter Männern* enacts the being of GDR gayness through a combination of private and public history with a distinct emphasis on the former. This documentary of being "among these men" becomes a monument in Foucault's sense, not just a reference to something that existed, but also what he called "its own volume."[69]

Notes

[1] For helpful feedback on earlier versions of parts of this essay, I gratefully acknowledge input from Katherine Bowers, Ilinca Iuraşcu, Gregory Mackie, and Vin Nardizzi.

[2] See, for example, Paul Cooke, "Ostalgie's Not What It Used to Be: The German Television GDR Craze of 2003," *German Politics & Society* 22, no. 4 (73)

(2004): 134–50; Anthony Enns, "The Politics of *Ostalgie*: Post-Socialist Nostalgia in Recent German Film," *Screen* 48, no. 4 (2007): 475–91; Aline Sierp, "Nostalgia for Times Past: On the Uses and Abuses of the *Ostalgie* Phenomenon in Eastern Germany," *Contemporary European Studies* 2 (2009): 47–60; Daphne Berdahl, *On the Social Life of Postsocialism: Memory, Consumption, Germany*, New Anthropologies of Europe (Bloomington: Indiana University Press, 2010); Claire Hyland, "'Ostalgie Doesn't Fit': Individual Interpretations of and Interaction with *Ostalgie*," in *Remembering and Rethinking the GDR: Multiple Perspectives and Plural Authenticities*, ed. Anna Saunders and Debbie Pinfold (Houndmills, Basingstoke, Hampshire: Palgrave Macmillan, 2013), 101–15.

[3] Elizabeth Freeman, *Time Binds: Queer Temporalities, Queer Histories* (Durham, NC: Duke University Press, 2010), 9–10.

[4] Although the film was co-directed by Ringo Rösener and Markus Stein, I will focus on Rösener's activity in this essay, since he was primarily responsible for the conceptualization of the film as well as the interactive, reflexive nature of the elements I discuss below, while also appearing in the film.

[5] For more on this "personality," see Angela Brock, "Producing the 'Socialist Personality'? Socialisation, Education, and the Emergence of New Patterns of Behaviour," in *Power and Society in the GDR, 1961–1979: The "Normalisation of Rule"?*, ed. Mary Fulbrook (New York: Berghahn Books, 2009), 220–52.

[6] Harry M. Benshoff and Sean Griffin, eds., *Queer Cinema: The Film Reader* (New York: Routledge, 2004), 2.

[7] Barbara Mennel, *Queer Cinema: Schoolgirls, Vampires and Gay Cowboys* (New York: Wallflower, 2012), 1.

[8] Alice A. Kuzniar, *The Queer German Cinema* (Stanford, CA: Stanford University Press, 2000), 5. See B. Ruby Rich, "The New Queer Cinema: Director's Cut," in *New Queer Cinema: The Director's Cut* (Durham, NC: Duke University Press, 2013), 16–32. This is the original version of Rich's essay that first publicly appeared in different form as "A Queer Sensation," *Village Voice*, March 24, 1992, 41–44.

[9] Kuzniar, *The Queer German Cinema*, 5.

[10] Les Wright, "From Outsider to Insider: Queer Politics in German Film, 1970–94," *European Journal of Cultural Studies* 1, no. 1 (1998): 97–98. Among other films, Wright mentions Rosa von Praunheim's *Nicht der Homosexuelle ist pervers, sondern die Situation in der er lebt* (It Is Not the Homosexual Who Is Perverse, but Rather the Situation in Which He Lives, 1971), Ulrike Ottinger's *Madame X—Eine absolute Herrscherin* (Madame X: An Absolute Ruler, 1977), Frank Ripploh's *Taxi zum Klo* (Taxi to the Toilet, 1980), Monika Treut's *Die Jungfrauen Maschine* (Virgin Machine, 1988), and Sönke Wortmann's *Der bewegte Mann* (Maybe, Maybe Not, 1994).

[11] Kuzniar, *The Queer German Cinema*, 15.

[12] Silke Arnold-de Simine, "Crossdressing, Remakes, and National Stereotypes: The Germany-Hollywood Connection," in *A Companion to German Cinema*, ed. Terri Ginsberg and Andrea Mensch (Malden, MA: Blackwell, 2012), 379–404; Robert M. Gillett, "A Documentarist at the Limits of Queer: The Films of Jochen

Hick," in *A Companion to German Cinema*, ed. Terri Ginsberg and Andrea Mensch (Malden, MA: Blackwell, 2012), 318–40.

[13] Feng-Mei Heberer, "How Does It Feel to Be Foreign? Negotiating German Belonging and Transnational Asianness in Experimental Video," in *The Autobiographical Turn in Germanophone Documentary and Experimental Film*, ed. Robin Curtis and Angelica Fenner (Rochester, NY: Camden House, 2014), 111–36.

[14] Gillett, "Documentarist," 318.

[15] Ibid., 319.

[16] See esp. Ibid., 319–20.

[17] Nora M. Alter, *Projecting History: German Nonfiction Cinema, 1967–2000* (Ann Arbor: University of Michigan Press, 2002). On Ottinger, see esp. 157–78. Alter also refers the reader to Kuzniar's book on queer cinema for more on "gender studies" (2n4).

[18] B. Ruby Rich, "Queering the Biopic Documentary," in *New Queer Cinema: The Director's Cut* (Durham, NC: Duke University Press, 2013), 123–29. Rich's essay was originally published in 1997.

[19] John Grierson, "The First Principles of Documentary," in *Grierson on Documentary*, ed. Forsyth Hardy (London: Faber, 1966), 147.

[20] Erik Barnouw, *Documentary: A History of the Non-Fiction Film*, 2nd ed. (New York: Oxford University Press, 1993), 297; see also Bill Nichols, *Blurred Boundaries: Questions of Meaning in Contemporary Culture* (Bloomington: Indiana University Press, 1994), 95.

[21] Bill Nichols, *Representing Reality: Issues and Concepts in Documentary* (Bloomington, IN: Indiana University Press, 1991), 32–75; Nichols, *Blurred Boundaries*, 92–106.

[22] Nichols, *Representing Reality*, 3–4.

[23] Bruzzi argues that especially recent documentaries, in which the intervention or even appearance of the filmmaker has become more common, demonstrate that the *document* in the *documentary* is crucially important. See, for example, Frederik Dhaenens, "Queer Cuttings on YouTube: Re-Editing Soap Operas as a Form of Fan-Produced Queer Resistance," *European Journal of Cultural Studies* 15, no. 4 (August 1, 2012): 442–56. On a recent integration of this form of self-broadcasting, transgender video diaries, into a feature film, see Kyle Frackman, "The Reality of the Body: Transgender, Transsexuality, and Truth in *Romeos*," *Colloquia Germanica* 46, no. 1 (2013): 64–87.

[24] Stella Bruzzi, *New Documentary: A Critical Introduction*, 2nd ed. (Abingdon: Routledge, 2006), 198.

[25] Ibid., 11.

[26] See, e.g., ibid., 13, 186.

[27] Elizabeth Cowie, *Recording Reality, Desiring the Real* (Minneapolis: University of Minnesota Press, 2011), 2.

[28] Sabine Hake, *German National Cinema*, 2nd ed. (London: Routledge, 2002), 197–98.

[29] Alisa Lebow, *First Person Jewish* (Minneapolis: University of Minnesota Press, 2008), xi.

[30] Robin Curtis and Angelica Fenner, "Introduction," in *The Autobiographical Turn in Germanophone Documentary and Experimental Film*, ed. Robin Curtis and Angelica Fenner (Rochester, NY: Camden House, 2014), 3.

[31] Ibid., 10; Bruzzi, *New Documentary*, 15.

[32] Nichols, *Blurred Boundaries*, 96–97.

[33] Bruzzi, *New Documentary*, 185–86.

[34] When thinking of abrasive potential, one can contrast these more recent works with ones that Rich wrote about earlier, works with "few aesthetic or narrative strategies in common, but what they seemed to share was an attitude. [Rich] found them 'irreverent' and 'energetic'." Michele Aaron, "New Queer Cinema: An Introduction," in *New Queer Cinema: A Critical Reader*, ed. Michele Aaron (New Brunswick, NJ: Rutgers University Press, 2004), 3.

[35] Bruzzi, *New Documentary*, 248.

[36] Michael Renov, "Introduction: The Truth about Non-Fiction," in *Theorizing Documentary*, ed. Michael Renov (NY: Routledge, 1993), 3.

[37] Because of space constraints for this essay, I cannot offer a satisfying contextualization of these German documentaries within the field of also non-German documentary films beyond the text in this section. For more information on documentary film, including outside of the German-language context, the reader is directed to the following, for example: Alter, *Projecting History*, Thomas Austin and Wilma De Jong, eds., *Rethinking Documentary: New Perspectives, New Practices* (NY: McGraw-Hill/Open University Press, 2008); Jim Lane, *The Autobiographical Documentary in America* (Madison: University of Wisconsin Press, 2002); Brian Winston, *Claiming the Real: The Griersonian Documentary and Its Legitimations* (London: British Film Institute, 1995); Brian Winston, *Claiming the Real II: Documentary: Grierson and Beyond* (London, New York: Palgrave Macmillan/British Film Institute, 2008).

[38] Even this brief list clearly favors Anglophone film, especially what has been produced in the United States. It is true that the United States has produced the lion's share of films that would fall into the relevant genre and topic. Other non-Anglophone or non-US-focused films of this type include *Woubi Chéri* (Darling Woubi, 1998, dir. Lauren Bocahut and Philip Brooks), *Dangerous Living: Coming Out in the Developing World* (2003, dir. John Scagliotti), *Männer, Helden, schwule Nazis* (Men, Heroes, Gay Nazis, 2005, dir. Rosa von Praunheim), *Tintenfischalarm* (Octopus Alarm, 2006, dir. Elisabeth Scharang), *A Jihad for Love* (2007, dir. Parvez Sharma), *East/West—Sex & Politics* (2008, dir. Jochen Hick), *Tongzhi in Love* (2008, dir. Ruby Yang), *Die Jungs vom Bahnhof-Zoo* (Rent Boys, 2011, dir. Rosa von Praunheim), *Les Invisibles* (The Invisible Ones, 2012, dir. Sébastien Lifshitz), *Call Me Kuchu* (2012, dir. Malika Zouhali-Worrall and Katherine Fairfax Wright), and *Der Kreis* (The Circle, 2014, dir. Stefan Haupt).

[39] Bruzzi, *New Documentary*, 15; see Michel Foucault, *The Archaeology of Knowledge*, trans. A. M. Sheridan Smith (New York: Vintage, 2010), esp. 206–7.

[40] Harry M. Benshoff and Sean Griffin, *Queer Images: A History of Gay and Lesbian Film in America* (Lanham, MD: Rowman & Littlefield, 2006), 214. They also list a number of selected queer documentaries with some annotation (276–77). A recent film that blends some of these genre characteristics is the Swiss *Der Kreis* (*The Circle*, 2014, dir. Stefan Haupt), a docudrama with third- and first-person narrative elements in interviews as well as re-enacted and fictional scenes. For more on *Der Kreis* and its approach to docudrama, see Kyle Frackman, "To Be Gay in 1950s Zurich," *kultur360*, May 27, 2016, http://www.kultur360.com/to-be-gay-in-1950s-zurich/.

[41] Mennel, *Queer Cinema*, 51; see also Thomas Waugh, *The Fruit Machine Twenty Years of Writings on Queer Cinema* (Durham, NC: Duke University Press, 2000).

[42] Thomas Waugh, "Walking on Tippy Toes: Lesbian and Gay Liberation Documentary of the Post-Stonewall Period 1969–1984," in *The Fruit Machine: Twenty Years of Writings on Queer Cinema* (Durham, NC: Duke University Press, 2000), 246–71; Mennel, *Queer Cinema*, 51; Benshoff and Griffin, *Queer Images*. Much of what arose out of these "events" or periods, it should be noted, evinced a male-centric attention that many will have recognized.

[43] For example, Richard Dyer, *Now You See It: Studies on Lesbian and Gay Film*, 2nd ed. (London: Routledge, 2003), 229; Emanuel Levy, *Cinema of Outsiders: The Rise of American Independent Film* (NY: New York University Press, 1999), 444.

[44] Levy, *Cinema of Outsiders*, 447.

[45] This could also partly have to do with changing funding structures for filmic work, depending as they more frequently do at present on the collaboration with television studios. Past queer films have received funding from German public television; one notable example is Rosa von Praunheim's *Nicht der Homosexuelle*. The film's funders and broadcasters changed because of controversies surrounding the project, but it was variously supported by ARD and the Cologne station WDR. See Kuzniar, *The Queer German Cinema*, 93–94.

[46] Hick's other films include feature films *Via Appia* (1990) and *No One Sleeps* (2000) and documentaries *Menmaniacs—The Legacy of Leather* (1995), *Sex/Life in L.A.* (1998), and *Cycles of Porn: Sex/Life in L.A. Part 2* (2005).

[47] Klaus Kreimeier, "Dokumentarfilm, 1892–2005," in *Geschichte des deutschen Films*, ed. Wolfgang Jacobsen, Anton Kaes, and Hans Helmut Prinzler, 2nd ed. (Stuttgart: J. B. Metzler, 2004), 432.

[48] Ringo Rösener to Author, "Interviewfragen!," May 13, 2014.

[49] The respective enforcement of §175 in the FRG and GDR differed, in that there were more arrests and public activities in the FRG than in the GDR. Josie McLellan has called the "story of East German homosexuality . . . one of failed liberalisation" (114), since the eventual decriminalization did not have the effect of increased tolerance; instead, it led to queer invisibility (118). See Josie McLellan, *Love in the Time of Communism: Intimacy and Sexuality in the GDR* (Cambridge: Cambridge University Press, 2011), 114–18; Jennifer V. Evans, "Decriminalization, Seduction, and 'Unnatural Desire' in East Germany," *Feminist Studies* 36, no. 3 (2010): 553–77; W. Jake Newsome, "Homosexuals after the Holocaust:

Sexual Citizenship and the Politics of Memory in Germany and the United States, 1945–2008" (PhD Dissertation, University at Buffalo, State University of New York, 2016), 68. For GDR enforcement statistics up to 1959 (others have not been published), see Klaus Berdl and Vera Kruber, "Zur Statistik der Strafverfolgung homosexueller Männer in der SBZ und DDR bis 1959," *Invertito—Jahrbuch für die Geschichte der Homosexualitäten*, no. 12 (2010): 58–124.

[50] There is an additional interview with Jürgen Lemke (b. 1943), a psychotherapist who published an important contribution to (East German) so-called *Protokolliteratur* (transcript literature), a blend of authentic interviews and authorial reshaping into novel-like prose. See Jürgen Lemke, *Ganz normal anders: Auskünfte schwuler Männer* (Berlin: Aufbau-Verlag, 1989). I do not count Lemke as one of the protagonists, because of the different style in which he is depicted, including the use of on-screen text to identify him, which does not occur for the other interviewees.

[51] See Bert Thinius, "Vom grauen Versteck ins bunte Ghetto: Ansichten zur Geschichte ostdeutscher Schwuler," in *Schwuler Osten: Homosexuelle Männer in der DDR*, by Kurt Starke (Berlin: Ch. Links Verlag, 1994), 11–90. *Coming Out* was the GDR's first feature film showcasing homosexuality. In the year prior (1988), the GDR's first and only documentary, *Die andere Liebe* (The Other Love), a short film directed by Helmut Kißling and Axel Otten, premiered in theaters and circulation. For more on *Die andere Liebe*, see Kyle Frackman, "Shame and Love: East German Homosexuality Goes to the Movies," in *Gender and Sexuality in East German Film: Intimacy and Alienation*, ed. Kyle Frackman and Faye Stewart (Rochester, NY: Camden House, 2018), 225–48.

[52] Waugh, "Walking on Tippy Toes," 254.

[53] Ibid.

[54] Andrey Borzenko, "Brotherly Love: 25 Years On, the Artist Behind the Iconic Berlin Wall Mural Tells His Story," *The Calvert Journal*, November 11, 2014, http://calvertjournal.com/articles/show/3356/Dmitri-Vrubel-Berlin-Wall-Brezhnev-Honecker-Kiss. The work was originally painted in 1990 and then repainted in 2009 after the city's erasure of it and much of the other art on the remaining Wall segments in order to save the remnants themselves from the twenty years of covering graffiti, environmental pollution, and deterioration.

[55] The photo does not often appear in scholarly discussions, though it does show up in media treatments of the Wall, as it did in articles surrounding the twenty-fifth anniversary of the fall of the Wall or reports about the 2009 repaintings, including in one piece on the National Public Radio website which found it necessary to call the action in the mural a seemingly alleged "'kiss'." See, e.g., Irene Noguchi, "Historic Art, Luxury Apartments Battle Over Berlin's Famous Wall," *NPR.org*, accessed October 9, 2015, http://www.npr.org/sections/parallels/2015/10/03/445583612/historic-art-luxury-apartments-battle-over-berlins-famous-wall. The painting came back into public discourse because of a 2016 Lithuanian homage to the painting by artist Mindaugas Bonanu in which Russian President Vladimir Putin and US President Donald Trump are in the positions of Brezhnev and Honecker, respectively.

[56] Bruzzi, *New Documentary*, 197.

[57] On the use of photographs, including in digital media, as historical evidence, see Jennifer Tucker, "Entwined Practices: Engagements with Photography in Historical Inquiry," *History and Theory* 48, no. 4 (December 1, 2009): 1–8 and its special issue.

[58] For many today it is a surprising aspect of the development of East German gay rights that it blossomed under the umbrella of the Lutheran Church—an association that made the secularist GDR government doubly suspicious of the potential discord that the gay activists would represent. For more on this, see, e.g., Kurt Starke and Eduard Stapel, "Vom Arbeitskreis 'Homosexualität' der Evangelischen Studentengemeinde in Leipzig zum Schwulenverband in Deutschland: Interview von Kurt Starke mit Eduard Stapel am 19. April 1994," in *Schwuler Osten: Homosexuelle Männer in der DDR*, by Kurt Starke (Berlin: Ch. Links Verlag, 1994), 91–110; and Bert Thinius, "Erfahrungen schwuler Männer in der DDR und in Deutschland Ost," in *Homosexualität in der DDR: Materialien und Meinungen*, ed. Wolfram Setz (Hamburg: Männerschwarm, 2006), 37–44.

[59] Olaf Brühl, "Sozialistisch und schwul: Eine subjektive Chronologie," in *Homosexualität in der DDR: Materialien und Meinungen*, ed. Wolfram Setz (Hamburg: Männerschwarm, 2006), 121–25.

[60] Eduard Stapel, *Warme Brüder gegen Kalte Krieger: Schwulenbewegung in der DDR im Visier der Staatssicherheit* (Magdeburg: Landesbeauftragte für die Unterlagen des Staatssicherheitsdienstes der ehemaligen DDR Sachsen-Anhalt, 1999), 99.

[61] For more information on the Stasi and their methods, see Paul Betts, *Within Walls: Private Life in the German Democratic Republic* (Oxford: Oxford University Press, 2010); Mike Dennis, *The Stasi: Myth and Reality* (Harlow: Longman, 2003); Jens Gieseke, *Die Stasi: 1945–1990*, 3rd ed. (Munich: Pantheon, 2011); and Elisabeth Pfister, *Unternehmen Romeo: die Liebeskommandos der Stasi* (Berlin: Aufbau-Verlag, 1999).

[62] On considerations of the strange and aberrant, see Jennifer V. Evans, "Introduction: Why Queer German History?," *German History* 34, no. 3 (2016): esp. 371–72 and its special issue on queer German history.

[63] For a skilled discussion of genre questions and their relation to queerness, see Richard Dyer, "Queer Noir," in *Queer Cinema: The Film Reader*, ed. Harry M. Benshoff and Sean Griffin (New York: Routledge, 2004), 89–104.

[64] One late-GDR exception is the aforementioned collection of interviews: Lemke, *Ganz normal anders: Auskünfte schwuler Männer*. A volume of interviews with lesbians appeared after the *Wende*: Kerstin Gutsche, *Ich ahnungsloser Engel: Lesbenprotokolle* (Berlin: Reiher, 1991). While the rural/urban divide is not unique or new to discussions of queer cultural production more broadly, including in films like Jochen Hick's *Ich kenn keinen—Allein unter Heteros* (2003), this depiction in *Unter Männern* of the GDR divide is remarkable, because nearly all previous depictions of East German LGBTQ life focus on the metropolis. An exception is the 1999 short documentary piece "Ein homosexuelles Pärchen in Cottbus," which aired on the ZDF program *Blickpunkt*.

[65] Originally the "Info-Schau," Panorama is a part of the Berlinale program each year showcasing mainly new (and usually singular) independent films. Since 1992,

the section's curator is Wieland Speck, a German director and actor who himself has a place in the history of queer film related to the GDR. Speck directed *Westler* (1985), a feature film about two gay men, one from East Berlin and one from West Berlin, who fall in love. The outdoor sequences in East Berlin were shot surreptitiously without official permission.

[66] Lynda McAfee, "Film and Videography," in *Between the Sheets, In the Streets: Queer, Lesbian, Gay Documentary*, ed. Chris Holmlund and Cynthia Fuchs (Minneapolis: University of Minnesota Press, 1997), 242. For more on (queer) film distribution, including in film festivals, see Michael Barrett et al., "Queer Film and Video Festival Forum, Take One: Curators Speak Out," *GLQ: A Journal of Lesbian and Gay Studies* 11, no. 4 (2005): 579–603; Tim Bergfelder, "National, Transnational or Supranational Cinema? Rethinking European Film Studies," *Media, Culture & Society* 27, no. 3 (May 1, 2005): 315–31; and Randall Halle, *The Europeanization of Cinema: Interzones and Imaginative Communities* (Urbana: University of Illinois Press, 2014).

[67] For more on methods, forms, and implications of nonfiction filmmaking in recent years with newer media, see Maxine Baker, *Documentary in the Digital Age* (Burlington, MA: Focal Press, 2006).

[68] Gillett, "Documentarist," 320.

[69] Foucault, *Archaeology*, 139.

Part II.

Queering the Other

The Culture of Faces: Reading Physiognomical Relations in Thomas Mann's *Der Tod in Venedig*

John L. Plews, Saint Mary's University

THIS CHAPTER TRACES the lesson for cultural types implied in the relationship between the descriptions of the faces observed in Thomas Mann's *Der Tod in Venedig* (1912; Death in Venice, 1928) and the observers' behavior and cultural standing.[1] Mann's novella begins with Gustav von Aschenbach, a Munich-based author, breaking from his work by taking a late-afternoon stroll in the English Garden. While waiting for the streetcar home, he is distracted by the appearance of a man who stands in the portico of the mortuary chapel of the Northern Cemetery, facing into the sun. Caught staring at the unexpected figure, Aschenbach looks away, senses a newfound desire to travel, and decides to postpone his book project by taking a holiday on the Mediterranean in order to put the spark back into his life and work. That evening, instead of writing, Aschenbach looks over maps and timetables. This sudden about-face is remarkable. The journey—through nature, the bustling city, reading the Greek crosses and religious inscriptions on the chapel's Byzantine facade—that would return Aschenbach to cultural production is entirely rerouted because of a desire awakened by encountering a man whom, after reflecting upon his appearance, Aschenbach chooses to avoid. Something in Aschenbach's appreciation of the stranger both disturbs him and causes him to reset his ways. This man is not the only such individual whom Aschenbach encounters and estimates during the novella. On his holiday in Istria and Venice, several men intrude uninvited into Aschenbach's world and, for the most part, cause him discomfort. In each case, Aschenbach reacts, sets his course again, and makes strategic decisions; and, in one instance, he is moved to write again. He always knows how to respond. He either avoids or pursues the figures based on his physiognomical understanding of them. In each case, concurrent facial descriptions and character assessments pave the way for Aschenbach's response. In this way, faces in *Der Tod in Venedig*—their physiognomical reception—motivate Aschenbach's attempt to retrieve and reinvigorate his cultural creativity.

Physiognomy matters in *Der Tod in Venedig*. In addition to the frequency of verbs of seeing and looking, there is a range of common to more technical words denoting "appearance" or the "face."[2] Descriptions draw on further particulars—such as the shape of the nose or the color of the hair—that help to appraise the face positively or negatively. The significance of such descriptions comes to the fore when the narrator explains Aschenbach's preoccupation with the human form by evoking the same theocritical convictions underlying Johann Caspar Lavater's extensive physiognomical project in the late eighteenth century:[3]

> Standbild und Spiegel! Seine [Aschenbachs] Augen umfaßten die edle Gestalt dort am Rande des Blauen, und in aufschwärmendem Entzücken glaubte er mit diesem Blick das Schöne selbst zu begreifen, *die Form als Gottesgedanken, die eine und reine Vollkommenheit, die im Geiste lebt und von der ein menschliches Abbild und Gleichnis hier leicht und hold zur Anbetung aufgerichtet war . . . So auch bediente der Gott sich, um uns das Geistige sichtbar zu machen, gern der Gestalt und Farbe menschlicher Jugend*, die er zum Werkzeug der Erinnerung mit allem Abglanz der Schönheit schmückte und bei deren Anblick wir dann wohl in Schmerz und Hoffnung entbrannten. (553–54; my emphasis)

> [Mirror and image! His [Aschenbach's] eyes took in the proud bearing of that figure there at the blue water's edge; with an outburst of rapture he told himself that what he saw was beauty's very essence; *form as divine thought*, the single and pure *perfection which resides in the mind, of which an image and likeness, rare and holy, was here raised up for adoration . . . so, too, the god, in order to make visible the spirit, avails himself of the forms and colours of human youth*, gilding it with all imaginable beauty that it may serve memory as a tool, the very sight of which then sets us afire with pain and longing.][4]

Clearly, it is appropriate in the world of this narrative to allude to the physical appearance of the face for meaningful knowledge. But the allusion to Lavater further implies that the narrative taps into a well-established discourse that assumes the preordination of human character and colludes with existing social hierarchies. In the first physiognomical portrait, that of the man "im Portikus, oberhalb der beiden apokalyptischen Tiere, welche die Freitreppe bewachen, . . . dessen nicht ganz gewöhnliche Erscheinung seinen [Aschenbachs] Gedanken eine völlig andere Richtung gab" (502; in the portico, above the two apocalyptic beasts that guarded the staircase, and something not quite usual in this man's appearance gave his thoughts a fresh turn: 8), the narrator quickly itemizes the portico-figure's physical and sartorial features to substantiate his unusualness (502–3). According to Lavaterian physiognomy, the nature of the "slightly unusual-looking" man in the portico must be known since he possesses particular structural features that allow the observer to classify him because, as a whole, they obtain meaning from a prior understanding of that individual's social position or identity in relation to the part of society to which the observer belongs. In the case of the unusual-looking portico-man, the elements of his appearance—his beardlessness, snub nose, red hair, fair complexion, exotic hat, pale eyes, long teeth—are generally those of someone who is, to Aschenbach, recognizably "durchaus nicht bajuwarischen Schlages" (502; [absolutely] not Bavarian: 8), "from far away," and thus *an itinerant non-Bavarian*. In the first sentence of the novel the narrator mentions the "gefahrdrohende Miene" (501; a menace: 7—literally, *a menacing face*) of the political climate in Europe, a direct allusion to the 1911 Agadir Incident between Germany and France. This passing remark is sufficient to provide the social function of the unusual figure's identity as an *itinerant foreigner*.[5] From the perspective of Aschenbach's culture, a foreigner is regarded as someone who *poses a danger or threat to national or personal interests*. This identity-function predicates the facial and bodily features of the portico-man, which in turn supply the substance of his nature. Sure enough, the concept of *danger* is readily fused with the unusual appearance of the portico-man. He is cast between "apocalyptic beasts." Like a mystical creature himself, he is at once red, speckled, milky, and colorless. Like some predator, he is armed with an iron point that stabs the ground and with fang-like teeth bared by retracted lips. His hat, stick, and position upon a threshold are reminiscent of Hermes the summoner of souls. Erich Heller believes the figure resembles "Dürer's image of Death."[6] The danger in confronting the portico-man becomes apparent when he returns Aschenbach's glances in a manner that is "so kriegerisch, so gerade ins Auge hinein, so offenkundig gesonnen, die Sache aus Äußerste zu treiben und den Blick des andern zum Abzug zu zwingen" (503; so directly, with such hostility, such plain intent to force the withdrawal of the other's eyes: 9). By reading the features of the portico-man as agreeing with an identity-function, Aschenbach will suppose to know him: the man bears the sign of the unusual and exotic appearance and is thus seen to be "domineering," "bold," "wild"—that is, aggressive and threatening by nature.

The portico-man is not the only "unusual" person whom Aschenbach observes. The author-figure encounters a series of characters—the old sailor, the man with a goatee, the old dandy clerk, the gondolier, the hotel manager, the elevator boy, the hotel barber, a beggar, an antiques dealer, the buffo-baritone guitarist, and the travel agent—whose appearances, through a variety of re-occurring features and gestures, are analogous with the first figure and each other.[7] Dorrit Cohn believes these figures are meaningful "by way of their serial *re*appearances," and several critics see them as interchangeable.[8] Just as with the portico-man's outward appearance, the peripheral figures' external features are regarded as a measure of the perceived social function of their respective identities. Since their appearances—their tilted hats, snub noses, red hair, pale and beardless or only half-bearded faces, slight builds, etc.—resemble the portico-man's, their identities surely have something in common with his. The old sailor, the man with the goatee, and the old dandy clerk are ethnic Italians from Austrian-administered Istria; and the dandy clerk prattles in French. The gondolier is "durchaus nicht italienischen Schlages" (525; [absolutely] of non-Italian stock: 26). The hotel manager wears French-styled clothes. The elevator boy is a French-speaking Swiss. The hotel barber becomes Aschenbach's German conversation partner since especially the Germans are leaving the resort. The baritone guitarist is "nicht venezianischen Schlages" and more likely Neapolitan (573; scarcely a Venetian type: 67). Finally, the travel agent is British. Like the portico-man, the peripheral figures are all foreign nationals to Aschenbach and, since they are all implicated in travel and in some way foreign to their current and immediate environment, they can be considered *itinerant foreigners*.

As we know from the discussion of the portico-man in the context of Lavaterian physiognomy, it is the qualitative affect of the function of his identity—from Aschenbach's cultural perspective—as an *itinerant foreigner*, that is, to pose a danger, that substantiates the unusual man's appearance that supposedly reveals his nature. In the same way, the dangers associated with foreignness and itinerancy also determine the physiognomical dimensions of the other unusual figures that affirm their natures. The international crisis in Agadir, evoked at the onset of the novel and instrumental in establishing the threatening function of the first foreigner encountered, is once again defining in regard to the character of the threat posed by the peripheral aliens. This incident, in addition to appearing aggressive, was all about deception. On July 1, 1911, the Germans sent the gunboat *Panther* to the Moroccan port of Agadir ostensibly to protect German nationals and commercial interests during a local disturbance. However, the real intention was to counteract what Germany regarded as French colonial expansionism in Morocco. Essentially, Germany was playing a game of military bluff in order to force a renegotiation of an earlier convention on Morocco in which German interests in northwest Africa had remained unsatisfied, which was also the case after the second incident. A similar atmosphere of compulsive deception has taken hold of affairs in Aschenbach's foreign destination of Venice. For instance, after Aschenbach encounters the antiques dealer who invited the passer-by to stop in order "ihn zu betrügen" (567; [that he] be duped: 63) the narrator remarks that "Das war Venedig, die schmeichlerische und verdächtige Schöne,—diese Stadt . . . halb Fremdenfalle" and that Aschenbach remembered "daß die Stadt krank sei und es aus Gewinnsucht verheimliche" (567; Yes, this was Venice, this the fair frailty that fawned and that betrayed . . . half snare; that the city sickened and hid its sickness for love of gain: 63).

The apparent hostility and trickery that comprise the presumed dangerous function of itinerant foreigners are factored into the peripheral figures' appearances. The method used goes back to Polemo and today is called "diminution."[9] The itinerant foreigners are hunchbacked and showy caprine, feline, or anuran ("buffo" coming from "bufo" meaning toad, 571) creatures that blabber and bleat or caw and make the mocking noises of a bird ("Pechvogel," literally meaning "bird of misfortune," 577).[10] They are physically crooked and off-balance with pointing digits and jerky expressions and movements. They smolder, glow red, and give off foul odors. They are pieced together artificially, made over, and dyed. They are more at home in the circus (517), on the comical stage (518, 571, 573), or among criminals, swindlers, and pimps (526, 567, 573). Especially the old sailor, the man with the goatee, and the gondolier are Charonic.[11] By reading the peripheral figures' appearances as animalistic, asymmetric, excessive, phoney, and melodramatic or unlawful, that is, concurring with their identity-function as foreign itinerants, Aschenbach knows them all to be "threatening" and "suspicious" by nature.[12]

The physiognomies that serve the assumed natures of the men Aschenbach observes also make the protagonist's reactions self-explanatory. Aschenbach reacts distinctly and consistently to the negative types he observes and defines. For example, he initially undertakes a "halb-zerstreute[ ], halb-inquisitive[ ] Musterung" (503; inquisitive and tactless [gaze]: 9) of the portico-man, but when the protagonist realizes that the unusual and threatening figure is returning his glances, he feels "peinlich berührt, sich abwandte . . . [entschied sich], des Menschen nicht weiter achtzugeben . . . und den Blick am Boden . . . gefesselt stehen blieb" (503–4; an unpleasant twinge, and turn[ed] his back . . . hastily resolv[ed] to give the man no further heed . . . rooted to the spot, his eyes on the ground: 9). After daydreaming, he "wich das Gesicht" ([wiped his face]— omitted by Lowe-Porter) and walks on "mit einem Kopfschütteln" (504; shaking his head: 10), but later checks for the man in spite of deciding earlier not to do so (507). Similarly, Aschenbach shudders (519) and his brow darkens (522) at the sight of the deceptive dandy clerk, he "bedeckte seine Stirn mit der Hand und schloß die Augen" (519: put his hand to his brow, he covered his eyes: 22), hallucinates about the figure in his sleep (520), feels lightheaded (522), and later tries to evade the man's drunken farewells (523). Aschenbach turns to face the gondolier only when he is obliged to address him (524). Otherwise he feels as if in a trance and keeps his back to the unlawful character (526). The author-figure is so unsettled by the encounters with the old dandy and the gondolier that as soon as he is alone in his hotel room he "badete sein Gesicht" (529: washed [his face]: 30). The overbearing baritone guitarist causes

Aschenbach to sit still with "einem fix gewordenen und schon schmerzenden Lächeln" (571; with his face set in a fixed and painful smile: 66) and "aufgerichtet wie zum Versuche der Abwehr oder der Flucht" (576; poised [as if preparing to defend himself or] for flight: 69), and again to feel as if caught in a spell (576). When he approaches the travel agent, he does so "mit der Miene des mißtrauischen Fremden" (577; posing as the suspicious foreigner: 70), and, after receiving the man's news, has "einen furchtbaren Traum" (582ff.; a fearful dream: 74). In sum, Aschenbach is disturbed or disgusted by the object of his gaze, makes little or no effort to hide this, and yet tries to avoid the other's attentions by averting his own glances.

Aschenbach's reactions show that he first takes a position in the world of this novella in direct opposition to those he defines as unusual, foreign, and threatening. His *undisguised disapproval*, cleansing himself after contact, and shutting himself off signal a distance from the threatening itinerant foreigners that prevents the knowledge of their appearances from reflecting on him in any way. This is important since—like the gunboat *Panther* off the Moroccan coast—Aschenbach in his Venetian setting is also itinerant and foreign. But, apparently, he is not one of them, and a man in his position should not consort with them or consider the threat they pose to be one he can confront, although, as the dreams and tiger(/panther?)-imagery testify, that sense of danger triggered by encountering strangers also stirs in his own subconscious. Thus, the first basic component of the physiognomical negotiation of the author-figure's cultural standing is establishing the necessary physical evidence that enables him to locate and avoid the unusual and the dangerous.

* * *

Not all the figures encountered by Aschenbach are shown to be negative in character. His first observation of Tadzio—the figure at the center of the Lavater-like reflection on the divine use of the human form—when compared to the peripheral figures, leaves an almost entirely favorable impression of the Polish lad. The initial description of "ein[em] langhaarige[n] Knabe[n] von vielleicht vierzehn Jahren" (529; a long-haired boy of about fourteen years: 30) typifies physiognomical procedures in that it begins with an itemization and gradually becomes more creative.[13] Repeatedly, Tadzio is likened to or referred to as some figure or other from classical culture (see below). In sum, Tadzio possesses a "wahrhaft gottähnliche Schönheit" (534; [truly] godlike beauty: 34) or "ein gottgleiches Antlitz, ein[en] vollkommene[n] Leib" (554; a godlike face or a form which is a good image of beauty: 52); he is "der schöne Knabe" (537; the lovely boy: 36), a "holde[ ] Erscheinung" (551; lovely apparition: 48) and "teure[ ] Erscheinung" (562; dear form: 58), and an "edle Gestalt" (553; the proud bearing of that figure (50)—literally *noble figure*).

As with determining the negative character of the peripheral figures, physiognomy holds that Tadzio's positive nature is ready for Aschenbach to decode in his facial features. External appearances are seen to concur with the function of identity as it is preconceived by that part of society represented by the observer, thus enabling the individual to be classified and the knowledge of their nature to be substantiated. Tadzio enjoys a particular status among the holidaymakers observed by Aschenbach that predicates his face and body in a way that allows him to be known apart from the other children and characters in the novella. His white skin, blond hair, straight nose, child's hands, delicate figure, relaxed pose, gray eyes, slender legs, and uneven teeth broadly constitute an appearance that a Wilhelminian German such as Aschenbach recognizes as belonging to the fourteen-year-old son of a Polish woman who could very well be married to a German senior official (531), and thus *an adolescent* among children, *a son* among daughters, and a *Germanized* Pole[14] among vacationing American, Russian, English, German, French, Polish, and other Slavic and Balkan people (529, 536, 538). Since Tadzio is his parents' favorite (531), popular among the other children at the beach, from whom he receives kisses of allegiance (539), frowns at his Russian foes (537), and testifies to divine inspiration, the function of the *part-German male adolescent* from Aschenbach's perspective is surely to serve as *darling, example, and little chieftain.* Certainly, the sense of *favorite, model, and leader* is transparent in Tadzio's appearance. He is made of such sweet or precious and regal material as honey, marble, ivory, and gold. He is the monumental stuff of sculpture and modernity's inheritance incarnate of ancient culture. By reading his features as agreeing with an identity-function, Aschenbach or the narrator may arrange the boy as differentiated from the "gutmütig-häßliche[n]" Russian children (536; ugly but good-natured: 36) and know him to be more than that. Tadzio the beautiful little chieftain bears the sign of the "perfect," "godlike," and "noble" face and is thus seen to be "graceful," "unique," "lovely," and "spoilt" by nature.

Aschenbach's reactions to Tadzio repeat and contrast the protagonist's reception of the other males encountered. The same physiognomy that accords Tadzio's positive nature provides the reason why Aschenbach should—in this case—pursue the boy. Early in the author-figure's perception of and encounters with the boy, the narrator labels Aschenbach's response to the fourteen-year-old as composed of "jener fachmännisch kühlen Billigung, in welche Künstler zuweilen einem Meisterwerk gegenüber ihr Entzücken, ihre Hingerissenheit kleiden" (535; the patronizing air of the connoisseur to hide, as artists will, their ravishment over a masterpiece: 35). By likening Aschenbach's response to Tadzio to the appreciative relation between an artist and a great painting the narrator considers the author-figure's deliberations on the boy in terms of a well-rehearsed dynamic that benefits the observer. Just as the artist uses the painting as the object of his approval to demonstrate his specialized ability to recognize the cultural value of the painting and thus also assert his own professional and symbolic superiority as someone entitled to pass such judgments, so Aschenbach's appraisal of Tadzio's ideal exterior indicates the comparative professional rigor of physiognomical evaluation and draws attention to his expertise in such matters. More specifically, Susan von Rohr Scaff regards such behavior as part of Aschenbach's adherence to Platonic principles, for "[b]y professing his perception of essential loveliness through Tadzio . . . Aschenbach elevates himself to one of the higher stages of Platonic comprehension."[15]

The narrator's definition of Aschenbach's appreciation of Tadzio also reveals the fact that artists and physiognomists use the ways of their profession—that is, the advantage of the authority garnered from the apparent ability of knowing "the likeness of spiritual perfection" when they see it— to disguise the pleasure they have in mere looking, a pleasure that is best concealed for the sake of professionalism. Aschenbach draws on a similar sense of social decorum when he notices Tadzio's hate for the Russians on the boy's darkening brow (537)—reminiscent of the protagonist's reaction to the old dandy. Aschenbach responds by turning away due to "Eine[r] Art Zartgefühl oder Erschrockenheit, etwas wie Achtung und Scham," although he is "erheitert und erschüttert . . . beglückt" (537; A feeling of delicacy, a qualm, almost like a sense of shame . . . moved and exhilarated . . . delighted: 37). Aschenbach pursues Tadzio, yet when wanting to touch and speak to the boy (in French like the old dandy), he fears becoming conspicuous and "versagt, verzichtet und geht gesenkten Hauptes vorüber" (557; gave up, abandoned his plan, and passed him with bent head: 54). The narrator explains this behavior by referring to the "Wesen und Gepräge" required of a professional artist, that is, to "die tiefe Instinktverschmelzung von Zucht und Zügellosigkeit" (557; the puzzle . . . that mingling of discipline and licence: 54). In line with the hotel management and Venice city administration, Aschenbach keeps up an appearance that masks excitement with resignation (547), that in Tadzio's presence is "ernst[ ]" (539; grave and serious: 38), "tiefernst" (561; profoundly serious: 57), and "gebildet[] und würdevoll[]" (561: dignified and cultured: 57), and in which "nichts eine innere Bewegung [verriet]" (561; let nothing appear of his inward state: 57). On one occasion, he is not quick enough in mounting his guard of "Ruhe und Würde" ([calm and dignity]—omitted by Lowe-Porter) and so bares his "Freude, Überraschung, Bewunderung" (562; joy, surprise, and admiration: 58); at this he flees. Similarly, he feels both "Triumph" and "Entsetzen" (horror: 66) at Tadzio's developing interest in him, but avoids making eye contact for fear he has aroused the suspicions of the boy's mother and governess (572). At one point, he is so moved by the boy's mimicry of his serious attitude toward the baritone guitarist that it takes all his strength not to drop his reserve and "sein Gesicht in den Händen zu verbergen" (576; hid[e] his face in his hands: 70). In sum, Aschenbach delights in Tadzio's appearance, but feels compelled to temper his enjoyment and caution his gaze. He presents his neutrality to the object of his attention and the surrounding world. As can be deduced from Aschenbach's reactions to Tadzio, the author's position and function relies on a self-regulated appreciation for the boy. Sure enough, Aschenbach's interest in Tadzio takes a productive turn when he decides to use the possible part-German Polish boy's physical contours as the foundation of a small prose treatise.[16] Yet he is mindful not to reveal to his readership the impetus for his new output, and thus transforms his impression of Tadzio into literature only in terms that are acceptable to mainstream society.[17] His *disguised approval* imposes the semblance of distance that supposedly limits the boy's significance in Aschenbach's affairs. However, the apparent distance in effect occasions proximity to the graceful adolescent male that enables the author to take full professional advantage of the model and inspiration of cultural production, a model not unlike the physically frail part-German, part-Bohemian who was Aschenbach as a child (508–9). The second basic component of the physiognomical negotiation of the author-figure's cultural standing is therefore providing the necessary physical evidence that enables the artist to assert his personal—and even narcissistic—idea of exemplary form while remaining within the bounds of professional aesthetic standards and established social manners.

* * *

Fundamental to substantiating the portico-man's and Tadzio's physiognomies is identifying the former as a *non-Bavarian* and implying, by the Polish boy's mother's marriage, that the latter is *part-German*. Also, Tadzio's likeness to various classical figures underlines the fact that, like the rediscovered articles of antiquity, he must, as a cultural item, fall within the sphere of *German* influence.[18] However, such readings of the *non-Bavarian* portico-man and the *part-German* Tadzio, by a narrator who presumably mirrors Aschenbach's perspective—it is the narrator who identifies Aschenbach's perspective as artistic connoisseurship (535) and who evokes Lavater (553–54)—are the result of conjecture. The description of the man in the Munich cemetery as someone with red hair, pale eyes, and white and freckled skin, and carrying "den landesüblichen Rucksack" (503; the indigenous rucksack: 8) would be more fitting for what we are told he is not: *a Bavarian*.[19] Likewise, the text gives no *other* indication that Tadzio could be anything but *a Pole*.[20] Evidently, the reader is to assume that accounts of the outward appearances of the portico-man, Tadzio, and the other male characters—and therefore their physiognomical meanings—are constructions of Aschenbach's mind and that the impressions they make have little to do with their real faces or even with their "apparent" identities.[21]

The physiognomies of the men lining Aschenbach's way are either mistaken identities or his willed perceptions. They are interpreted as a foreign threat or as a "colonized" inspiration in order to explain, by way of their apparent material being, the protagonist's required reaction of avoidance or pursuit. Seeing these male faces in such ways helps Aschenbach—and the narrator—to give the impression that the protagonist has not been distracted from his revered cultural vocation, that he is on a journey guided by established national, professional, and social principles. Indeed, Aschenbach would act differently if he were to assign meanings to the faces according to what they "really" are. If the portico-man were openly deemed a Bavarian, Aschenbach would have no reason—as the apparently part-German Tadzio shows—to feel threatened and avoid this figure. They would be compatriots and allies. Likewise, if there were no possibility of imagining Tadzio to be part-German, the protagonist would feel compelled—as the apparent non-Bavarian proves—not cautiously to pursue the boy and express his admiration for him, but rather to scuttle any interest and keep contact to a minimum. For a Pole in the eyes of a Wilhelminian German represents, if not a foe, a colonial and geopolitical inferior and not someone to exalt. Aschenbach would act similarly to Tadzio's aggression aimed at the Russian family on the beach (357). But he does not act in these ways: he avoids the apparently non-Bavarian Bavarian in the chapel portico and—with some hesitation—pursues the apparent part-German who is a Pole. Since the portico-man is likely to be a Bavarian and since Tadzio is utterly Polish, the physiognomical readings that steer Aschenbach as a man of culture away from some and toward another must be a foil for something that has nothing to do with foreignness and nothing to do with Germanization. If the knowledge of faces puts Aschenbach back on track, but the declared national or ethnic identities that substantiate that knowledge are willfully assigned, then some other aspect of how Aschenbach relates to these others must be responsible for substantiating the knowledge—the threat or the standard—contained in those faces. Some dangerous identity other than foreignness must be at the root of Aschenbach's sense of those unusual types who are threatening, shrill, and flamboyant. Some ideal identity other than one affected by Germanization must be at bottom of his regard for the perfect and graceful lad. And these identities must be so disturbing or so precious that they are invisibly contained within common physiognomy under the guises of foreignness or cultural Germanization (which includes a link to the classical Greek ideal) while remaining the genuine cause of the protagonist's strategies of avoidance and pursuit that direct his cultural self-interest.

Since it is Aschenbach's intention to break from routine that causes him to invoke a cover-up by assigning foreignness or Germanization and so cope with the disturbing or ideal faces that distract or motivate him, analyzing the resulting physiognomies reflects less on those faces and more on the observer. Such an analysis shows his will to greater cultural authority and the role physiognomy plays in facilitating that endeavor. Lavater's physiognomical treatises comprise a complex system that, while claiming to decode external features, in fact encodes the face in order to reproduce existing hierarchies. The resulting physiognomical knowledge and the sociocultural hierarchies it supports reflect the ambition and prejudice of the physiognomist or that part of society to which he belongs. Lavaterian physiognomy tailors the facts of people's appearances to suit particular roles, and always in the interests of the cultural establishment. It is a tactic designed to gain influence by fashioning opinion on the meaning, place, and worth of the different members of humanity. Physical descriptions compiled by the observer are rhetorical sites in which the observer defines others and so declares his own authority as the type of person best suited for making pronouncements on others. Ultimately, the attempt to know others turns faces into cultural products that one constructs in order to assert and know one's own function and position. The face of the person observed is a screen for the special interests of the observer as he projects his self-definition as an authority on society.

Similarly, in his study of the literary portrait, Peter von Matt argues that, in this genre, the role of the real-life face that motivates description is significantly limited.[22] To explain, Matt evokes the philologist Wilhelm von Humboldt's assertion that language is not complete enough to convey all the subtleties of the human face and character (97). Matt maintains that, once confronted with this insufficiency of language to communicate an individual's face, authors can only enumerate certain features and thereby produce not the face, but an additional layer of signs (97). Matt also draws on the satirist Georg Christoph Lichtenberg's criticism of the physiognomist's tendency to speak in a specialized language understood only by other physiognomists and unintelligible to the uninitiated (97). Matt suggests—presumably because of the simultaneous inadequacy and overspecialization of language—that authors intent on revealing the impressions of faces necessarily go beyond mere surface to compose literary portraits and physiognomies that in the end tell less about the people observed than they do about the author (97–98).[23]

Matt's approach to explaining an author's communication of the face implicitly evokes the dialectic of reading discussed by exponents of *Rezeption-aesthetik* (reception theory) and reader-response criticism (cf. 192–93) such as Wolfgang Iser and Stanley Fish, respectively. Essentially, in order not to provide a physiognomy only for physiognomists' sake, that is, ostensibly to communicate the meaning of a face effectively to a wide audience, the author/physiognomical observer relies on a number of associations or stock cultural allusions. These allusions are brought to the face by the face-reader from the catalogue of his/her experiences in the effort to interpret, that is, fill in the "gaps" or the "indeterminacy" in the text of, the basic features of, the actual face with his/her "own faculty for making connections" or will to understand and formulate the unformulated, thus, along the lines of Wolfgang Iser.[24] Since these allusions are not realized in the actual face, but virtually and exclusively in the imagination of the author/observer, they eventually supplant the basic facts of the real face. Furthermore, while these allusions are, on the one hand, formulations of the self that strive toward understanding, once subsequently articulated as a literary excursion, they serve, on the other hand, as "interpretive strategies" that the author/observer expects to resonate with the reading public or "interpretive community" because that public as well draws on memories and experiences, ones they may share with the observer, thus, as Stanley Fish has written.[25] As such, the allusions or strategies represent common ways of thinking about particular topics and thus indicate a series of social norms and expectations. As Matt claims, the descriptive portrait of the face is a construction comprised of social and psychological projections that are universally taken for granted (202). Matt argues that physiognomical description is "the expression of the way [the author or observer] sees himself socially and artistically" (1), that it reflects "the relation between author [i.e., observer] and social reality" (53), and that the moral and social norms inextricably linked with describing faces make the observer present in the physiognomy of the observed (98).

Closer examination of the narrator's accounts of Aschenbach's observations shows the basic details of the face to be supplanted by associations or cultural allusions. These allusions expand on the bare facts of the faces and act as triggers in the reader's imagination to help establish meaningful physiognomical connotations (cf. Matt 193). Of course, it is in the nature of the genre of physiognomy that, when conveying the impression of a face, the observer accumulates allusions and constructs details that, while approximating the face observed, are nonetheless born of the observer's own socially contingent experiences. Accordingly, the allusions summoned in Aschenbach's observations provide the critical reader with explicit revelations with which to analyze not the characters to whom those faces belong, but rather Aschenbach and how he negotiates his own position in society. The supplementary details born of Aschenbach's faculty for making connections—his reiteration of existing thought and culture in the descriptions of the observed—tell us most of all how this authority on the nature of people formulates himself. Aschenbach reads the faces of the portico-man, the old dandy, Tadzio, and so on, not for what they are, but for how someone in Aschenbach's position, as a literary author and celebrated member of a specialized community of cultural producers, is disposed and expected to see them. His perspective reveals elements of his own life experiences—the set of norms and universal truths by which he conducts his life. Thus the physiognomical descriptions discussed above are sites from which one may analyze the protagonist in his role as physiognomist and author.

The supplementary allusions underscoring the physiognomical assertion of the portico-man's frightening and problematic foreignness, though misleading by willfully turning a compatriot into a foreigner, bear witness not just to Aschenbach's capacity to imagine foreignness, but specifically to the author-figure's experience of the genuine threat posed by the unexpected figure, a threat intrinsically dangerous to his social position. The text begins the description of the basic features of the portico-man's face with animal terms and focuses on his fanglike teeth, indicating that the threat involves a savage appetite that gnaws at Aschenbach. Likewise, the fashion statement of the wide-brimmed straw hat, red scarf, and yellow suit bring to mind a dandy style that reveals the threat as being contrary to convention. Meanwhile, the walking stick and the rucksack provide a popular-culture reference to the *Wandervogel*, a predominantly male youth movement of hikers, indicating that the threat concerns the question of masculinity. But perhaps most significant is the subtle evocation of the opening chapter of Adelbert von Chamisso's *Peter Schlemihls wundersame Geschichte* (Peter Schlemihl's Miraculous Story, 1814).[26] By including in this episode the words "d[as] Fremdländische[ ]" and "de[r] Fremde[ ]" (503; distinctly exotic: 8; the stranger: 9), by staging the scene in a cemetery next to a public garden with a setting sun (502), by making the figure grimace and return Aschenbach's glances, and then by having Aschenbach feel both embarrassed and transfixed (503) and, finally, decide to embark on a journey to a southern resort, the narrator locates Aschenbach's perspective on the unusual man within the realm of the fictional Schlemihl's infamous encounter with the Gray Man, where he is seduced into selling his shadow, an act that the earlier literary character soon comes to regret, since his shadowlessness entails that he must suffer the pain of public scorn or turn to deception to maintain a respectable position in society.

Clearly, deception is also involved in the associations employed in the physiognomical reading of the portico-man. While imported fashion, the explorer, and the migrant from overseas, the cultural meanings of animals, dandyism, the *Wandervogel* movement, and *Peter Schlemihl* construct foreignness by evoking other species, they in fact betray some other matter occupying Aschenbach's fantasy. The threat that is foisted on the reader as foreign aggression and deceit has little to do with foreignness per se. Concerned with physical craving, unconventionality, masculinity, and seduction, the declaration of foreign physiognomy is rather a screen for "improper" sexual predatoriness. Robert Tobin points out how the encounter with the portico-man pivots about the German word *treiben* (drive) and that the whole scene operates like a sexual come-on.[27] The allusions summoned in the account of the portico-man, as well as Aschenbach's assertion of the man's face as threateningly foreign and his impulse to avert his gaze and wipe his face, are triggered by a homosexual aspect of the encounter. The animal hunger is carnal desire. The red scarf, Tobin has also pointed out, is a sartorial code for homosexuals and male prostitutes.[28] The dandy has long been considered one of the visual manifestations of the homosexual man.[29] Various *Wandervogel* groups were accused of being homoerotic outfits.[30] As well, I have shown elsewhere how *Peter Schlemihl* traces the social consequences of open same-sex sexual attraction.[31] Finally, Aschenbach's daydream following the encounter involves a geography that is as erotic as it is exotic.[32] In fact, on closer inspection, the body that Aschenbach declares *non-Bavarian* is reminiscent of the nineteenth-century homosexual activist Karl Heinrich Ulrichs's and the sexologist Magnus Hirschfeld's theorizations of the Uranian or third sex. It is both effeminate (beardless; the waist and hips as focal point) and exaggeratedly masculine (protruding Adam's apple; heightened, domineering pose). The androgynous mix of the *sexuelle Zwischenstufen* (intersexual variants) is reverberated in the transverse of the snub nose and the furrowed brow, while the suggestion of a facial deformity connects with the medicalization of "queer" bodies.[33]

The account of Aschenbach's reception of the portico-man exemplifies how physiognomical practices can be summoned by a cultural producer to deflect danger, and in this case the social recrimination of a man who pursues same-sex sexual attraction. Highly attuned to his times, Aschenbach would be aware of the proscription against homosexuality. In Mann's experience of German society of the day, open homosexuality was not tolerated by men occupying public positions of influence (even if some of them were homosexual).[34] This group included among others such men as royal confidant Alfred Krupp, Center Party leader Chaplain Dasbach, Prince Philipp zu Eulenburg, Count Kuno von Moltke, Prince Friedrich Heinrich of Prussia, and Chancellor Bernhard von Bülow, men who in the first decade of the twentieth century were the object of some accusation or public scandal of a homosexual kind that also raised concerns of national interests.[35] Also included were men like Aschenbach's forefathers, "Offiziere, Richter, Verwaltungsfunktionäre . . . im Dienste des Königs, des Staates" (508; officers, judges, departmental functionaries . . . in the service of king and state: 12), or like the "hohe[r] deutsche[r] Beamte[ ]" (532; German high official: 32) to whom Aschenbach imagines Tadzio's mother is married; thus, men like Aschenbach or other important nationally recognized cultural producers.[36] Consequently,

Aschenbach knows he must recoil from homosexual encounters if he is not to jeopardize his cultural recognition. But such is the climate of suspicion that, as he recoils, he must take care not to incriminate himself by giving away his ability to intuit others' homosexual tendencies or situations where he encounters homosexuals. Thus, sensing a possible homosexual interlude, Aschenbach willfully interprets the queer physiognomy of the Bavarian in the portico of a Munich cemetery chapel as that of a non-Bavarian to explain his reaction and cover his intuition.

This pattern prevails in Aschenbach's subsequent encounters with similarly unusual and negatively cast males. The allusions used to relay the physiognomical assertion of the hostile and tricky itinerant aliens also reveal that the emphasis on their foreignness is a willful interpretation orchestrated to deflect from the real cause of the threat to *von* Aschenbach, a bourgeois German writer. For instance, the old sailor's, the gondolier's, the elevator boy's, and the baritone guitarist's grins or grimaces (517, 525, 548, 573, 574, 575), the designation of the old sailor and the man with the goatee as "Schattenhaft sonderbare Gestalten" (520; Strange, shadowy figures: 23), and the old dandy clerk's and gondolier's colorful attire (518, 525) repeat the impression of the portico-man's appearance and carry forward the references contained in that first figure to the queer encounter in Chamisso's *Peter Schlemihl* and to the implication of people of the third sex inherent in dandy fashion. Indeed, the threat that both confirms and is confirmed by these characters' physiognomically underscored foreignness finds its origins in the recurring opportunity they present Aschenbach to realize the kind of illicit sexual desire that would compromise the author's cultural standing. The focus on the way the dandy clerk manipulates his tongue, salivates, and sucks his fingers (522–23), in combination with his loud speculation that Aschenbach is about to meet his lover (here, the diminutive neuter "[das] Liebchen," 523), are surely an anticipation of oral sex. The gondolier's forceful and full-bodied stroke (525), his gentle rocking of Aschenbach from behind, and the protagonist's thoughts of having fallen into the hands of a criminal (526) amount to the simulation of anal penetration and the projection of a seduction fantasy akin to storylines of gay erotica or pornographic animation.[37] The guitarist's antics with his tongue (573, 577) and the swollen veins on his head (573) again provide a sexual undertone to Aschenbach's observation. As well, the speculation that the comical, pimp-like buffo-baritone is likely Neapolitan possibly evokes the *femminielli*, or male transvestite prostitutes of the Spanish Quarter of Naples.[38] Put on the spot by homosexuality—a disposition that, if it were to come to light, would make Aschenbach's cultural celebrity untenable—the author-figure consistently calls upon physiognomy to emphasize the foreignness of the men he encounters and thus hide the real threat from which, for the sake of maintaining his power and influence, he is obliged to withdraw.

As with the negatively cast men, the physiognomical descriptions of Tadzio are less an expression of the boy's character than they are a projection of Aschenbach's circumstances. While the narrator expends a significant amount of text outlining Tadzio's figure, the resulting portrait remains rather generic: Tadzio has a face, hair, a nose, eyes, legs, etc., that are—in Aschenbach's eyes—appealing and divine. With words alone the narrator fails to replicate the boy fully and precisely. As the narrator remarks, Tadzio's smile is indescribable (541) or, "Er war schöner, als es sich sagen läßt" (562; lovelier he was than words could say: 58;); and Aschenbach is painfully aware "daß das Wort die sinnliche Schönheit nur zu preisen, nicht wiederzugeben vermag" (562: that language could but extol, not reproduce, the beauties of the sense: 58). Consequently, the patchy detail of the actual face is supplemented with stock cultural allusions. John Frey remarks that Aschenbach's "physical look . . . turns into a spiritual seeing" that "conjures up images from antiquity and myth" (187). In the narrator's account of Aschenbach's observation of Tadzio, the allusions include references to history of art (Spinario or "the slave boy extracting a thorn," Greek sculpture, half profile, Parian marble), mythology (Spinario, Eros), fashion and manners (long hair, an English sailor's suit, black patent leather shoes, a pose unlike his sisters', downcast eyes), pathology ("was he poorly?," looking paler, bad teeth, anemia), and child rearing ("softness and tenderness," "pampered favorite"). Once again, since the allusions associated with the face reflect the observer's cultural experiences, Aschenbach's physiognomical regard for Tadzio serves as a resource for analyzing the author-figure's negotiation of his position in society. Primarily, Tadzio's face and figure—as seen through the discourses of art, mythology, fashion and manners, pathology, and pedagogy—provide a ready means for Aschenbach to exercise his knowledge of *the boy* as the locale of cultural ideals and thus express the degree of his own cultural learning.

Aschenbach demonstrates familiarity with the artistic appreciation of the male form particularly as initiated by Johann Joachim Winckelmann in his art-historical treatises (and whose final days find rough parallels in Aschenbach's Hadean encounter with the criminal gondolier, the gladly abandoned attempt to return north to Germany, and his death in a northern Italian city on the Adriatic). Not only does Tadzio's face resemble Greek sculpture, or his skin have the quality of marble, but Aschenbach's attempt to get to know "jede Linie und Pose" (552; every line and pose: 49) of Tadzio's body turns the boy into a sculpture. The description of Tadzio on the beach contains references to the drapery, tools, posing, lighting, and materials familiar to the manufacture and exhibition of sculpture.[39] It also evokes the sexual indeterminacy, the imagery of water and fluidity, the dreamy state between sleep and consciousness, and the fondness for the fluff upon the adolescent's skin that commentators on

Winckelmann have noted as the hallmarks of his descriptions of statues and their ideal pubescent models.[40]

As the figures of Spinario and Eros indicate, the narrator is also keen to interject allusions to classical mythology and legend into Aschenbach's interest in Tadzio. The narrator equates Tadzio's smile with that of Narcissus and, presumably following Aschenbach's thought processes, loses sight of the Polish boy in the reference to the tragic ancient Greek figure.[41] Aschenbach refers to Tadzio as a Phaeacian (534) and Hyacinthus (560), and suggests that he is the son of Alcibiades while Jaschu is Critobulus (539). He draws a parallel between their potential relationship and that of Socrates and Phaedrus (554–55) in a way that includes attention to physical appearances—"ein Ältlicher und ein Junger, ein Häßlicher und ein Schöner, der Weise beim Liebenswürdigen" (554; an elder with a younger, ugliness paired with beauty and wisdom with grace: 51). He imagines the effect of Tadzio's existence on his creativity in the terms of the story of Ganymede and Zeus—"wie der Adler einst den troischen Hirten zum Äther trug" (556; as once the eagle bore the Trojan shepherd aloft: 53). Other figures and stories evoked by the narrator, either directly or as Aschenbach daydreams and imagines, include those of Helios (549), Oceanus in Elysium (550), Amor (554), Acheloüs (554), Semele and Zeus (555), Eos and Tithonus (558), Cleitus, Cephalus, the Olympians, Orion, Poseidon (559), Pan, Apollo, Zephyr (560), and Hermes (592). The abundance of such allusions tells the reader one thing above all: Aschenbach is undeniably well-read in the classics.[42] But the descriptions of Tadzio are a projection of Aschenbach not merely insofar as they embody the breadth of the author-figure's reading—of the classics and their reception by August von Platen and Friedrich Nietzsche.[43] They also reflect Aschenbach's interest in the meaning of certain aspects of those classical and fine art texts. The effect of the allusions connected with Tadzio has not been to pin the boy down as the readily imaginable and exact likeness of any one of the figures invoked either in appearance or in character. Rather, any sense of the "real" boy is dispersed among Aschenbach's wide knowledge of ancient Greek and Roman culture as a vague reminiscence of an ephebic youth. By deliberating on Tadzio's appearance, Aschenbach summons to the fore of *his own* consciousness and circumstances a way of regarding youth, that is, a way of regarding an older man's relation to male youth, that was supposedly peculiar to the customs of classical culture.

The allusions that depart from Tadzio's basic physique to assert his graceful part-Germanness—an ethnic conversion further cemented from the German perspective by modern German culture's inheritance of ancient Greek culture—ultimately reveal how the Germanization of the Pole is a strategy designed at once to bolster the author-figure's claim to cultural authority and to deflect the real cause of his interest in the boy.

Several critics have pointed out that many of the classical allusions in *Der Tod in Venedig* are homosexual references. For example, Robert Tobin has pointed to the presence of Hyacinthus, Ganymede, Socrates, and Plato as homosexual markers (234) and how "Aschenbach is specifically thinking of certain elements of Greek culture that were . . . open to forms of same-sex desire" (239).[44] Robert K. Martin remarks that "The model of Plato's *Symposium* . . . would serve Mann as the basis for the sexual aesthetics of *Death in Venice*" (59) and that "The friendship tradition evoked in *Tonio Kröger* is enlarged in *Death in Venice* to focus on the Greek tradition, seen as the basis of intellectual growth, of erotic love between an older man and a youth" (63).[45]

The suggestion that classical allusions serve as a location of homosexual references can also be made in regard to each of the other discourses alluded to in the Tadzio descriptions. The traditions of art history, fashion, pathology, and pedagogy all incorporate aspects that, when evoked in male-male contexts and in combination with each other, have the potential to add up to indices of queerness. By echoing Winckelmann's manner of discussing the plastic arts, the allusions to sculpture evoke a treatment of beauty in art by a man who, as Paul Derks insists, was able to conceive an ideal of beauty in the way he did only because he was a homosexual.[46] In fact, the homosexual valency of Tadzio's sculpture-like pose is twice accented since, with his hands clasped behind him and with the tight covering of skin across his torso, this seminude replicates depictions of Saint Sebastian who, along with Ganymede, as Martin rightly claims, comprises one of "The two greatest subjects of homosexual art."[47] By selecting only those clothes that the wardrobe of aristocratic childhood has appropriated from the navy or shares in common with the dandy, the allusions to fashion suggest recognized yet covert locales of homosexuality. In the readiness to diagnose Tadzio with chlorosis, the text possibly indicates, as Tobin argues for the novella's undercurrent theme of cholera, "an awareness of the importance of medical discourses in creating modern notions of sexuality" ("Life and Works" 238; see also Hayes/Quinby 167, 171).[48] Finally, by isolating Tadzio's demeanor as indicative of a favorite child and thus barely removed from Socrates' favorite pupil Phaedrus evoked later, even the passing comments on the boy's upbringing tie in with a pedagogical tradition built on male-male erotic relations.[49]

Aschenbach's perception of Tadzio saturates the boy's looks with extraneous contexts, all concerning aspects of cultural heritage historically selected by gay men to represent their psyche. Tadzio is rendered not as a Polish lad on vacation but as a classically cultured part-German, an ancient Greek demigod, a dead ringer for Sebastian, or a sailor boy, who is popular with the boys and possibly suffers from a poor constitution, not because he is anything but a Polish lad on vacation, but because in speaking of his own learning Aschenbach selects areas of culture that resonate the most with him. That is, he draws on aspects of art history, classical mythology, pathology, etc., that remind him that he is an authoritative member of the cultural community, enable him to realize a culturally necessary homosexual sensitivity, and perhaps, as Tobin maintains, to teach him to "construct" his own sexuality.[50]

Aschenbach's reflections on Tadzio's face and figure thus amount to a projection of the learned self whose professional interest in that learning is concomitant with finding a concrete manifestation of his own possible homosexual sensibility. Indeed, it is only by taking on the responsibility for assembling Tadzio's physiognomy that Aschenbach comes to his self-realization. He wonders whether the controlled force that produces the sculpture-like boy—that is, the Winckelmannian desire that invented the modern ideal of beauty—is also at work in him:

> Der strenge und reine Wille jedoch, der, dunkel tätig, dies göttliche Bildwerk [Tadzio] ans Licht zu treiben vermocht hatte,—war er nicht ihm, dem Künstler, bekannt und vertraut? Wirkte er nicht auch in ihm, wenn er, besonnener Leidenschaft voll, aus der Marmormasse der Sprache die schlanke Form befreite, die er im Geiste geschaut und die er als Standbild und Spiegel geistiger Schönheit den Menschen darstellte? (553)

> [And yet the pure, strong will which had labored in darkness and succeeded in bringing this godlike work of art to the light of day—was it not known and familiar to him, the artist? Was not the same force at work in himself when he strove in cold fury to liberate from the marble mass of language the slender forms of his art which he saw with the ye of his mind and would body forth to men as the mirror and image of spiritual beauty? (50)]

The above quotation is a pointed confession of the homosexual inspiration underlying the prevailing understanding of the ability to recognize beauty and modern artistic production.[51] Perhaps it avows that classicized Western culture is underpinned by queer sentiment.[52] Certainly, Aschenbach's four most recent works—a prose epic on Frederick the Great, the novel *Maja*, the tale *An Abject Man*, and a theoretical treatise on spirit and art that is compared by critics to works by Schiller[53]—indicate his possible homosexual sympathy if not only for the fact that they feature the type of hero best symbolized by Sebastian or, as Eugene McNamara blithely puts it, "the suffering homosexual."[54] But Aschenbach does not simply make a theme out of homosexuality, and nor does Tadzio merely remain a fixture of his private fantasy. The Polish boy's physiognomical image becomes the foundation for creative writing. In this, Aschenbach apes Winckelmann's conception of the male aesthetic ideal after the physique of Friedrich Reinhold von Berg. Since Aschenbach's works generally concern queer figures, and his very latest work summons Winckelmann's queer project not just in terms of depicting Tadzio or biographical parallels but specifically in the way Aschenbach performs the process of writing, it has to be stressed that in considering Aschenbach's physiognomy of Tadzio one is especially concerned with the projection of the type of homosexuality responsible for literary production, a homosexuality, it seems, that is peculiar to such important figures as authors and cultural producers. The good fortune of Tadzio's appearance coalesces with the projection of *the writer as homosexual*.

However, in the cultural collage comprising Tadzio's physiognomy, the coincident projection of Aschenbach the writer-and-homosexual is also no unmitigated version of this observer-protagonist. The expression of Aschenbach delivered in the descriptions of Tadzio takes on a form that agrees with the social proscriptions regulating the circumstances of a writer-and-homosexual.[55] As a result of the intolerance of influential men for men-loving men at the time, the specter of homosexuality relayed—along with that of the canonical author—through another's physiognomy comes to shape only in a carefully mediated or sublimated manner. Though it is hard to imagine how his readers would not see it, Aschenbach certainly has no intention of revealing to them in any direct way the exceptional impetus for his output.[56] Ignace Feuerlicht remarks that in *Der Tod in Venedig* Mann's "choice of classical Greek elements is explained indirectly by his assertion that the homoerotic Platen cultivated the Persian ghazal, the Renaissance sonnet, and the Pindaric ode because these genres also dealt with pederasty and gave it literary legitimacy. Thus the erotic feelings in Platen's works could be viewed by his readers as traditional, impersonal, and inoffensive."[57] Similarly, to avoid courting suspicion, Aschenbach transforms Tadzio into literature only in terms that, while locating homosexual desire, at once divert that desire to ends that are useful to mainstream society. Aschenbach draws on those queer contexts that are sanctioned and available only because they also already sustain the predominance of male-oriented authority. Winckelmann's aesthetic ideal of male youth, classical stories of the gods' love for beautiful youth, the nineteenth-century sexologists' theorizing of sexual inverts, the single-sex signifier of uniforms or dandy attire, and the Socratic tradition represent the type of systems used in the broader culture to promote the so-called "civilizing and healthy potential of male bonds" or the "unsurpassable standard of the male."[58] Thus the physiognomical descriptions of Tadzio both accommodate Aschenbach's homosexuality and, in accordance with hegemonic prohibition, immediately limit it. The rendition of Tadzio reflects the only way society permits a man such as Aschenbach—a writer-and-homosexual—to be and still function as a creative individual. Consequently, Aschenbach is not the genius of the pure knowing subject proposed by Arthur Schopenhauer.[59] The allusions drawn upon by Aschenbach's physiognomical take on Tadzio show his turning a foreigner into a part-German to be motivated by a homosexuality that in other instances the author-figure is obliged to avoid. Aschenbach provides Tadzio with an air of classicism that bespeaks cultured Germanness only because he needs a decoy for the homosexual aspect of his self-interested pursuit of cultural authority. Whereas with the negatively cast men Aschenbach uses physiognomy to avoid the issue of homosexuality altogether, with Tadzio he realizes he may use the discourse of the beautiful face to shield a homosexuality that is necessary as far as modern aesthetics are concerned.

Aschenbach knows what he is doing. This is not a case of self-deception.[60] Any writer must appeal to the broader will of society if s/he is to find professional success. Certainly the narrator is aware that artists are compelled to respond favorably to the dictates of the establishment.[61] By drawing on, yet shrouding, homosexuality in dualistic discourses, Aschenbach knows he will keep the honor the nation bestows upon his works (506) and further the consensus he shares with his generation (510). He gives a society that privileges males exactly what it expects: through his eyes, Tadzio strikes a pose "von lässigem Anstand und ganz ohne die fast untergeordnete Steifheit, an die seine weiblichen Geschwister gewöhnt schienen" (531; of easy grace, quite unlike the stiff subservient mien which was evidently habitual to his sisters: 31). Critics have pointed out that Mann and Aschenbach alike are quick to realize in the realm of fiction the opportunity for the subsistence—even success—to be had by queers should they take on the role of supporting the norm. Robert K. Martin points out how in *Tonio Kröger* the effeminate dance instructor Knaak "turns his status as outsider to his advantage and provides an example of the way society uses such marginal figures as part of a structure of social control": "Knaak, with his assumption of the role of what Michel Foucault calls 'surveillance,' illustrates the fragility of gender definition as well as the phenomenon of the 'house-nigger,' in which society can claim tolerance by allowing isolated figures the appearance of freedom, provided of course that they serve only to perpetuate the system of exclusion from which they are temporarily exempt."[62] Similarly, Robert Tobin insists that there is "something gay in almost every element of Aschenbach's writing" and that Aschenbach "consistently writes about the artistic benefits of the repression or sublimation of homosexuality; he sings the productivity of the closet."[63] Vacationing in Venice, Aschenbach again seizes his same-sex attraction in order to add to his contributions to the literary canon. He invests in a sociocultural system that reinforces public opinion by integrating the most distinct and different as a standard to represent conventional beliefs.[64] Aschenbach secures an esteemed position by a strategy of "nüchterner Leidenschaft" (553; cold fury: 50) or what the narrator refers to as "jene[] fachmännisch

kühle[ ] Billigung" (535; the patronizing air of the connoisseur: 35). That
is, his literary success is preconditioned by his being queerly physiognomically sensitive and at the same time by contributing to the system that
demands he control his feelings and not admit the queer underpinning of
culture. Aschenbach—like Winckelmann before him—sustains the fantasy
of a homosexual interest *in* men but diverts the notion of acting out that
desire in reality in a physical or flagrant manner by subordinating it to
serve the interests *of* men, by providing the graceful ideal image of their
apparent physical and intellectual superiority. In short, Tadzio's physiognomy is a blueprint of Aschenbach's success in a conventional world.

By studying Aschenbach's practice of physiognomy—his way of willfully reading faces to secure his cultural standing—it is possible to see the
underlying paradox in the culture-producing echelons of Aschenbach's
society that requires a successful member at once to suppress and embrace
aspects of same-sex sexuality. Just as the connotations of grotesque "foreign" figures reveal the common denominator of a sexuality from which
Aschenbach tends to recoil, so do the connotations associated with the
classicized/Germanized Tadzio turn out to have a sexual undercurrent, but one that is seen to make a positive contribution to the culture
that Aschenbach supports as a writer.[65] Aschenbach's physiognomizing thus shows the protagonist to have taken a position in the debate
on homosexual emancipation. On the one hand, Aschenbach shows contempt for, and distances himself from, the types he deems threateningly
foreign yet who resemble the sexual invert or third sex as proposed by
Ulrichs and later by Hirschfeld and his Wissenschaftlich-humanitäres
Komitee (Scientific-Humanitarian Committee). On the other hand, the
way in which Aschenbach praises, and argues his pursuit of, the accultur-
ated Tadzio aligns the author-figure with the perspective of such men as
Adolf Brand and Benedict Friedländer.[66] These founding members of the
rival Gemeinschaft der Eigenen (Community of the Special) rejected the
congenital third-sex model and the rights movement that had built up
around it. They considered themselves "bisexual homosexuals" and advocated Hellenic man-boy erotic (i.e., nonsexual) relations between males,
believing that such pedophile relations were conducive to the construction of the political state and aesthetically superior to either homosexual
or heterosexual relations.[67] This difference in opinion—and the disturbing distraction the third-sex homosexual represents to the proponents
of the apparently more culturally superior Hellenic model—is intimated
early in *Der Tod in Venedig* when Aschenbach's pedantic interest in the
Greek inscriptions in the cemetery is interrupted by the "new direction
of thought" spurred by the appearance of the "unusual" portico-man.
While physiognomy helps Aschenbach to regulate his encounters with
men, its analysis reveals a duality in the proscription upon homosexuality
that the protagonist may exploit. His sense of his own cultural superiority

precludes him from engaging sexually with men close to his age. Yet it requires him or gives him a certain leeway to recognize the homoerotic appeal of the younger male and so allow his interest *in* men to be co-opted in the service of the interests *of* men.[68]

A consideration of physiognomy in the text also shows the narrator practicing on Aschenbach in the same Lavaterian way as Aschenbach regards others, providing a lengthy description of Aschenbach's face.[69] Having identified Aschenbach from the outset as a *writer*, the novella-narrator gives meaning to the arbitrary components of this fellow cultural producer's face by insisting that his features bear witness to his occupation as a *servant to art*. In the narrator's opinion, art is "an enhanced life" that causes both deep happiness and rapid debilitation in the producer. By correlating Aschenbach's face with the preconceived function of the artist as someone who *suffers for the cause*, the narrator confirms the knowledge of the protagonist's nature. Aschenbach's temples and high forehead, his aristocratic nose, his grooved cheeks, and his manly chin are lent signification by the inflection of strenuous effort, experience, and dedication and so testify that Aschenbach is "finicky," "over-refined," "weary," "hyper-stimulated," but also "educated" and "dignified" by nature.

However, close examination of the narrator's descriptions of Aschenbach reveals an unflattering portrayal. While there are some positive terms ("gold," "aristocratic," "dignified," "cultured"), the narrator makes greater use of expressions that are negative and suggest the author-figure is both undersized ("below average," "delicate," "narrow," "lean") and oversized ("too big," "lofty," "thick," "large," "high"), worn ("thin," "gray," "slack," "tired," "sunken"), cracked ("lined," "knotted," "cut," "furrowed," "cleft"), stiff ("tense," "serious"), off balance ("leaning to one side"), and angular ("hooked," "keen"). D. J. Farrelly ascribes Aschenbach's facial dichotomy to the close, yet antagonistic, relationship of Apollo and Dionysus.[70] Peter von Matt interprets the sideward tilt of Aschenbach's head as an allusion to the pose of Christ suffering on the cross and an indication of the artist as "the only authentic martyr of bourgeois society, the secularized saint."[71] But Aschenbach's dilapidated hatchet face on a big head leaning to one side has a far greater kinship with the unusual fellows he regards so negatively.[72] The narrator's positive verdict on Aschenbach as the exhausted aesthete is as willful as any of the physiognomical assessments Aschenbach makes of the men he encounters. As Arthur Burkhard has shown, Mann tends to cast artist-figures as people who are recognizably "not normal," as "dubious, disreputable, questionable or genuinely suspicious characters" who lead "a life made difficult in consequence, with 'something always to conceal or to defend.'"[73] Burkhard notices resemblances between "[t]hese isolated, branded, marked men"; that they have "awkward bodies," a "lack of masculinity," and symbolically "queer" names.[74] E. L. Marson suggests that

Aschenbach's physiognomy, marked by "excessive passion," recalls the "classic picture of the legendary physical effects of onanism."[75] In *Der Tod in Venedig*, the emphasis on Aschenbach's educated writer's looks is deceptive, for all along he bears the signs of the third-sex homosexual deemed incompatible with the (bourgeois) projects of nation and culture. The narrator uses the image of the exhausted aesthete to mask someone who underneath is a tired queen.

Just as reviewing the faces that Aschenbach observes reveals how he manipulates them in order to maintain his esteemed position in society, so too does the narrator's description of Aschenbach serve as a site for analyzing not the protagonist, but the way the narrator negotiates his own cultural status. The narrator's decoding of Aschenbach's face is an encoding motivated by self-interest. It is a demonstration of the narrator's power and need to read a kindred spirit as positive no matter how that other person "really" is or appears externally. For, instead of confirming a homosexual, the narrator appraises Aschenbach's physiognomy as that of an excessively diligent and long-suffering artist. The narrator benefits from such a strategy in two ways. First, as someone who shares the same vocation and initially many of the same cultural attitudes as Aschenbach[76] and who is compelled to follow this celebrity's every step, the narrator's attempt to misconstrue the signs of homosexuality enables him to engage himself with the revered author-figure and so, by association, take advantage of his socially esteemed position without having any negative aspersions reflect back on him. Second, the narrator gains kudos by being seen to possess the ability to recognize the artistic greatness of an individual simply by inspecting that person's face. By imparting an artist's professional suffering on the basis of Aschenbach's dilapidated features, Mann's narrator reaps the same reward as Lavater once did by appraising the positive nature of the poet from Goethe's apparent beauty.

However, the unflattering undertone to the narrator's description of Aschenbach recalls not so much Lavater's praise of Goethe as the less than glowing physiognomical assessment of Lavater that Goethe used to distance himself from the Swiss physiognomist.[77] The narrator hedges his bets in making an example of Aschenbach for the sake of his own position. As the story develops, Aschenbach's interest in Tadzio shifts more clearly from aesthetic to sexual, from Hellenic to homosexual, a fact—explicit in Aschenbach's second dream (582–84)—that is contrary to bourgeois values and compromises the protagonist's and, correspondingly, the narrator's social standing. Aschenbach's observation of Tadzio becomes less guarded[78] and, likewise, his relation to the negative types changes from passive observer, to addressee, respondent, addresser, and, finally, confidant. Consequently, in order to maintain and demonstrate his dignified position, the narrator must re-evaluate his relation to the protagonist from one of proximity to one of distance. So long as Aschenbach avoids men such as the one in the portico and pays only professional attention to the boy, the narrator maintains his association, for it is to his own advantage to be in such company. But he becomes detached from the protagonist as soon as Aschenbach gives up his charade. Dorrit Cohn has traced the narrator's use of ever more negative nomenclature for Aschenbach and a gradual divergence both in aesthetic and in moral stances between the narrator and the protagonist as ways in which the narrator begins to separate himself from the author-figure (125–26, 129; see also Pike 136; Reed, *Uses* 148, 163).[79] Physiognomy is another such strategy. After willfully seeing only commendable self-sacrifice in Aschenbach's face, the narrator later re-encodes the protagonist by sending him for a physiognomical makeover at the hotel barber's. This removes Aschenbach's educated physiognomy and further emphasizes the growing distance between the straying protagonist and the "reliable" narrator. We are told that Aschenbach attends to his outward appearance because those physical characteristics so indicative of the "educated and dignified nature of the writer and servant to art"—the ageing body, gray hair, and sharp features—revolt him and make him feel ashamed and hopeless (585). The barber repairs Aschenbach's "Vernachlässigung" by dyeing his gray hair black again (585) and applying makeup.[80]

Holger Pausch and Diana Spokiene interpret the made-up Aschenbach as a lovesick attempt at rejuvenation or an effort to appeal to a younger generation by getting with the fashion,[81] a move that presumably only makes the author-figure out to be yet another fashion victim who is reluctant to accept the transitoriness of his own existence.[82] Yet this interpretation is only part of the story. For makeup is not only an article of the modern fashion discourse, it is a weapon in the arsenal of physiognomy. Makeup enables warriors to appear more fearsome, actors or clowns to belabor their tragedy, and women to accentuate their features. So too does Aschenbach's makeover only reveal him to be threatening, tragic, and effeminate. The makeover emphasizes Aschenbach's queerness; the apparent cover-up uncovers him. While pointing out that Aschenbach's sartorial and cosmetic metamorphosis is anticipated in the old dandy clerk,[83] Pausch and Spokiene do not address the fact that, despite the deflection of the narrator's initial positive assessment, the language-system of Aschenbach's own physical features has all along shown the author-figure to have something in common with the types he regards so negatively. As Margaret Gullette accurately points out, Aschenbach must be pretty ugly, as no one seems to be particularly attracted to him.[84] The change that overcomes Aschenbach is no change at all; it is a shift in the strategy of the narrator. The narrator's first description of Aschenbach is the cover-up; his final one is a mean-spirited, self-interested outing, which Aschenbach is forced to watch face-to-face in the mirror. Rather than covering up

Aschenbach's mortality, the trip to the barber's only exaggerates the protagonist's ugliness and proximity to the negative grotesque types. It extends the distance between the soul-searching protagonist and the narrator eager to maintain his narrative control and cultural authority. Just as Aschenbach had once distanced himself from homosexuals by painting them as foreigners and turning away, the narrator now ensures that his previous proximity to the protagonist that abetted the narrator's position is revised. Now the narrator can gain in prestige by turning away from Aschenbach. By the same strokes as Aschenbach once used—and as echoed by the baritone guitarist's initial encroachment upon his audience and then re-establishment of the artistic distance between them—the narrator puts a new face on Aschenbach—that of a foreigner and queer—to establish some distance between him and the now supposedly disgraced author-figure.[85] What has been intimated yet excused throughout the novel is now emphasized by Mann's narrator: Aschenbach is exactly the type of man whom a cultural producer such as the narrator knows demonstrably to avoid in order to be successful. And who is to say that the narrator has not known this all along? Close examination reveals that the narrator first sets up Aschenbach physiognomically in order to promote himself, and then betrays his central character in order to supersede him.[86]

No longer projecting the social and moral standard, indeed, finally only erasing that standard with a makeover, Aschenbach is forced to show his other side, a same-sex interest that, almost as immediately as it reveals itself, brings an end to his esteemed place in society: the announcement of his death is received by the world the same day. This and more: Tadzio, revealed as the project of homosexual desire, has his face rubbed in the sand by his former friend and stereotypically more masculine Jaschu, only finally to re-emerge in Aschenbach's eyes as Hermes, the Hellenic symbol of creativity (590–92). The lesson is clear: Mann's text maintains that certain queer drives and desires, while essential to cultural production, are at once incompatible with social and intellectual success, that not just their deflection, but their sustained repression is necessary if one wishes to maintain one's standing in the public eye and be economically viable as an intellectual, canonical author, and national treasure. Mann uses physiognomy—the reasoning of the attraction of some faces and the repulsion of others—to demonstrate the double bind informing cultural production in the modern age. That bind is a homosocial imperative concerning the concomitant homoerotic underpinning of art discourse and the homophobic economy of symbolic recognition. Mann's novella warns of the grave consequences of failing to contain within art musings one's interest *in* men within the interests *of* men. It warns cultural producers of the discriminatory dynamics of the cultural field and of their part in maintaining that discrimination. As Russell Berman points out, the narrator ignores Aschenbach's ultimate ethical choice "to refrain from acting on a desire incompatible with social norms."[87] Because of this, Berman maintains that "the text demonstrates the inappropriateness of the narrator's evaluation of the writer" and that secondary literature's "evaluation of Aschenbach's death, the final scene on the beach, urgently needs reconsideration."[88] Indeed, Aschenbach dies of cholera from eating tainted strawberries, an erotic symbol described by Bernhard Frank as "testicular";[89] he does not die of moral decay (at most, he has stepped in as a crypto-incestuous father-figure). But more to the point, Aschenbach is extinguished by a physiognomizing narrator, driven to secure his own place in the symbolic economy of culture, and making use of a system of outing and belittling others that Mann has used extensively elsewhere in his early works.[90] While Berman talks of the "defeat . . . of the authoritarian narrator, who emerges as deeply mistaken in his moralizing judgment,"[91] one cannot help but wonder whether that moral defeat translates into success and celebrity for the narrator. One cannot help but speculate on whether Mann holds up *Der Tod in Venedig* as a mirror to his peers to make them countenance the repressive and contradictory dynamics of cultural production and cultural recognition of the time. One wonders whether Mann's text is itself a physiognomy—both mask and uncovering—an outward representation of the internal social-sexual struggles and cultural complicity of a certain revered author Thomas Mann.

Notes

[1] This chapter is adapted from my doctoral dissertation, "The Specter of the Face. Reading Physiognomy and Power in Modern German Prose Works. Lavater—Chamisso—Mörike—Stifter—Th. Mann." University of Alberta, Edmonton, 2001.

[2] These include "Erscheinung" (502, 503, 528, 551, 562), "Gesicht" (504, 519, 528, 530, 531, 531, 532, 540, 570, 573), "Gestalt" (515, 520, 530, 553, 554), "Antlitz" (516, 530, 554, 572), "Miene" (529, 546, 561, 562, 577), "Ausdruck" (530), "Züge" (548, 573, 574), "Angesicht" (556), and "Gesichtszüge" (585, 590); the more technical include "physiognomische Entstellung" (503), "physiognomische Durchbildung" (515), "Physiognomie" (517, 524), "Gesichtsbildung" (525), "Form" (530), "Halbprofil" (530), "Profil" (534), and "Mienenspiel" (573). All references to the novella are to "Der Tod in Venedig," *Große kommentierte Frankfurter Ausgabe*, vol. 2.1, edited by T. J. Reed. Frankfurt am Main: Fischer, 2004, 501–92.

[3] See Johann Caspar Lavater, *Physiognomische Fragmente zur Beförderung der Menschenkenntniß und Menschenliebe*, 4 vols. (Leipzig: Weidmann, Reich, and Steiner, 1775–78).

[4] All translations of *Der Tod in Venedig* are H. T. Lowe-Porter's from *Death in Venice. Tristan. Tonio Kröger* (First published 1928; London: Penguin, 1955), though I indicate where she has omitted details from the original. Here: 50–51,

my emphasis. Susan von Rohr Scaff sees in these words Aschenbach's evocation of Platonic thought ("Plato and Nietzsche in *Death in Venice*," in *Approaches to Teaching Mann's* Death in Venice *and Other Short Stories*, ed. Jeffrey B. Berlin [New York: MLA, 1992]. 140–45; here, 142).

[5] See also Kurt Fickert, "Truth and Fiction in *Der Tod in Venedig*," *Germanic Notes* 21 (1990): 25–31; here, 27; and John R. Frey, "'Die stumme Begegnung': Beobachtungen zur Funktion des Blicks im *Tod in Venedig*," *German Quarterly* 42, no. 1 (1968): 177–95; here, 179.

[6] Heller, *Thomas Mann: The Ironic German. A Study* (Cleveland, OH: Meridian, 1961), 104.

[7] The straw hat worn by the unusual portico-man is reflected in the tilted hat worn by the man with the goatee (517), in the old dandy's tilted Panama (518), in the gondolier's tilted straw hat (525), in the hat the beggar extends (567), and in the baritone guitarist's felt hat (573). The portico-man, the gondolier, and the baritone guitarist all have snub noses, retracted lips that bare white teeth, and red hair and eyebrows (502–4, 524–25, 572–74). The baritone guitarist also has the same pale, beardless face and protruding Adam's apple, lean neck, sport-shirt, pronounced furrows, and grimaces as the portico-man (572–74). The portico-man and the old dandy each wear a yellow suit (503, 518) made of a woolen material similar to the fabric of the travel agent's clothes (577); further parallels are established through the persistent yellow color of the gondolier's sash (525), the fingers of the man with the goatee (517), and the old dandy's false teeth (519). Links with the portico-man include the repetition of his colorless eyes in the whites of the beggar's eyes (567) and the reflection of his red hair in the travel agent's blushes (577), while the old dandy and the baritone guitarist are associated by the former's use of makeup and phoney youthful looks (519) and the latter's artificially white-lit face and indeterminate age (570, 573). The peripheral figures also smirk and grin (517, 548, 573, 574, 575), bow and grovel (518, 523, 567, 574, 574, 575, 576; "katzbuckelnd," literally meaning arching like a cat), or are hunched, staggering, or squatting (517, 521, 567), are dirty and smell (517, 573, 574), smoke cigarettes (517, 521), lick the corner of their mouths (522, 523, 573) or stick their tongues out (577), have boney, old fingers (517, 519, 522) that paw (522) or point at others (576), have a decorative half-beard or mustache (517, 519, 523, 525, 528)—whether genuine or false—are slight yet energetic (525, 573), or, finally, chatter (517, 525, 563, 585), make noises (523), are shrill (518), or giggle and laugh (522, 575).

[8] Cohn, "The Second Author of *Der Tod in Venedig*," in *Critical Essays on Thomas Mann*, ed. Inta M. Ezergailis (Boston: Hall, 1988), 124–43; here, 136. See Frederic Amory, "The Classical Style of *Der Tod in Venedig*," *Modern Language Review* 59 (1964): 399–409; here, 405; André Cadieux, "The Jungle of Dionysus: The Self in Mann and Nietzsche," *Philosophy and Literature* 3 (1979): 53–63; here, 60; Werner Deuse, "'Besonders ein antikisierendes Kapitel scheint mir gelungen': Griechisches in *Der Tod in Venedig*," in *"Heimsuchung und süßes Gift": Erotik und Poetik bei Thomas Mann*, ed. Gerhard Härle (Frankfurt am Main: Fischer, 1992), 41–62; here, 48–49; Bernhard Frank, "Mann's *Death in Venice*," *Explicator* 64.2 (2006): 99–101; here, 99; André von Gronicka, "'Myth Plus Psychology.' A Style Analysis of *Death in Venice*," *Germanic Review* 31 (1956): 191–205;

here, 197–99; Anthony Heilbut, *Thomas Mann: Eros and Literature* (New York: Knopf, 1996), 253, 256; Heinz Kohut, "Thomas Manns 'Tod in Venedig.' Zerfall einer künstlerischen Sublimierung," *Psycho-Pathographien. I: Schriftsteller und Psychoanalyse*, ed. Heinz Kohut and Alexander Mitscherlich (Frankfurt am Main: Suhrkamp, 1972), 142–67; here, 144, 145, 148, 152–53; Fritz Martini, "Thomas Mann. *Der Tod in Venedig*," *Das Wagnis der Sprache: Interpretationen deutscher Prosa von Nietzsche bis Benn* (Stuttgart: Klett, 1956), 176–224, here, 190; Franz H. Mautner, "Die griechischen Anklänge in Thomas Manns *Tod in Venedig*," *Monatshefte* 44 (1952): 20–26; here, 20; Hannelore Mundt, *Understanding Thomas Mann* (Columbia: University of South Carolina Press, 2004), 89; Hans W. Nicklas, *Thomas Manns Novelle* Der Tod in Venedig: *Analyse des Motivzusammenhangs und der Erzählstruktur* (Marburg: Elwert, 1968), 63–65; T. J. Reed, *Thomas Mann: Der Tod in Venedig; Text, Materialien, Kommentar mit den bisher unveröffentlichten Arbeitsnotizen Thomas Manns* (Munich: Hanser, 1983), 154; *Death in Venice: Making and Unmaking a Master* (New York: Twayne, 1994), 43–44, 62–63); Heidi M. and Robert J. R. Rockwood, "The Psychological Reality of Myth in *Der Tod in Venedig*," *Germanic Review* 59 (1984): 137–41, here 138, 140; Claus Sommerhage, *Eros und Poesis: Über das Erotische im Werk Thomas Manns* (Bonn: Bouvier, 1983), 73; Martin Swales, *Thomas Mann: A Study* (London: Heinemann, 1980), 38; Robert Tobin, "The Life and Works of Thomas Mann: A Gay Perspective," in *Thomas Mann* Death in Venice. *Complete, Authoritative Text with Biographical and Historical Contexts, Critical History, and Essays from Five Contemporary Critical Perspectives*, ed. Naomi Ritter (Boston: Bedford, 1998), 230; and Vernon Venable, "Structural Elements in *Death in Venice*," in *Thomas Mann*, ed. Harold Bloom (New York: Chelsea House, 1986), 23–34; here, 27.

[9] See also Edward Diller, "The Grotesque Animal-Heroes of Thomas Mann's Early Works," *German Life and Letters* 20 (1967): 225–33; here, 229.

[10] Marc A. Weiner discusses the dangerous acoustical impressions of the negative figures in "Silence, Sound, and Song in *Der Tod in Venedig*: A Study in Psycho-Social Repression," *Seminar* 23 (1987): 137–55; here 142–45, 147. The acoustical inferiority of their "noise" signals their social inferiority and thus the threat they pose to an author of high social standing (137–39, 150–51).

[11] By such measures, the old dandy clerk is seen to be "angeregt[ ]" (518; thrilled: 21), "kühn" (518; rakish: 21), "neckisch" (519; playful: 22), "widerlich" (521; repulsive: 24), "kläglich" (521; pitiabl[e]: 24), "jammervoll" (522; deplorabl[e]: 24), "schauderhaft[ ]" (523; ghastly: 25). Similarly, the gondolier is viewed as "ungefällig[ ], ja brutal[ ]" (524; unpleasing, even brutish: 26), "verwegen" (525; rakish: 26), "schroff[ ], überheblich" (525; gruff, overbearing: 27), "unleidlich" (525; intolerable: 27), "sonderbar unbotmäßig[ ], unheimlich entschlossen[ ]" (525; tongue-tied, obstinate, uncanny: 27), "eigenmächtig[ ]" (526; despotic: 27), and "schlecht[ ]" (527; bad: 28), while the hotel manager is "schmeichelnd höflich" (528; caressing: 29). Likewise, the baritone guitarist is regarded as "frech[ ]" (573; impudent: 67), "brutal und verwegen, gefährlich und unterhaltend" (573; brutal, blustering . . . unpleasant and entertaining: 67), "etwas Zweideutiges, unbestimmt Anstößiges" (573; an equivocal meaning, yet vaguely offensive: 67), "trotzig, herrisch, fast wild" (573; of defiance and self-will,

almost of desperation: 67), "verdächtig[ ]" (573; suspicious: 67), "So frech . . . so demütig" (574; as cringing as . . . forward: 68), "tückisch" (574; servile: 68), "drohend" (574; very marked: 68), "täuschendst[ ]" (575; most deceptive: 69), and "unverschämt" (575; [unashamedly]—omitted by Lowe-Porter; it would have appeared on page 69 of her translation).

[12] Even the British travel agent is not to be trusted entirely. On the one hand, he seems to show Aschenbach a kinder face as a foreigner: "noch jung, mit in der Mitte geteiltem Haar, nahe bei einander liegenden Augen und von jener gesetzten Loyalität des Wesens, die im spitzbübisch behenden Süden so fremd, so merkwürdig anmutet" (577; "young . . . with his eyes set close together, his hair parted in the middle, and radiating that steady reliability which makes his like so strange a phenomenon in the *gamin*, agile-witted south" 71). He abandons the official silence concerning the cholera outbreak and provides Aschenbach with an honest answer to his questions. On the other hand, the implication of the discovery of a traditional ally in the fellow northern European amounts, in the context of the Agadir Incident, to a historical and practical miscalculation on Aschenbach's part. In the diplomacy that followed Agadir, the British did not support the German position. Indeed, the British travel agent has blue eyes (577) that in idiomatic German declare him to be *blauäugig* or naive.

[13] The full description reads: "Mit Erstaunen bemerkte Aschenbach, daß der Knabe vollkommen schön war. Sein Antlitz,—bleich und anmutig verschlossen, von honigfarbenem Haar umringelt, mit der gerade abfallenden Nase, dem lieblichen Munde, dem Ausdruck von holdem und göttlichem Ernst, erinnerte an griechische Bildwerke aus edelster Zeit, und bei reinster Vollendung der Form war es von so einmalig-persönlichem Reiz, daß der Schauende weder in Natur noch bildender Kunst etwas ähnlich Geglücktes angetroffen zu haben glaubte . . . Weichheit und Zärtlichkeit bestimmten ersichtlich seine Existenz. Man hatte sich gehütet, die Scheere an sein schönes Haar zu legen; wie beim Dornauszieher lockte es sich in die Stirn, über die Ohren und tiefer noch in den Nacken. Ein englisches Matrosenkostüm, dessen bauschige Ärmel sich nach unten verengerten und die feinen Gelenke seiner noch kindlichen, aber schmalen Hände knapp umspannten, verlieh mit seinen Schnüren, Maschen und Stickereien der zarten Gestalt etwas Reiches und Verwöhntes. Er saß, im Halbprofil gegen den Betrachtenden, einen Fuß im schwarzen Lachschuh vor den andern gestellt, einen Ellenbogen auf die Armlehne seines Korbsessels gestützt, die Wange an die geschlossene Hand geschmiegt, in einer Haltung von lässigem Anstand und ganz ohne die fast untergeordnete Steifheit, an die seine weiblichen Geschwister gewöhnt schienen. War er leidend? Denn die Haut seines Gesichtes stach weiß wie Elfenbein gegen das goldige Dunkel der umrahmenden Locken ab. Oder war er einfach ein verzärteltes Vorzugskind, von parteilicher und launischer Liebe getragen?" (529–31; Aschenbach noticed with astonishment the lad's perfect beauty. His face recalled the noblest moment of Greek sculpture—pale, with a sweet reserve, with clustering honey-coloured ringlets, the brow and nose descending in one line, the winning mouth, the expression of pure and godlike serenity. Yet with all this chaste perfection of form it was of such unique personal charm that the observer thought he had never seen, either in nature or art, anything so utterly happy and consummate. . . . Tenderness and softness, it was plain, conditioned his existence.

No scissors had been put to the lovely hair that (like the Spinnario's) curled about his brows, above his ears, longer still in the neck. He wore an English sailor suit, with quilted sleeves that narrowed round the delicate wrists of his long and slender though still childish hands. And this suit, with its breast-knot, lacings, and embroideries, lent the slight figure something "rich and strange," a spoilt, exquisite air. The observer saw him in half profile, with one foot in its black patent leather advanced, one elbow resting on the arm of his basket-chair, the cheek nestled into the closed hand in a pose of easy grace, quite unlike the stiff subservient mien which was evidently habitual to his sisters. Was he delicate? His facial tint was ivory-white against the golden darkness of his clustering locks. Or was he simply a pampered darling, the object of a self-willed and partial love? 30–31).

Elsewhere, Tadzio is described as having "dämmergraue[] Augen" (532, 587, 592; "twilit grey" 32, 79, 83), which he is in the habit of casting down and then up again (534, 541, 544, 561); his head is that of Eros "vom gelblichen Schmelze parischen Marmors" (535; with the yellowish bloom of Parian marble, 35) and is poised "in unvergleichlichem Liebreiz" (534; in incomparable loveliness, 35); his skin color is "marmorhaft gelblich" (561; creamy marble, 58), though on one day "schien er blässer . . . als sonst" (562; he did look a little pale, 58); his eyebrows are "fein[ ] und ernst[ ]" (535; fine serious, 35), "ebenmäßig[ ]" (562; shapely, 58), and "schärfer" (562; delicate[ ], 58); his curly hair grows over his temples and ears (535); he has "schlanke[ ] Beine" (537; slender legs, 36); his smile is "unbeschreiblich lieblich[ ]" (541; indescribably lovely, 40), "sprechend, vertraut, liebreizend und unverhohlen" (562; unabashed and friendly . . . speaking, winning, captivating, 58), or he looks "mit einem Ausdruck, der kaum ein Lächeln, nur eine entfernte Neugier, ein höfliches Entgegennehmen war" (572; with an expression that was hardly a smile, but rather a distant curiosity and polite toleration, 66); he strikes a pose "in unvermeidlicher und anerschaffener Grazie, den linken Unterarm auf der Brüstung, die Füße gekreuzt, die rechte Hand in der tragenden Hüfte" (572; in all his innate, inevitable grace, with his left arm on the balustrade, his legs crossed, the right hand on the supporting hip, 66); and yet his teeth were "nicht recht erfreulich . . . etwas zackig und blaß, ohne den Schmelz der Gesundheit und von eigentümlich spröder Durchsichtigkeit wie zuweilen bei Bleichsüchtigen (541; imperfect, rather jagged and bluish, without a healthy glaze, and of that peculiar brittle transparency which the teeth of chlorotic people often show, 40).

[14] Cf. John Burt Foster Jr., "Why Is Tadzio Polish? *Kultur* and Cultural Multiplicity in *Death in Venice*" in *Thomas Mann* Death in Venice, ed. Ritter, 192–210; here, 195, 199–201.

[15] Scaff, "Plato and Nietzsche in *Death in Venice*," 142. Richard White demonstrates, however, that "*Death in Venice* may be viewed as a challenge to every idealizing impulse, including that of Plato, which seeks to justify the erotic impulse or the pursuit of beauty for the sake of something higher." This would include intellectual realization and professional ambition. White, "Love, Beauty, and Death in Venice," *Philosophy and Literature* 14.1 (1990): 53–64; here, 61.

[16] "Und zwar ging sein Verlangen dahin, in Tadzios Gegenwart zu arbeiten, beim Schreiben den Wuchs des Knaben zum Muster zu nehmen, seinen Stil den Linien dieses Körpers folgen zu lassen, der ihm göttlich schien, und seine Schönheit ins

Geistige zu tragen, wie der Adler einst den troischen Hirten zum Äther trug." (556) (He would write, and moreover he would write in Tadzio's presence. This lad should be in a sense his model, his style should follow the lines of this figure that seemed to him divine; he would snatch up this beauty into the realms of the mind, as once the eagle bore the Trojan shepherd aloft. [52–53])

17 "Es ist sicher gut, daß die Welt nur das schöne Werk, nicht auch seine Ursprünge, nicht seine Entstehungsbedingungen kennt; denn die Kenntnis der Quellen, aus denen dem Künstler Eingebung floß, würde sie oftmals verwirren, abschrecken und so die Wirkungen des Vortrefflichen aufheben" (556; Verily it is well for the world that it sees only the beauty of the completed work and not its origins nor the conditions whence it sprang; since knowledge of the artist's inspiration might often but confuse and alarm and so prevent the full effect of its excellence: 53).

18 See Foster, "Why Is Tadzio Polish?" 194.

19 Cf. Edward S. Brinkley, "Fear of Form: Thomas Mann's *Der Tod in Venedig*," *Monatshefte* 91 (1999): 2–27; here, 8.

20 Cf. Foster, "Why Is Tadzio Polish?" 199.

21 For remarks on the figures as products of Aschenbach's imagination, see also Amory, "The Classical Style of *Der Tod in Venedig*, 405; Frey, "'Die stumme Begegnung,'" 178, 179; Gronicka, "'Myth plus Psychology,'" 199; Kohut, "Thomas Mann's *Tod in Venedig*," 158; Rodney Symington, "The Eruption of the Other: Psychoanalytic Approaches to *Death in Venice*," in *Thomas Mann* Death in Venice, ed. Ritter, 127–41; here, 136, and Isadore Traschen, "The Uses of Myth in *Death in Venice*," in *Thomas Mann*, ed. Harold Bloom (New York: Chelsea, 1986), 87–101; here, 90). Mann maintained that the figures appearing in *Der Tod in Venedig* were based on individuals he had encountered (Mann, "Lebensabriß," *Gesammelte Werke in zwölf Bänden*, vol. 11 (Frankfurt am Main: Fischer, 1960), 98–144; here, 124); see also Gilbert Adair, *The Real Tadzio: Thomas Mann's* Death in Venice *and the Boy Who Inspired It* (New York: Carroll & Graf, 2003), 11–15.

22 Peter von Matt, . . . *fertig ist das Angesicht: Zur Literaturgeschichte des menschlichen Gesichts* (Munich: Hanser, 1983). See also Michael Niehaus, "Physiognomie und Literatur im 19. Jahrhundert (von Poe bis Balzac)," in *Geschichten der Physiognomik: Text, Bild, Wissen*, ed. Rüdiger Campe and Manfred Schneider (Freiburg im Breisgau: Rombach, 1996), 411–30; here, 425.

23 Cf. John Graham, "Contexts of Physiognomic Description: *Ut Pictura Poesis*," and Christopher Rivers, "'L'homme hiéroglyphié': Balzac, Physiognomy, and the Legible Body," both in *Faces of Physiognomy*, ed. Shookman, 139–43 and 144–60 respectively.

24 Wolfgang Iser, "The Reading Process: A Phenomenological Approach," *New Literary History* 3 (1972): 279–99.

25 Stanley E. Fish, "Interpreting the *Variorum*," *Critical Inquiry* 2 (1976): 465–85.

26 T. J. Reed provides a further link to Chamisso by suggesting that Mann's admiration for the earlier author's ability to move on from his hit story to become

a mature, recognized cultural and scholarly figure in the eyes of a later generation was the same status Mann wished to attain and the same process Aschenbach
was undergoing in *Der Tod in Venedig* (*Thomas Mann: Der Tod in Venedig; Text,
Materialien, Kommentar*, 133–34, 149; *Death in Venice: Making and Unmaking
a Master*, 7).

[27] Robert Tobin, "Why Is Tadzio a Boy? Perspectives on Homoeroticism in *Death
in Venice*," *Death in Venice: A New Translation, Backgrounds and Contexts*, trans.
and ed. Clayton Koelb (New York: Norton, 1994). 207–32; Tobin, "Life and
Works of Thomas Mann: A Gay Perspective," 229–30.

[28] Tobin, "Life and Works," 235.

[29] Ina Hartwig, "Noten zu Homosexualität," *Merkur* 49 (1995): 904–14. James
P. Wilper argues that the old dandy—and Aschenbach—allude to Oscar Wilde
(*Reconsidering the Emergence of the Gay Novel in English and German* [West
Lafayette, IN: Purdue UP, 2016], 159–64 and "Wilde and the Model of Homo-
sexuality in Mann's *Tod in Venedig*," *CLCWeb: Comparative Literature and Cul-
ture* 15.4 (2013): 1–8; here, 4).

[30] James D. Steakley, *The Homosexual Emancipation Movement in Germany* (New
York: Arno, 1975), 54–56.

[31] John L. Plews, "'Aus dem Gesicht verloren': The Physiognomical Shade and
Chamisso's Peter Schlemihl's Coming-out Story," *Seminar* 40 (2003): 327–48.
See Brinkley, "Fear of Form," on how the description of the portico-man alludes
to the portrait in Oscar Wilde's *The Picture of Dorian Gray* (8). I maintain that
the allusion harks back to the earlier literary figure of Chamisso's Schlemihl and,
thus, to a text that not only occurs within German literature, but also likely influenced Wilde's text.

[32] See also Jean Jofen, "A Freudian Commentary on Thomas Mann's *Death in
Venice*," *Journal of Evolutionary Psychology* 6 (1985): 238–47; here, 240. There are
"Blätter[ ], so dick wie Hände . . . riesige[ ] Farne[ ] . . . fette[s], gequollene[s]
und abenteuerlich blühende[s] Pflanzenwerk . . . haarige Palmenschäfte . . . wun-
derlich ungestalte Bäume, deren Wurzeln dem Stamm entwuchsen und sich durch
die Luft in den Boden, ins Wasser senkten . . . groß, milchweiße Blumen; Vögel
von fremder Art, hochschultrig, mit unförmigen Schnäbeln . . . ein klapperndes
Wetzen und Rauschen . . . knotige[ ] Rohrstämmen eines Bambusdickichts"
(504; [leaves as thick as hands—omitted by Lowe-Porter] . . . Hairy palm-trunks
. . . lush brakes of fern . . . crass vegetation, fat, swollen, thick with incredible
bloom . . . trees, mis-shapen as a dream, that dropped their naked roots straight
through the air into the ground or into water . . . mammoth milk-white blossoms
. . . strange high-shouldered birds with curious bills . . . [a clattering grinding and
whooshing—omitted by Lowe-Porter] . . . knotted joints of a bamboo thicket:
9–10).

[33] Traschen reminds us that Socrates had a snub nose, as did the satyrs ("The
Uses of Myth in *Death in Venice*," 90). See Steakley on Ulrichs's consideration
of effeminate men (*Homosexual Emancipation*, 6, 8, 15–17). See also James W.
Jones on the third sex: *"We of the Third Sex": Literary Representations of Homosexuality in Wilhelmine Germany* (New York: Lang, 1990). See Steakley, "Iconog-
raphy of a Scandal: Political Cartoons and the Eulenburg Affair in Wilhelmine

Germany," in *Hidden from History: Reclaiming Gay and Lesbian Past*, ed. Martin Bauml Duberman, Martha Vicinus, and George Chauncey, Jr. (London: Penguin, 1991). 233–63, for a discussion of the graphic representation of the third sex as "bug-eyed, wasp-waisted aliens" (242) with "elongated head[s]" (248) and "alien physiognom[ies]" (see also figs. 6 [260] and 10 [262]). See Steakley (*Homosexual Emancipation,* 13) for the shift in the German debate on homosexuality from the judicial realm to the medical one. See also Tobin, "Queering Thomas Mann's *Der Tod in Venedig*," *Thomas Mann,* ed. Stefan Bornchen, Georg Mein, and Gary Schmidt (Munich: Fink, 2014), 67–79; here, 72–73). For medical discourse and homosexuality, see Foucault's *The History of Sexuality, Volume I: An Introduction,* trans. Robert Hurley (New York: Vintage, 1990).

[34] For a general understanding of the experiences of homosexuals at the time, see Patrick Higgins, ed., *A Queer Reader* (London: Fourth Estate, 1993), 135–36, James W. Jones, *"We of the Third Sex,"* Harry Oosterhuis, ed. *Homosexuality and Male Bonding in Pre-Nazi Germany: The Youth Movement, the Gay Movement, and Male Bonding before Hitler's Rise. Original Transcripts from "Der Eigene," the First Gay Journal in the World,* trans. Hubert Kennedy. [*Journal of Homosexuality* 22.1/2 (1991).] (New York: Haworth, 1991), Steakley, *Homosexual Emancipation,* and Angela Taeger, "Homosexual Love Between 'Degeneration of Human Material' and 'Love of Mankind': Demographical Perspectives on Homosexuality in Nineteenth-Century Germany," in *Queering the Canon,* ed. Christoph Lorey and John L. Plews (Columbia, SC: Camden House, 1997), 20–35. The degree of tolerance or intolerance of homosexuality in Germany at Mann's time is also reflected in the reception of Mann's novella (see Karl Werner Böhm, *Zwischen Selbstsucht und Verlangen: Thomas Mann und das Stigma Homosexualität; Untersuchungen zu Frühwerk und Jugend* [Würzburg: Königshausen & Neumann, 1991], 17–59).

[35] See Steakley, *Homosexual Emancipation.* For references pertaining to Mann's interest in the Eulenburg trial, see Böhm, *Zwischen Selbstsucht und Verlangen,* 302–5, and John Margetts, "Die 'scheinbar herrenlose' Kamera. Thomas Manns 'Tod in Venedig' und die Kunstphotographie Wilhelm von Gloedens," *Germanisch-Romanische Monatsschrift* 39 (1989): 326–37; here: 337, fn. 24. See also Norman Domeier, *The Eulenburg Affair: A Cultural History of Politics in the German Empire* (Rochester, NY: Camden House, 2015).

[36] Aschenbach equates the nature of his professional life with theirs: "Auch er hatte gedient, auch er sich in harter Zucht geübt; auch er war Soldat und Kriegsmann gewesen, gleich manchen von ihnen,—denn die Kunst war ein Krieg, ein aufreibender Kampf, für welchen man heute nicht lange taugte. Ein Leben der Selbstüberwindung und des Trotzdem, ein herbes, standhaftes und enthaltsames Leben, das er zum Sinnbild für einen zarten und zeitgemäßen Heroismus gestaltet hatte,—wohl durfte er es männlich, durfte es tapfer nennen" (568–69; It had been a service, and he a soldier, like some of them; and art was war—a grilling, exhausting struggle that nowadays wore one out before one could grow old. It had been a life of self-conquest, a life against odds, dour, steadfast, abstinent; he had made it symbolical of the kind of over-strained heroism the time admired, and he was entitled to call it manly, even courageous: 64).

[37] See also Jofen, "A Freudian Commentary on Thomas Mann's *Death in Venice,* 242; Tobin, "Why Is Tadzio a Boy?" 225, "Life and Works of Thomas Mann: A Gay Perspective," 234, and "Queering Thomas Mann's *Der Tod in Venedig,*" 73–74).

[38] See also Heilbut, *Thomas Mann: Eros and Literature,* 257. For an account of modern-day *femminielli,* see Frank Browning, *A Queer Geography: Journeys toward a Sexual Self* (New York: Noonday, 1996), 39–86.

[39] "Er lag ausgestreckt, das Badetuch um die Brust geschlungen, den zart gemeißelten Arm in den Sand gestützt, das Kinn in die hohlen Hand . . . Er stand am Rande der See, allein . . .—aufrecht, die Hände im Nacken verschlungen, langsam sich auf den Fußballen schaukelnd, und träumte ins Blaue, während kleine Wellen, die anliefen, seine Zehen badeten. Sein honigfarbenes Haar schmiegte sich in Ringeln an die Schläfen und in den Nacken, die Sonne erleuchtete den Flaum des oberen Rückgrates, die feine Zeichnung der Rippen, das Gleichmaß der Brust traten durch die knappe Umhüllung des Rumpfes hervor, seine Achselhöhlen waren noch glatt wie bei einer Statue, seine Kniekehlen glänzten, und ihr bläuliches Geäder ließ seinen Körper wie aus klarem Stoffe gebildet erschienen. Welch eine Zucht, welche Präzision des Gedankens war ausgedrückt in diesem gestreckten und jugendlich vollkommenen Leibe!" (552–53; he would lie at full length, with his bath-robe around him, one slender young arm resting on the sand, his chin in the hollow of his hand . . . he might be at the water's edge, alone . . . standing erect, his hands clasped at the back of his neck, rocking slowly on the balls of his feet, day-dreaming away into blue space, while little waves ran up and bathed his toes. The ringlets of honey-coloured hair clung to his temples and neck, the fine down along the upper vertebrae was yellow in the sunlight; the thin envelope of flesh covering the torso betrayed the delicate outlines of the ribs and the symmetry of the breast-structure. His armpits were still as smooth as a statue's, smooth the glistening hollows behind the knees, where the blue network of veins suggested that the body was formed of some stuff more transparent than mere flesh. What discipline, what precision of thought were expressed by the tense youthful perfection of this form!: 50).

[40] See Catriona MacLeod, "The 'Third Sex' in an Age of Difference: Androgyny and Homosexuality in Winckelmann, Friedrich Schlegel, and Kleist," in *Outing Goethe and His Age,* ed. Alice A. Kuzniar (Stanford, CA: Stanford University Press, 1996), 194–214; here, 199–201; Kevin Parker, "Winckelmann, Historical Difference, and the Problem of the Boy," *Eighteenth-Century Studies* 25 (1992): 523–44, here, 540–41; Simon Richter, *Laocoon's Body and the Aesthetics of Pain: Winckelmann. Lessing. Herder. Moritz. Goethe* (Detroit: Wayne State University Press, 1992), 55. See also Richter, ch. 2: "Winckelmann: Laocoon and the Eunuch" (38–61). Amory demonstrates Mann's use of various classical writing styles in *Der Tod in Venedig* ("The Classical Style of *Der Tod in Venedig*"). See also T. J. Reed on the use of "statuesque language" in Mann's novella (*Thomas Mann: The Uses of Tradition* [Oxford: Clarendon, 1974], 146–48). Heinz Gockel explains Tadzio's becoming a sculpture in the context of the affect upon Mann of Nietzsche's understanding of Apollonian forces ("Aschenbachs Tod in Venedig," in *Erzählungen und Novellen,* ed. Rudolf Wolff [Bonn: Bouvier, 1984], 27–41; here, 37–38).

[41] "Es war das Lächeln des Narziß, der sich über das spiegelnde Wasser neigt, jenes tiefe, bezauberte, hingezogene Lächeln, mit dem er nach dem Widerschein der eigenen Schönheit die Arme streckt,—ein ganz wenig verzerrtes Lächeln, verzerrt von der Aussichtslosigkeit seines Trachtens, die holden Lippen seines Schattens zu küssen, kokett, neugierig und leise gequält, betört und betörend" (562; With such a smile it might be that Narcissus bent over the mirroring pool, a smile profound, infatuated, lingering, as he put out his arms to the reflection of his own beauty; the lips just slightly pursed, perhaps half-realizing his own folly in trying to kiss the cold lips of his shadow—with a mingling of coquetry and curiosity and a faint unease, enthralling and enthralled: 58).

[42] For further information on the classical allusions in *Der Tod in Venedig*, see Amory, "Classical Style"; Willy R. Berger, "Thomas Mann und die antike Literatur," in *Thomas Mann und die Tradition*, ed. Peter Pütz (Frankfurt am Main: Athenäum, 1971). 52–100; here, 58–63, 75; George Bridges, "The Problem of Pederastic Love in Thomas Mann's *Death in Venice* and Plato's *Phaedrus*," *Selecta: Journal of the Pacific Northwest Council on Foreign Languages* 7 (1986): 39–46; Diskin Clay, "Phaedrus on the Lido: Tod in Venedig," *Arion: A Journal of Humanities and the Classics* 21 (2013): 63–76; Werner Deuse, "'Besonders ein antikisierendes Kapitel scheint mir gelungen': Griechisches in *Der Tod in Venedig*," in *"Heimsuchung und süßes Gift": Erotik und Poetik bei Thomas Mann*, ed. Gerhard Härle (Frankfurt am Main: Fischer, 1992), 41–62; Bernhard Frank, "Mann's *Death in Venice*," *Explicator* 45.1 (1986): 31–32; Frank, "Mann's *Death in Venice*." *Explicator* 64 (2006): 99–101; Gronicka, "Myth plus Psychology, 203–5; Lorraine Gustafson, "Xenophon and *Der Tod in Venedig*," *Germanic Review* 21 (1946): 209–14; Alice van Buren Kelley, "Von Aschenbach's *Phaedrus*: Platonic Allusion in *Der Tod in Venedig*," *Journal of English and Germanic Philology* 75 (1976): 228–40; Herbert Lehnert, "Note on Mann's *Death in Venice* and the *Odyssey*," *PMLA* 80 (1965): 306–7; E[ric] L[awson] Marson, *The Ascetic Artist: Prefigurations in Thomas Mann's "Der Tod in Venedig,"* (Bern: Lang, 1979); Mautner, "Die griechischen Anklänge in Thomas Mann's *Tod in Venedig*," *Monatshefte* 44 (1952): 20–26; Wolfgang F. Michael, "Stoff und Idee im 'Tod in Venedig,'" *Deutsche Vierteljahrsschrift für Literaturwissenschaft und Geistesgeschichte* 33 (1959): 13–19; Nicklas, *Thomas Manns Novelle* Der Tod in Venedig (45–52); Reed, *The Uses of Tradition*, 156–75; Ritter, "A Critical History of *Death in Venice*," *Thomas Mann*, ed. Ritter, 91–109, here, 95ff.; Scaff; Tobin, "Why Is Tadzio a Boy?" 227, 229–30 and "Life and Works," 234; Traschen, "The Uses of Myth in *Death in Venice*"; Hans Rudolf Vaget, "*Der Tod in Venedig*," in *Thomas Mann—Kommentar zu sämtlichen Erzählungen* (Munich: Winckler, 1984), 170–200; here, 170–75; and White, "Love, Beauty, and Death in Venice."

[43] For the influence of Platen on *Der Tod in Venedig*, see Frank Busch, *August Graf von Platen—Thomas Mann: Zeichen und Gefühle* (Munich: Fink, 1987); Mautner, "Die griechischen Anklänge in Thomas Manns *Tod in Venedig*," 23–24; Nicklas, *Thomas Manns Novelle* Der Tod in Venedig, 37–39; and Joachim Seyppel, "Adel des Geistes: Thomas Mann und August von Platen," *Deutsche Vierteljahrsschrift für Literaturwissenschaft und Geistesgeschichte* 33 (1959): 565–73. For the influence of Nietzsche's thought on Aschenbach and *Der Tod in Venedig*, see Albert

Braverman and Larry David Nachman, "The Dialectic of Decadence. An Analysis of Thomas Mann's *Death in Venice*," *Germanic Review* 45 (1970): 289–98; here, 292; Cadieux, "The Jungle of Dionysus"; Adrian Del Caro, "Philosophizing and Poetic License in Mann's Early Fiction," in ed. *Approaches to Teaching Mann's Death in Venice and Other Short Stories*, ed. Jeffrey B. Berlin (New York: MLA, 1992), 39–48; Manfred Dierks, *Studien zu Mythos und Psychologie bei Thomas Mann* (Bern: Francke, 1972), 18–59; D. J. Farrelly, "Apollo and Dionysus Interpreted in Thomas Mann's *Der Tod in Venedig*," *New German Studies* 3 (1975): 1–15; Gockel, "Aschenbachs Tod in Venedig," 35–40; Daniel Marshall, "Beating Space and Time: Historical Gay Sex and Queer Cultural Geographies of Masculinities," *Angelaki* 20.1 (2015): 33–51; here 36–38; Roger A. Nicholls, *Nietzsche in the Early Work of Thomas Mann* (New York: Russell and Russell, 1976), 77–91; Ford B. Parkes, "The Image of the Tiger in Thomas Mann's *Tod in Venedig*," *Studies in Twentieth-Century Literature* 3 (1978): 73–83; Reed, *The Uses of Tradition*, 155, 171 and *Death in Venice: The Making and Unmaking of a Master*, 76–79; Scaff, "Plato and Nietzsche in *Death in Venice*"; Traschen, "The Uses of Myth in *Death in Venice*," 97–100; and White, "Love, Beauty, and Death in Venice," 63.

[44] Tobin, "The Life and Works of Thomas Mann: A Gay Perspective."

[45] Robert K. Martin, "Gender, Sexuality, and Identity in Mann's Short Fiction," in *Approaches to Teaching Thomas Mann's Death in Venice and Other Short Stories*, ed. Jeffrey B. Berlin (New York: MLA, 1992), 57–67. Ernst A. Schmidt sees a correlation between *Der Tod in Venedig* and Virgil's Corydon-*Eclogue* in the constellation of the artist and man-boy love ("Künstler und Knabenliebe: Eine vergleichende Skizze zu Thomas Manns *Tod in Venedig* und Vergils zweiter Ekloge," *Euphorion* 68 (1974): 437–46) and Claus Sommerhage reveals by way of psychoanalysis the homoerotic dimension of the Socratic source of Aschenbach's dreams and daydreams (*Eros and Poesis*, 91–97).

[46] Derks, *Die Schande der heiligen Päderastie: Homosexualität und Öffentlichkeit in der deutschen Literatur, 1750–1850* (Berlin: Rosa Winkel, 1990), 208. See also Heinrich Detering, *Das offene Geheimnis: Zur literarischen Produktivität eines Tabus von Winckelmann bis zu Thomas Mann* (Göttingen: Wallstein, 1994), 335.

[47] Martin, "Gender, Sexuality, and Identity in Thomas Mann," 64. Venable considers the dandy clerk as "a loathsome travesty of the Sebastian-like hero-type" ("Structural Elements in *Death in Venice*," 28). See also Heilbut (*Thomas Mann: Eros and Literature*, 252); and Tobin ("Why Is Tadzio a Boy?" 222).

[48] Tobin, "Life and Works," 238; see also Tom Hayes and Lee Quinby, "The Aporia of Bourgeois Art: Desire in Thomas Mann's *Death in Venice*," *Criticism* 31 (1989): 159–77; here, 167, 171.

[49] See also Tobin, "Life and Works" 239.

[50] Tobin, "Life and Works" 237–42.

[51] The reference is surely to Winckelmann's 1763 letter to Friedrich Reinhold von Berg, *Abhandlung von der Fähigkeit der Empfindung des Schönen in der Kunst, und dem Unterrichte in derselben* (Treatise on the Ability to Recognize Beauty in Art and on the Schooling in that Ability). Johann Joachim Winckelmann, "Abhandlung von der Fähigkeit der Empfindung des Schönen in der Kunst, und

dem Unterrichte in derselben," in *Kleine Schriften: Vorreden; Entwürfe*, ed. Walther Rehm (Berlin: de Gruyter, 1968), 211–33.

[52] See Martin, "Gender, Sexuality, and Identity in Thomas Mann," 64.

[53] See Hans Wysling, "Aschenbachs Werke. Archivalische Untersuchungen an einem Thomas Mann-Satz," *Euphorion* 59 (1965): 272–314.

[54] Eugene McNamara, "'Death in Venice': The Disguised Self," *College English* 24 (1962): 233–34; here, 233; see also Tobin "Why Is Tadzio a Boy?" 222–24 and "Life and Works," 232.

[55] Cf. Hayes and Quinby, "The Aporia of Bourgeois Art," 162.

[56] "Es ist sicher gut, daß die Welt nur das schöne Werk, nicht auch seine Ursprünge, nicht seine Entstehungsbedingungen kennt; denn die Kenntnis der Quellen, aus denen dem Künstler Eingebung floß, würde sie oftmals verwirren, abschrecken und so die Wirkungen des Vortrefflichen aufheben" (556; Verily it is well for the world that it sees only the beauty of the completed work and not its origins nor the conditions whence it sprang; since knowledge of the artist's inspiration might often but confuse and alarm and so prevent the full effect of its excellence: 53).

[57] Ignace Feuerlicht, "Thomas Mann and Homoeroticism," *Germanic Review* 57 (1982): 89–97; here, 94. Cf. Marson, *The Ascetic Artist*, 122; cf. Swales, *Thomas Mann: A Study*, 42.

[58] See George L. Mosse, *The Image of Man: The Creation of Modern Masculinity* (New York: Oxford University Press, 1996).

[59] Cf. Braverman and Nachman, "The Dialectic of Decadence," 292–93; see also Heilbut, *Thomas Mann: Eros and Literature*, 247; White, "Love, Beauty, and Death in Venice," 62–63.

[60] Cf. Lilian R. Furst, "The Potential Deceptiveness of Reading in *Death in Venice*," in *Thomas Mann* Death in Venice, ed. Ritter, 158–70; here, 162.

[61] "Fast jedem Künstlernaturell ist ein üppiger und verräterischer Hang eingeboren, Schönheit schaffende Ungerechtigkeit anzuerkennen und aristokratischer Bevorzugung Teilnahme und Huldigung entgegenzubringen" (531; For in almost every artist nature is inborn a wanton and treacherous proneness to side with the beauty that breaks hearts, to single out aristocratic pretensions and pay them homage: 31–32).

[62] Martin, "Gender, Sexuality, and Identity," 60, 61.

[63] Tobin, "Life and Works," 232; also 236; cf. Frank Baron, "Sensuality and Morality in Thomas Mann's *Tod in Venedig*," *Germanic Review* 45 (1970): 115–25.

[64] See Christoph Lorey and John Plews, "Defying Sights in German Literature and Culture: An Introduction to Queering the Canon," in *Queering the Canon*, ed. Lorey and Plews, xiii–xxiv; here, xiv–xviii.

[65] Cf. Reed, who argues—by referring to Mann's knowledge of the purely sexual and the higher cultural uses of homosexuality conceived by Plato—that Aschenbach is stalled at the sexual level, idolizing Tadzio as opposed to turning him into divine thought (*The Uses of Tradition*, 156–75; *Thomas Mann*, Der Tod in

Venedig: *Text, Materialien, Kommentar,* 160–62). Cf. Christoph Koné, who sees a variation in the gaze between the encounters and "fetishistic scopophilia" in the way Aschenbach regards Tadzio (Koné, "Aschenbach's Homovisual Desire: Scopophilia in *Der Tod in Venedig* by Thomas Mann," in *Thomas Mann,* ed. Bornchen, Mein, and Schmidt, 95–106; here, 101).

66 The distinction I make (see also Plews, "The Specter of the Face") has also been pursued by Tobin ("Queering Thomas Mann's *Der Tod in Venedig*").

67 See Steakley, *The Homosexual Emancipation Movement in Germany,* 43–44, 46, 54, 61.

68 Harry Oosterhuis discusses Mann's linking of homoeroticism and the German nation in the essays *Betrachtungen eines Unpolitischen* (Reflections of a Nonpolitical Man, 1918) and *Von deutscher Republik* (On the German Republic, 1922) (in "The Dubious Magic of Male Beauty: Politics and Homoeroticism in the Lives and Works of Thomas and Klaus Mann," in *Queering the Canon,* ed. Lorey and Plews (Columbia, SC: Camden House, 1998, 181–206; here, 189–92, 194). Oosterhuis indicates that, while Mann was little interested in homosexual emancipation and rejected Hirschfeld's position, his initial political understanding of homoeroticism and the tradition of male-male associations in German culture meant his views approximated those of Brand and archconservative intellectual Hans Blüher (see also Detering, *Das offene Geheimnis,* 285–90; Feuerlicht, "Thomas Mann and Homoeroticism," 93). I am also struck by the proximity between Mann's and Friedländer's thought after reading the following remarks by Ritter about the essay *Über die Ehe* (On Marriage, 1925): "Mann equated 'virtue and morality' with heterosexual marriage, and 'aestheticism' with homosexual artists. He seemed to see in gay [*sic*] love only a narcissistic death wish. Yet, confusingly enough, he also insisted in his diaries that his particular 'abstract' homoerotic desire represented a healthier instinct than his far more powerful drive for a bourgeois family" ("A Critical History of *Death in Venice*," 91–92). While Heilbut perhaps goes a little far in asserting that Mann speaks "for homosexuals" (*Thomas Mann: Eros and Literature,* 251), it certainly appears that Aschenbach is accompanied by Mann in sharing Brand and Friedländer's viewpoint. Feuerlicht has catalogued Mann's sustained interest in adolescent males and young men ("Thomas Mann and Homoeroticism," 91–92).

69 "Gustav von Aschenbach war ein wenig unter Mittelgröße, brünett, rasiert. Sein Kopf erschien ein wenig zu groß im Verhältnis zu der fast zierlichen Gestalt. Sein rückwärts gebürstetes Haar, am Scheitel gelichtet, an den Schläfen sehr voll und stark ergraut, umrahmte eine hohe, zerklüftete und gleichsam narbige Stirn. Der Bügel einer Goldbrille mit randlosen Gläsern schnitt in die Wurzel der gedrungenen, edel gebogenen Nase ein. Der Mund war groß, oft schlaff, oft plötzlich schmal und gespannt; die Wangenpartie mager und gefurcht, das wohlausgebildete Kinn weich gespalten. Bedeutende Schicksale schienen über dies meist leidend seitwärts geneigte Haupt hinweggegangen zu sein, und doch war die Kunst es gewesen, die hier jene physiognomische Durchbildung übernommen hatte, welche sonst das Werk eines schweren, bewegten Lebens ist. Hinter dieser Stirn waren die blitzenden Repliken des Gesprächs zwischen Voltaire und dem Könige über den Krieg geboren; diese Augen, müde und tief durch die Gläser blickend, hatten das blutige Inferno der Lazarette des Siebenjährigen Krieges gesehen.

Auch persönlich genommen ist ja die Kunst ein erhöhtes Leben. Sie beglückt tiefer, sie verzehrt rascher. Sie gräbt in das Antlitz ihres Dieners die Spuren imaginärer und geistiger Abenteuer, und sie erzeugt, selbst bei köstlicher Stille des äußeren Daseins, auf die Dauer eine Verwöhntheit, Überfeinerung, Müdigkeit und Neugier der Nerven, wie ein Leben voll ausschweifendster Leidenschaften und Genüsse sie kaum hervorbringen vermag" (515–16; Gustave von Aschenbach was somewhat below middle height, dark and smooth-shaven, with a head that looked rather too large for his almost delicate figure. He wore his hair brushed back; it was thin at the parting, bushy and grey on the temples, framing a lofty, rugged, knotty brow—if one may so characterize it. The nose-piece of his rimless gold spectacles cut into the base of his thick, aristocratically hooked nose. The mouth was large, often lax, often suddenly narrow and tense; the cheeks lean and furrowed, the pronounced chin slightly cleft. The vicissitudes of fate, it seemed, must have passed over his head, for he held it, plaintively, rather on one side; yet it was art, not the stern discipline of an active career, that had taken over the office of modelling these features. Behind his brow were born the flashing thrust and parry of the dialogue between Frederick and Voltaire on the theme of war; these eyes, weary and sunken, gazing through their glasses, had beheld the blood-stained inferno of the hospitals in the Seven Years' War. Yes, personally speaking too, art heightens life. She gives deeper joy, she consumes more swiftly. She engraves adventures of the spirit and the mind in the faces of her votaries; let them lead outwardly a life of the most cloistered calm, she will in the end produce in them a fastidiousness, an over-refinement, a nervous fever and exhaustion, such as a career of extravagant passions and pleasures can hardly show: 19).

Elsewhere Aschenbach is said to have gray hair (540, 544, 576), a "müdes und scharfes Gesicht" (540; keen and weary face: 39), and a high forehead (544) and to look serious (539; twice sharing this expression with Tadzio: 561, 576). When discussing encounters between Aschenbach and Tadzio, the narrator refers not only to "jene[] fachmännisch kühle[] Billigung" (535; the patronizing air of the connoisseur: 35), but also to "d[ie] gebildete[] und würdevolle[] Miene des Älteren" (561; The elder's dignified and cultured mien: 57).

70 Farrelly, "Apollo and Dionysus Interpreted in Thomas Mann's *Der Tod in Venedig,*" *New German Studies* 3 (1975): 1–15; here, 5.

71 Matt, . . . *fertig ist das Angesicht,* 197–98.

72 See also Rockwood and Rockwood, "The Psychological Reality of Myth in *Der Tod in Venedig,*" 138; and Tobin, "Life and Works," 228.

73 Arthur Burkhard, "Thomas Mann's Appraisal of the Poet," *PMLA* 46 (1931): 880–916; here, 881, 883, 886.

74 Burkhard, "Thomas Mann's Appraisal," 890, 892, 895, 896, 897.

75 Marson, *The Ascetic Artist,* 20; see also 20–21, n17.

76 Cohn, "The Second Author of *Der Tod in Venedig,*" 126–27.

77 Cf. Matt, . . . *fertig ist das Angesicht,* 81–82. Mann used Goethe as one of several models for Aschenbach. Other models include novelist Gustave Flaubert, composers Gustav Mahler and Richard Wagner, philosopher Friedrich Nietzsche, and poet August von Platen. For allusions to Platen in Aschenbach, see Fred E.

Oppenheimer, "Auf den Spuren Gustav Aschenbachs: Schlüsselfiguren zu Gustav Aschenbach in Thomas Manns *Der Tod in Venedig*," in *Studies in Modern and Classical Languages and Literature*, ed. Fidel Lopez Criado (Madrid: Origenes, 1988), 145–53; here, 146–52.

[78] See Frey, "'Die stumme Begegnung,'" 191.

[79] Cohn, "The Second Author of *Der Tod in Venedig*," 125–26, 129. See also Burton Pike, "Thomas Mann and the Problematic Self," *Publications of the English Goethe Society* 37 (1967): 120–42; here, 136; and Reed, *The Uses of Tradition*, 148, 163.

[80] "Aschenbach . . . sah . . . seine Brauen sich entschiedener und ebenmäßiger wölben, den Schnitt seiner Augen sich verlängern, ihren Glanz durch eine leichte Untermalung des Lides sich heben, sah weiter unten, wo die Haut bräunlich-ledern gewesen, weich aufgetragen, ein zartes Karmin erwachen, seine Lippen, blutarm soeben noch, himbeerfarben schwellen, die Furchen der Wangen, des Mundes, die Runzeln der Augen unter Crème und Jugendhauch verschwinden,— erblickte mit Herzklopfen einen blühenden Jüngling" (586; He watched it in the mirror and saw his eyebrows grow more even and arching, the eyes gain in size and brilliance, by dint of a little application below the lids. A delicate carmine glowed on his cheeks where the skin had been so brown and leathery. The dry, anaemic lips grew full, they turned the colour of ripe strawberries, the lines round eyes and mouth were treated with a facial cream and gave no place to youthful bloom. It was a young man who looked back at him from the glass—Aschenbach's heart leaped at the sight: 78).

[81] Holger A. Pausch and Diana Spokiene, "Walter Benjamin, Roland Barthes und die Dialektik der Modesprache im Werk Thomas Manns," *Wirkendes Wort* 49 (1999): 86–104; here, 96–98.

[82] Cf. Pausch and Spokiene, "Walter Benjamin, Roland Barthes und die Dialektik der Modesprache im Werk Thomas Manns," 91, 99. Margaret Morganroth Gullette makes the same point in her discussion of the "protagonist's illusory attempt to circumvent his ageing . . . by trying to possess youth vicariously through the bodies of the young" ("The Exile of Adulthood: Pedophilia in the Midlife Novel," *Novel: A Forum on Fiction* 17.3 (1984): 215–32; here, 215). See also Swales, *Thomas Mann: A Study*, 41. Viktor Žmegač sees Mann's use of makeup in the context of Charles Baudelaire's antithesis between nature (the imitation of nature) and the civilizing process of cultural artifice (Žmegač, "Zu einem Thema Goethes und Thomas Manns: Wege der Erotik in der modernen Gesellschaft," *Goethe Jahrbuch* 103 (1986): 152–67; here, 164).

[83] Pausch and Spokiene, "Walter Benjamin, Roland Barthes und die Dialektik der Modesprache," 97.

[84] Gullette, "The Exile of Adulthood," 223.

[85] "Die Aufhebung der physischen Distanz zwischen dem Komödianten und den Anständigen" (574; overstep[ping] the physical distance between [the comedian] and respectable people: 68); "bei wiederhergestelltem künstlerischen Abstand zwischen ihm und den Herrschaften" (575; he was farther off from his audience: 69—literally: *having restored the artistic distance between him and the audience*).

[86] Burton Pike maintains that "Aschenbach is diminished so that the narrator may triumph" ("Thomas Mann and the Problematic Self," 137).

[87] Russell A. Berman, "History and Community in *Death in Venice*," in *Thomas Mann* Death in Venice, ed. Ritter, 263–80; here, 275.

[88] Berman, "History and Community," 275.

[89] Bernhard Frank, "Mann's *Death in Venice*," 2006, 99.

[90] See Edward Diller, "The Grotesque Animal-Heroes of Thomas Mann's Early Works," *German Life and Letters* 20 (1967): 225–33.

[91] Berman, "History and Community," 276.

Seeing the Human in the (Queer) Migrant in Jenny Erpenbeck's *Gehen, Ging, Gegangen* and Terézia Mora's *Alle Tage*

Nicholas Courtman, Jesus College, Cambridge

ORE THAN A MILLION MIGRANTS have come to Germany since the
beginning of 2015, many of them refugees fleeing from conflict in Syria or other parts of the globe.[1] One of the many
responses to this influx of people has been the establishment of a number of housing centers specifically for LGBTQ refugees, a phenomenon
that has been covered by a number of mainstream press outlets. While
Germany has been home to queer migrants and refugees long before
2015, the media reports on these centers constitute one of the few times
that these migrants' existence has been acknowledged in German public
discourse, which Fatima El-Tayeb claims has long been, and still is, dominated by patterns of thought in which migrants and racialized "communities [. . .] appear as by default heterosexual, the queer community as by
default white."[2] Several authors and filmmakers have produced German-
language films and texts that undermine this simplistic dichotomy by
exploring the experience of migrant and racialized LGBTQ people,[3] yet
many authors—and critics—perpetuate the discursive tendency to erase
the existence of queer migrants. In this essay, I will analyze and compare
two novels that engage with forced migration and displacement, namely
Terézia Mora's *Alle Tage* (All Days, 2004) and Jenny Erpenbeck's *Gehen,
Ging, Gegangen* (Going, Went, Gone, 2015),[4] to examine the place of
non-heterosexual sexuality in authors' attempts to render the experience
and existence of (queer) migrants visible.

Before summarizing the plot of these novels in greater detail, it is
necessary to explore some of the theory informing my methodology in
this chapter. In its exploration of the dynamics of visibility and erasure,
my analysis is informed by the work of Judith Butler, particularly those
strands of her work that focus, in Moya Lloyd's words, on "the relation
between normative violence and cultural intelligibility: how, that is, culturally particular norms define who is recognizable as a subject capable of
living a life that counts."[5] While her earlier writings explored this primarily in relation to gender and sexuality, Butler's focus broadened after 2000

to address a greater variety of cultural norms that mold collective understandings "of what constitutes [. . .] the distinctively human life, and what does not,"[6] with gender and sexuality functioning as two of many vectors of identity through which she examines what she terms the "differential production of the human and the less-than-human."[7] The military conflicts that followed 9/11 and their media coverage in the West were significant in driving this shift, as reflected in Butler's two collections of essays on these topics. In *Frames of War* (2009), Butler explicitly links her thought on the cultural delineation of the distinctively human life with the notion of (in)visibility, arguing that media and political discourses surrounding these conflicts are structured by epistemological frames that "work to differentiate the lives we can apprehend [as viably human] from those we cannot," frames that "not only organize visual experience but also generate specific ontologies of the subject."[8]

Butler describes these frames as "at once a material and perceptual issue, since those whose lives" cannot be accommodated within these frames, and thereby appear to be of a lesser viability or worth, are often forced into precarity, "made to bear the burden of starvation, underemployment, legal disenfranchisement, and differential exposure to violence and death,"[9] in blatant disregard of what Butler proposed, in *Undoing Gender*, as an ethical duty to attend to "what humans require to maintain and reproduce the conditions of their own livability,"[10] both at and beyond the level of material sustenance. The differential allocation of visibility to certain subjects and populations is, according to Robert Young, also one of the prime concerns of postcolonial theory in the twenty-first century. Responding to the proclamation of postcolonial theory's death, Young asserts that, in the twenty-first as in the late twentieth century, the "task of the postcolonial [. . .] is to make the invisible [. . .] visible."[11] Young argues that the postcolonial criticism of the previous century sought to do this by dismantling Eurocentric epistemological regimes that effaced the existence and political claims of indigenous or colonized peoples. Postcolonial criticism in the twenty-first century, however, faces a situation in which military conflicts, environmental crisis, and economic globalization have together fostered the development of "a new subaltern tricontinental of migrants [. . .] made up of refugees, internally displaced persons, stateless persons, asylum seekers, economic migrants, illegal aliens,"[12] subjects who function, Young argues, as the invisible support system of economies around the globe, while regularly being forced into the precarity described by Butler.[13]

Reading Young's article in 2017 with Germany in mind, where refugees and migrants have for the last two years been almost constantly present in media discourse and public debate, one may ask whether the "invisibility" of which Young speaks is now a thing of the past, replaced by an almost excessive visibility that simultaneously fuels, and is fueled by, growing right-wing populist nationalism. One certainly has the impression that Young's call for increased visibility would benefit from Butler's concern about the frames through—and conditions under—which visibility is bestowed. Indeed, Klaus Bade argues that the dehumanizing language which has been the stock and trade of numerous politicians, journalists, and citizens for years when speaking of Young's tricontinental, and has, to speak with Butler, thereby partially governed the terms under which those subjects attain cultural visibility, has laid the seeds for the widespread public aggression towards refugees that often finds expression in physical violence,[14] with some groups estimating there to have been well over 1,000 attacks on migrants and their lodgings in the twenty-four months since January 2015.[15]

This already complex situation is made even more complex for queer migrants when we consider that lesbian and gay rights have, over the last fifteen years, occasionally been co-opted by right-wing groups eager to cast migrants as endangering gay and lesbian rights, a phenomenon that has come to be frequently discussed under the term homonationalism.[16] It is worth stressing that these right-wing groups are seldom truly committed to the defense of LGBTQ people, as evidenced by the trans- and homophobia spouted by members of the Alternative für Deutschland (Alternative for Germany). Regardless of this, when such politicians pit migrants against queers in this manner, it only serves to fortify and further entrench the reductive binary thinking identified by El-Tayeb. The positioning of queers and migrants as binary opposites effectively erases the existence of those queer migrants who belong to both groups, an example of a phenomenon known as "intersectional invisibility."[17] One of the arenas in which we encounter this particular form of intersectional invisibility at work is in the interdisciplinary field of migration studies, which some have criticized for "virtually ignor[ing] the connections among heteronormativity, sexuality, and immigration,"[18] and often "relying upon heteronormative assumptions when establishing what kinds of socio-genetic affiliations and affective ties are thought to matter."[19]

This fraught discursive field provides the background to my analysis of the novels of Mora and Erpenbeck, which engage with waves of migration sparked by two different conflicts in the late twentieth and twenty-first century. *Alle Tage* explores the aftermath of conflicts in the former Yugoslavia through a narrative woven around the protagonist Abel Nema, who flees to Berlin to avoid military enlistment and remains there after the end of the conflict, living for several years as an undocumented migrant before entering a sham marriage for visa purposes. The labyrinthine narrative proceeds non-chronologically, each chapter focusing on (and partially focalized through) different characters who come into contact with Abel, many of whom are undocumented migrants or refugees. *Gehen, Ging, Gegangen* follows Richard, a recently retired East German professor of Classical Literature, as he befriends a number of refugees—mostly Muslim men, many of African descent, displaced by the Libyan civil war of 2011—involved with the refugee camp situated on Berlin's Oranienplatz following the clearance of the camp by the Berlin Senate,[20] and goes on to educate himself about their reasons for fleeing, their living conditions, and the laws regulating asylum in Europe.

In my analysis, I will first examine the similar way in which both texts try to make the dehumanizing effects of state treatment of refugees and undocumented migrants visible, with both authors presenting migrants as being stuck in a pathologically empty and extended present. Following on from this, I will examine Erpenbeck's attempts to undermine the discursive dehumanization of refugees through a positive reframing, drawing attention to the way in which the healthy, "natural" temporality that she develops as an alternative to this pathological extended present is itself imbricated in the exclusive privileging of heteronormative affiliations and the erasure of queer migrants. Finally, I will turn to *Alle Tage* to examine not only the intersections of deviant sexuality and migrant experience and identity, but also to examine the way in which queerness has been made almost entirely invisible in the majority of the secondary literature on the text. This reading of the readings to which the text has already been subjected will show how existing criticism has obscured the novel's heretofore overlooked exploration of the double displacement of queer migrants.

Migration and the Extended Present

Sarah Turnbull argues that the temporal experience of migrants awaiting decisions from state authorities that would grant them asylum, or rights of employment or freedom of movement comparable to those of citizens, is often one of being "stuck" in time, left waiting in an extended present without a sense of personal agency.[21] Turnbull focuses primarily on the experience of time within detention centers, but claims that many migrants outside of such centers who do not possess relevant documentation often report experiencing this pathological feeling of being stuck.[22] Mora and Erpenbeck's novels explore various facets of this extended present through a variety of spaces, some controlled by the state, others established by migrants who are attempting to evade or resist state control.

These spaces are portrayed as functioning according to their own temporal logics, bearing strong resemblance to the heterotopic spaces theorized by Michel Foucault. Foucault uses the term heterotopia to describe "real places [. . .] which are something like counter-sites, a kind of effectively enacted utopia in which all the other real sites that can be found within the culture, are simultaneously represented, contested, and inverted."[23] Modern heterotopias are predominantly "heterotopias of

deviation: those in which individuals whose behavior is deviant in relation to the required mean or norm are placed."[24] Foucault's examples
include prisons, hospital clinics, and psychiatric wards, a list to which one
can reasonably add temporary centers housing refugees. Foucault stresses
that "heterotopias are most often linked to slices in time," claiming that a
"heterotopia begins to function at full capacity when men [*sic!*] arrive at a
sort of absolute break with their traditional time."[25]

One such space in *Alle Tage* is the flat inhabited by Kinga, a volatile
woman whom Abel first encounters during a train journey in his home
country, meeting her again years later in Berlin. Kinga claims that if she
had stayed in her home country, she would have become a teacher and
lived in bourgeois respectability (*AT* 145). Due to her lack of papers,
however, she instead supports herself by working odd jobs as a babysit-
ter or cleaner and through occasional performances with her band (*AT*
146). Her bandmates, who originate from the same country as Abel and
Kinga, voice a longing for a life of bourgeois legality and the longevity and stability such a life promises, as indicated by Kinga's bandmate
Janda's expression of desire for "einen Ort [. . .] an dem ich mich in
Frieden niederlassen kann" (*AT* 147; a place where I can settle down in
peace). What Kinga has instead of such a place is the leftover rehearsal
space of the musicians, which she names *Anarchia Kingania* (*AT* 145).
In the following passage, Kinga portrays *Anarchia Kingania* as fundamentally opposed to the desire for longevity and stability harbored by
her and her bandmates:

> Wir leben hier in einer Enklave, sagte Kinga. Was folgt daraus?
> Daraus folgt zum einen, dass alles *jetzt* ist. Aussagen, die Zukunft
> betreffend, können zwar gemacht werden, aber das ist auch nicht
> mehr als ein Kaffeebohnenorakel. (*AT* 153; italics in original)

> [Here we live in an enclave, said Kinga. What does that mean? For
> one that means that everything is *now*. Statements regarding the
> future can be made, but they're not worth more than reading tea
> leaves.]

Anarchia Kingania and its focus on the present are not presented as
being entirely negative. As Anke Biendarra points out, it is the only
living space in the entire novel that "provides both sociality and community building,"[26] in which the otherwise solitary Abel is forced into
contact with Kinga's bandmates and with the guests that attend her wild
parties, which can be read as the purest expression of the space's align-
ment with a Dionysian embrace of the intensity of the moment. Yet it is
also made clear that this is not a present that can last. The frantic pace of
life in the flat, rather than providing a stream of new experiences, soon
gives way to monotony and repetition, with the narrator proclaiming

that "was nach Chaos aussah, war in Wirklichkeit eine Folge immer gleicher Tage" (*AT* 153; what looked like chaos was in reality a series of
days that were all the same). Eventually Kinga's mental health starts to
deteriorate, she begins pacing the hallway talking to herself (*AT* 290),
and doesn't wash herself for days on end (*AT* 293). Just as it prevented
her from seeking official employment, her lack of papers prevents her
from seeking medical treatment:

> Geh zum Arzt, ha! Ja, wo leben wir denn? DA HABEN WIR WOHL
> WAS VERPASST, *GENOSSE!* Geh zum Arzt. Wenn ich eine dieser
> . . . eine von *denen* wäre, könnte ich zum Arzt gehen. (*AT* 291; ital-
> ics in original)

> [Go to the doctor, ha! Where do you think we're living? WE'VE
> MISSED OUT ON SOMETHING THERE, *COMRADE!* Go to
> the doctor. If I were one of those . . . if I were one of *them*, I could
> go to the doctor.]

Prior to this outburst, Kinga is terrified by her reflection in a puddle, in
which she sees herself as a "haltlose Kreatur" (an ungrounded creature /
a creature adrift, *AT* 289), a description that suggests her lack of rooted-
ness in place and time to be one of the primary causes of her descent into
madness. At this point, she throws a final party in the flat, which seems
like a dystopian reimagining of the earlier affairs, as she renames *Anarchia
Kingania* "Titanic," locks the flat from inside, terrorizes the guests, and
threatens to jump off the roof. By the end of the novel she makes good
on the threat, killing herself by jumping out of a window after having left
it too late to seek professional treatment (*AT* 355).

In her presentation of *Anarchia Kingania*, Mora provides a model
of how migrants who find themselves consigned to illegality may relate
to time and space, while drawing attention to the limitations placed upon
the agency of undocumented migrants. While the focus upon the present
in the construction of an intense, hedonistic social hub can be seen as
a creative response to the impossibility of establishing a future through
avenues of legal employment, it is—as Kinga says herself—fundamentally futureless. Nonetheless, it is a space that Kinga and the musicians
create and manage themselves, a fact which Kinga purposefully stresses
in comparison to the alternative of living in a space of the same temporality but in the control of the state: "Das wichtigste ist, sagt Kinga,
nicht in ein Lager zu gehen. Wenn du in ein Lager gehst, bist du erledigt.
Unabhängig bleiben, egal wie" (*AT* 145; the most important thing is not
to go into a camp. If you go into a camp, then you're done for. Stay independent, no matter what).

Gehen, Ging, Gegangen also touches upon the question of the construction and use of space under conditions of restricted agency. The

earlier sections of the text show the refugee-run camp at Oranienplatz, while the later sections depict a series of refugee accommodation centers following the clearance of the camp, such that, in contrast to *Alle Tage*, we see both "independent" and state-controlled heterotopia of migration. The two novels also differ in their emphasis upon the significance of the migrants' inability to seek legal employment. The references in *Alle Tage* to the professions the characters would have pursued if they had a work permit are present, but not prominent in the text. In *Gehen, Ging, Gegangen*, on the other hand, the question of the right to work is foregrounded throughout, and is introduced the first moment that Richard passes a group of refugees protesting on the Alexanderplatz.

> An einem Donnerstag Ende August versammeln sich zehn Männer vor dem Roten Rathaus in Berlin. Sie haben beschlossen, heißt es, nichts mehr zu essen. [. . .] Ihre Hautfarbe ist Schwarz. [. . .] Was wollen die Männer? Arbeit wollen sie. Und von der Arbeit leben. (*GGG* 18)

> [On a Thursday at the end of August, ten men gather in front of the Red Townhall in Berlin. They have resolved, it is said, to not eat anything. [. . .] The color of their skin is black [. . .] What do the men want? They want work. And to live from the work.]

At this point in the narrative, the camp on the Oranienplatz is still in place, where the refugees are presented as living in an empty, extended present similar to that which we encountered in *Alle Tage*; when a journalist visiting the camp asks what the men do all day since they are not allowed to work, a white German associated with the camp replies, "Nichts. [. . .] Wenn das Nichtstun zu schlimm wird, organisieren wir eine Demo" (*GGG* 48; Nothing. When doing nothing gets too bad, we organize a demonstration). This recalls the opening scene of the novel, which documents Richard's experience of "eine ganz andere Art von Zeit" (*GGG* 10; a completely different type of time) in his first days of retirement, as he can no longer fill his time with work. The woman's words lead Richard to realize that "über das sprechen, was Zeit eigentlich ist, kann er wahrscheinlich am besten mit denen, die aus ihr hinausgefallen sind. Oder in sie hineingsperrt" (*GGG* 15; he can probably speak best about what time really is with those people who have fallen out of it. Or been locked into it). When he returns to the camp to speak with the refugees, however, the camp has already been dismantled and its inhabitants moved into state-run temporary residences. While the refugees agreed to enter these new centers in the hope that their applications for asylum would be processed at an accelerated rate, the state-run centers produce an even more pathological temporality, turning time against them: "[Mit] der Wunderwaffe der Zeit hacken sie auf die Ankömmlinge ein, stechen ihnen mit Tagen und Wochen die Augen aus, wälzen die Monate über sie hin [. . .]" (*GGG*

103; They hack at the arrivals with the miracle weapon time, prick out their eyes with days and weeks, roll the months out over them).

Richard goes to the centers and speaks with many of the refugees. In the course of these conversations, the idea of time filled with work appears as the natural alternative to the time imposed on them by the state. When Richard asks what the men do all day during his first visit to the center, they respond that "wir wollen arbeiten [. . .] aber wir bekommen keine Arbeitserlaubnis. [. . .] Ein Tag ist genau wie der andre" (*GGG* 63; we want to work [. . .] but we don't receive a work permit [. . .] Every day is just like every other), betraying a striking similarity with the "Folge immer gleicher Tage" in *Anarchia Kingania* (*AT* 153). That work provides the natural use of time is further emphasized by the text's narrator:

> In Wahrheit wollen sie vom Senat überhaupt nichts. In Wahrheit wollen sie auf Arbeitssuche gehen und sich ihr Leben selbst organisieren, so wie jeder, der bei Kräften und bei Verstand ist. (*GGG* 102)
>
> [Truth be told, they want absolutely nothing from the senate. Truth be told, they want to go and look for work and organize their own lives, just like anyone who is of sound body and mind.]

Of course, Foucault defined heterotopia as spaces in which precisely those who are not "bei Kräften und bei Verstand" are placed, such as the mentally ill, the severely handicapped, or the aged. The refugees, all men in the prime of their life, are repeatedly shown to be sleeping in the middle of the day (GGG 59, 65, 121, 145) and are placed by the Berlin Senate in a former retirement home (*GGG* 54), identified by Foucault as a prototypical heterotopia of deviation.[27] Erpenbeck goes to considerable lengths to tease out a variety of implications from this placement, and repeatedly styles the extended present in which the refugees find themselves as a type of premature infirmity or senility; Richard observes that the Germans employed by the state to act as the wardens of the center enter the refugees' rooms without knocking, "wie ein Arzt oder Pfleger auf einer Krankenstation" (*GGG* 59; like a doctor or nurse in a hospital ward), and he later finds himself "davon erschreckt, dass diese jungen Männer hier plötzlich so alt sein müssen. Warten und Schlafen. [. . .] Warten und Schlafen" (*GGG* 66; appalled that these young men must suddenly be so old. Waiting and sleeping [. . .] waiting and sleeping).

From Perverted Time to
Family Time: Reframing Refugees

In these passages, Erpenbeck seems to be trying to render the suffering caused by the German state's policies towards refugees visible by focusing on said policies' direct effects, primarily by suggesting that the state's actions lead to a perversion of a natural temporal order in which time is filled with, and given meaning by, work. To speak with Butler, we may identify these passages as part of Erpenbeck's attempt to draw attention to how said policies undermine the refugees' possibility of living a livable life. Erpenbeck is not only concerned with bestowing visibility upon the refugees' suffering, however; she also attempts to make the refugees visible as subjects in their own right, rendering them as individualized figures instead of presenting them as an undifferentiated and passive, suffering mass. One of the main ways in which Erpenbeck attempts to do this is through passages containing interview-style dialogues between Richard and various refugees.[28] In these exchanges, described by Erpenbeck in media interviews as often containing verbatim material from interviews she conducted with refugees in preparation for the novel,[29] the focus lies primarily upon the interviewees' lives prior to the events which forced them to flee and the structure of their everyday lives before these traumatic breaks.

It is the latter of these two foci, namely the recounting of everyday life in their places of origin, that provides examples of "natural" temporal orders that function as the alternative models to the perverted temporality into which the refugees are forced by the German state. In pursuing this effect, Erpenbeck regularly emphasizes the prior embeddedness of the refugees in the spatio-temporal structures of the family and the home, that is to say, those "heteronormative socio-genetic affiliations and affective ties" that, according to Kira Kosnick, dominate discussions in migration studies.[30] Thus in the passage in which Richard speaks with Awad, a Ghanaian national who grew up in Libya before being expelled during the 2011 civil war, Awad's relationship with his father is the focus:

Der Vater zieht die Jalousien auf der Südseite des Hauses, auf die tagsüber die Sonne scheint, erst abends nach oben. Der Vater bringt seinem Sohn bei, wie man sich nach dem Duschen den Rücken abtrocknet, mit einem schräg über den Rücken gespannten Handtuch. Sein Vater bringt ihm bei, wie man kocht. Sein Vater schenkt ihm den ersten Rasierapparat.
Mein Vater sagte mir, wer ich bin, sagt Awad. (*GGG* 76)

[The father doesn't pull up the blinds on the south-side of the house, on which the sun shines during the day, until the evening. The father teaches his son how to dry his back after showering by stretching a towel over his back at an angle. His father teaches him how to cook. His father gives him his first shaving razor as a gift.
My father told me who I am, says Awad.]

Erpenbeck aims in this passage to bring out the emotional significance that the seemingly banal details of everyday life within the family home can accrue, and effectively suggests that the transmission of these habits and knowledge from father to son is central in the formation of the son's very identity. The affective intensity of the passage is heightened by the repeated references to the father at the beginning of each sentence and by the shifts in the preceding article ("Der" ⇒ "Sein" ⇒ "Mein"), bringing the references from the realm of the general to the personal. It is worth noting, however, that the preponderance of general articles at the passage's beginning establish that which follows as paradigmatic in nature; the recounting of Awad's identity formation under his father thereby functions not only as an individual story of how Awad learns who *he* is from *his* father, but also as an example of how *the* son learns who he is through *the* father's tutelage. The link between father and son is shattered when Awad's father is killed following the outbreak of conflict, destroying Awad's sense of self in the process: "Ich weiß nicht mehr, wer ich bin" (*GGG*, 81; I no longer know who I am).

Many of the conversations between Richard and the refugees similarly detail the traumatic destruction of families, and Erpenbeck often uses similar literary techniques to increase the emotional impact of the passages. In another passage Raschid, for example, recounts how his children drowned when the boat in which they were travelling to Europe capsized. Before narrating this moment, however, he painstakingly reconstructs the daily routine in his household prior to the outbreak of war:

> Mein Sohn war beinahe drei, und meine Tochter schon fünf Jahre alt. [. . .] Um acht Uhr gingen wir aus dem Haus, ich brachte die Kinder zur Schule. Ahmed, beinahe schon drei, und Amina, fünf Jahre alt. [. . .] Halb eins oder eins, wenn die Schule vorbei war, kamen die Kinder zu mir. Ahmed und Amina. [. . .] Das Abendbrot hab immer ich gekocht. Der Kleine durfte von meinem Teller essen. Danach gingen die Kinder zu Bett. [. . .] Er hat immer viel geträumt. Ahmed. Dann ließ ich ihn bei mir schlafen, und meine Frau ging für den Rest der Nacht ins Kinderzimmer zu unserer Tochter. Amina. (*GGG* 236–37)

> [My son was almost three, and my daughter already five years old. [. . .] At eight in the morning we left the house, I took the children to school. Ahmed, almost already three, and Amina, five years old. [. . .] At half-past twelve or one o'clock, when school was finished, the children came to me. Ahmed and Amina. [. . .] I always cooked dinner. The little boy was allowed to eat from my plate. Then the children went to bed. [. . .] He always dreamt a lot. Ahmed. Then I let him sleep with me, and my wife went for the rest of the night to the children's bedroom to our daughter. Amina.]

The repetition of the children's names and ages serves here not only to increase the affective intensity of the passage, but also to impress the extent of the tragedy befalling those who die on the way to Europe's shores upon a general public that seems to care more when those drowning are children, as shown by the case of Alan Kurdi. As mentioned earlier, Erpenbeck has repeatedly insisted upon the factual veracity of these stories, stories that often remain obscured as a result of the frames through which the popular press, politicians, and citizens depict or discuss those who are seeking refuge in Europe, whether they be depicted as scroungers, extremists, anachronistic threats to European progressiveness, or threats to the nation's economic well-being.

Without negating the importance of providing alternatives to such dehumanizing narratives, however, it is worth pausing to reflect upon the form of Erpenbeck's corrective to these forms of framing. Indeed, it would seem that her corrective derives much of its force from heteronormative understandings of which temporalities and which kinship structures belong to a life worth living. Jack Halberstam has argued that "normative narratives of time [. . .] form the base of nearly every definition of the human in almost all of our modes of understanding."[31] Of the various heteronormative narratives of time which he identifies, "family time," defined as "the normative scheduling of daily life [. . .] that accompanies the practice of child rearing," and the "time of inheritance," defined as "an overview of generational time within which values, wealth, goods, and morals are passed through family ties from one generation to the next,"[32] are of particular relevance here; they are recognizably at work in Raschid and Awad's stories, and play a role of considerable importance in making them recognizable as viably human subjects within accepted frames of cultural intelligibility.

That Erpenbeck makes use of these heteronormative temporal narratives in her attempts at reframing refugees is, of course, not to be criticized in and of itself. What is problematic, however, is her tendency to present historically contingent norms as belonging to an ahistorical "natural" order, a tendency that is noticeable in her treatment of work in the novel. As already shown, the state's refusal to grant the refugees the right to work is presented in the text as the perversion of a natural temporal order which leaves them in a state of premature senility. The refugees' call for the right to work is often cast as a call for the restitution of the natural order of things; Raschid assuring Richard that "wenn du mich arbeiten sehen könntest, sähest du einen ganz anderen Raschid [. . .] Arbeiten ist für mich so natürlich wie Atmen" (*GGG* 241; if you could see me working, you would see an entirely different Raschid [. . .] working for me is as natural as breathing) is but one example of this. At other points in the text, the heterosexual family is subjected to a similar form of naturalization, often in concert with the naturalization of work: in the novel's final pages, Erpenbeck has the refugee that Richard nicknames Apollo state that "es muss eine Ordnung geben. Erst muss ich Arbeit haben, dann eine Wohnung, dann kann ich heiraten und dann Kinder bekommen" (*GGG* 345; there has to be an order. First I need to have work, then a flat, then I can get married and then I can have kids).

In this passage we see the establishment of a narrative sequence of work, abode, marriage, reproduction as an implicitly natural order of progression, deviation from which is explicitly to be avoided. This would not be problematic if Apollo's statement were presented as one particular perspective, simply one vision among many of what constitutes a "distinctively human life" worth living,[33] but this is not the case. Indeed, there is no suggestion, neither directly after Apollo's statement nor at any other point in the text, that any of the refugees' desires deviate significantly from this template. The novel instead abounds with passages in which the refugees equate normality with being surrounded by women and children (*GGG* 204) or where marriage is presented as the only form of relationship they desire (*GGG* 218). At times one has the sense that in her quest to fight the negative images of refugees circulating in the public sphere, Erpenbeck produces a counter-image that becomes constrictive in its adherence to standards of (heteronormative) bourgeois respectability, such that all the refugees are presented as would-be exemplary (re)productive citizens, men eager for nothing more than the chance to contribute to society through their labor, marry women, and have children.

The erasure of queer refugees that follows on from such discursive operations is an implicit one, a form of erasure by omission. There is one significant instance, however, in where such erasure takes a more active form. It begins with a passage depicting a protest organized by the refugees, during which Richard sees "wie einer der jungen Sympathisanten sein selbstgebasteltes Plakat hochhebt, auf dem steht: *Hoch leben die Schwulen und Lesben in Kenia!*" (*GGG* 268, italics in original; how one of the young sympathizers holds up a self-made placard which reads: *Long Live the Gays and Lesbians in Kenya!*). The term "Sympathisant" is significant here, as it recalls an earlier passage in which Richard observes the interaction between refugees and young, white, left-wing Germans, identified as "Sympathisanten" (*GGG* 44–45; Sympathizers). In this earlier passage, which veers between heterodiegetic and focalized narration, the "sympathizers" are cast as juvenile and naïve in their rebellion against the "heile Welt" of German bourgeois respectability, while the refugees are suggested to want nothing more than entry into the "heile Welt" against which the sympathizers are rebelling. The later uses of the term "Sympathisant" invariably evoke this earlier passage and its insinuation of fundamental differences in the worldviews and desires of the two groups.

There is no further comment upon the placard when Richard first sees it; it and its bearer are simply one of Richard's sights during the demonstration. Placard and placard-holder resurface a few pages later, however, when Richard reads a newspaper article reporting on the demonstration and the squatting of a building as a protest act by a number of other refugees, in which a number of white "Sympathisanten" were involved. This article goes on to argue that the refugees are simply

> Opfer dieser Sympathisanten, würden für deren politische Ziele instrumentalisiert, nur fehle es [den Flüchtlingen] an Intelligenz und Durchblick, um das zu erkennen. Richard erinnert sich an den jungen Mann mit dem Plakat, den er auf der Demonstration gesehen hat: *Hoch leben die Schwulen und Lesben von Kenia!* Wahrhaftig, Richard, ebenso wie die anderen Leser dieser wichtigen deutschen Zeitung beim Frühstück sitzend, in einem warmen Haus, vor sich Toast, Tee, Orangensaft, Honig und Käse, Richard sieht wahrhaftig eine düstere Zukunft über Deutschland heraufziehen, sollte sich dieser Unterstützer mithilfe der Flüchtlinge [. . .] ins Kanzleramt putschen. (*GGG* 273–74, italics in original)

> [The victims of these sympathizers who are exploiting them for their own political goals, only the refugees lack the intelligence and the savvy to recognize what's being done with them. Richard remembers the young man with the placard that he saw at the demonstration: *Long Live the Gays and Lesbians of Kenya!* Truly, Richard, sitting at breakfast just like the other readers of this important German daily newspaper, in a warm house with toast, orange juice, honey and tea in front of him, truly, Richard sees a dark future dawning on Germany should this supporter manage to putsch his way into the Chancellor's office with the help of the refugees.]

Clearly, with the emphasis placed upon Richard's domestic comfort and the outlandish reference to the dark future that might rise over Germany following the putsch of a gay rights protestor into the *Kanzleramt*, Erpenbeck is trying to ironize Richard's thoughts in this passage, and one could even read this irony as part of an attempt to draw attention to public tendencies to ignore the existence of queer refugees. Yet one would have to qualify this as a failed attempt, for a number of reasons. For one, the article does not mention the sympathizer demonstrating for gay and lesbian rights, such that the homophobic fears of a "dark future" should gay rights supporters come to power can be interpreted as Richard's alone, and not part of a satire of public homophobia.

Furthermore, and more significantly, the text as a whole predisposes the reader to concur with Richard, perhaps not in his fears of a dark future should queers come to power, but at least in his belief that the political interests of queers and refugees are indelibly separate. This is achieved in part through the absence of any mention of homosexuality or homophobia anywhere else in the novel; while Erpenbeck dedicates considerable textual space to thorough explorations of different reasons driving people to seek asylum abroad, including civil war, ethnic conflict, environmental disaster, and abject poverty, there is no passage where Richard learns about homophobia. This is compounded further by Erpenbeck's decision to identify the gay rights protestor as a "Sympathisant," a representative of the one group that is presented throughout the text as adherent to a worldview diametrically opposed to that of refugees. As a result, Erpenbeck's text, rather than drawing attention to the challenges facing queer refugees, runs the risk of reproducing the binary opposition of queers and migrants identified by El-Tayeb, and thereby partaking in the discursive erasure of their very existence.

The Invisible Elephant in the Room: Queerness in *Alle Tage*

The same charges of erasure cannot, given Mora's decision to give her novel a queer protagonist in the form of Abel Nema, be levelled against *Alle Tage*, even if they can, as we will see, be levelled against many critics who have written on the text. That is not to say that Abel's queerness is knowable or recognizable in a simple sense; indeed, while the novel's idiosyncratic form and narrative style are designed to make it difficult for the reader to get any concrete sense of who Abel is in general,[34] it is Abel's sexuality which proves perhaps most difficult to pin down. Abel seems to see himself and be seen by some others as a gay man,[35] and harbors an erotic fascination for men like Kinga's bandmates who successfully embody ideal heteronormative masculinity.[36] There are many signs within the text, however, that indicate that Abel may be more accurately described as a pederast. These include his statements during a drug-induced hallucination (*AT* 360, 369, 381, 393–94) and his purchase of an album filled with

> alte oder auf alt gemachte, bräunliche Fotos [. . .] eine Sammlung nackter Kerle. Jungs. Knaben. [. . .] die meisten sind nackt. Ihr reifer Penis wie angeklebt an ihren schönen, olivfarbenen Körpern (*AT* 210)

> [photos, brownish and old, or made to look old [. . .] a collection of naked blokes. Guys. Boys. [. . .] Most of them are naked. Their mature penises looking as if they were glued on to their beautiful, olive-colored bodies]

Yet these signs are not designed to be entirely conclusive,[37] especially in relation to Abel's sexual interactions with other men. One of the chapters deals with Abel's relationship with Danko, a young Roma boy from

Abel's country of origin who sleeps one night in Abel's flat after running away from his violent father; despite being "ganz überwältigt [. . .] von [Dankos] *Schönheit*" (*AT* 208, italics in original; entirely overwhelmed by Danko's beauty), Abel rejects Danko's attempt to kiss him (*AT* 211). Indeed, it is never suggested that Abel has sexual contact with a minor,[38] and the only sexual partner Abel is suggested to have prior to his amnesia—itself the result of a stroke he suffers upon being gay-bashed by members of Danko's former gang—is an adult man.[39]

Hopefully this brief overview makes it clear that Abel's sexuality offers ample and complex material for discussion. Yet studies of the novel display a striking silence on the question of Abel's sexuality. In many articles, the sexual side of Abel's sexuality is glossed over in favor of Abel's unrequited love for his childhood friend Ilia. Laura Bohn Case, for example, reads the entire novel following Ilia's refusal to return Abel's "words of love" as a search "for this missing response of love."[40] Yet for Case this search seems to have no sexual component; she makes no mention of Abel's visits to sex clubs, his relationship with Danko, the questionable photo albums, or his self-professed homosexuality, focusing instead on questions of linguistic and cultural integration, such that the problems created by Abel's feelings for other men, sexual or otherwise, are collapsed under the challenges he faces as a displaced person. Klaus Siblewski makes a similar argument when he contends that Abel's displacement begins the day that he is rejected by Ilia and thereby "aus dem Reich der Liebe vertrieben wird" (is exiled from the realm of love).[41] In both readings, the more complex and challenging facets of Abel's sexuality are first circumvented through an exclusive analytical focus on love, only for that experience of love to then be read as a precursor to the experience of migration and displacement, occluding the significance of sexuality as a distinct concern within the novel.

Somewhat shockingly, the erasure of sexuality in favor of a focus on geopolitical displacement can even be found in articles that purport to analyze sexuality within the novel, as illustrated by an article by Aurora Distefano.[42] Distefano begins her discussion by observing that Abel claims to be "homosexuell [. . .] wobei er tatsächlich an keiner Stelle der Geschichte homosexuell aktiv wird"[43] (homosexual [. . .] but he in fact is not homosexually active at any point in the story), a lack of "homosexual activity" which she implicitly offers as proof that he isn't gay. She then analyzes Abel's reactions to Kinga's sexual advances; while he allows her to kiss and fondle him, he at no point makes a move himself, and does not have sex with her (*AT* 157). Distefano interprets this disinterest as proof of "Unerfahrenheit, vergleichbar einem Jugendlichen, dem hierzu die Reife naturgemäß noch fehlt" (a lack of experience, comparable to an adolescent who is by nature still lacking the necessary maturity), remarking that "einen Gefallen, Geschmack, oder Vorzüge wie sie Männer im Verhältnis zu Frauen haben können, hat Abel nicht" (Abel does not have a liking, preference, or taste of the type that men can have for women).[44] Clearly, Distefano's argument is based upon a homophobic equation of natural and/or mature masculinity with the capacity for heterosexual desire. She claims that Abel, unable to produce this "mature" response, is stuck between boyhood and manhood as a result of losing the "identitätsbildend[e] Pole Heimat, Familie und Liebe"[45] (identity-constituting poles of homeland, family, and love) upon fleeing for Germany. It is at this point that we see sexuality once more subsumed under the rubric of geopolitical displacement, as Distefano argues that Abel's sexual desire for "Knaben" stems from the fact that they

> Verkörpern die Vergangenheit, nach der sich Abel sehnt, den Punkt in seinem Leben, als er noch ein Junge war und ihm der Krieg seine Heimat und Familie noch nicht genommen hatte.[46]

> [Embody the past that Abel is longing for, the point in his life when he was still a boy and war had not yet taken his homeland and his family away from him.]

Like many of the critics who have analyzed *Alle Tage*, Distefano seems to be intent on reading the novel solely through the lens of forced migration and its consequences, such that she seems blind to numerous passages that suggest that for queers, the homeland and the family home, supposedly the true objects of Abel's desire, may be anything but a source of comfort worth longing for. Indeed, *Alle Tage* depicts a world in which homophobia permeates the public and private spheres in which Abel and his fellow migrants live, in both Germany and their country of origin. This homophobia finds it most violent expression in Abel's crucifixion by the gang of young Roma boys to which Danko belongs and whose leader, Kosma, is shown to have a particular hatred of deviants and "perverts" (*AT* 194).[47] Mora writes the passage in which Kosma confronts Abel after Danko has disappeared so as to illustrate the dialectic of fascination and repulsion characteristic of homophobia.

> Kosma wurde rot und fing zu brüllen an. *Arschficker*! brüllte er. Soll ich dich aufschlitzen? Hä? Sollen wir dich aufschlitzen, du *Arsch*? Perverse Sau, Spitzel, Mörder! *Seinen Arsch aufschlitzen. Seine Eier abbeißen.* (*AT* 217–18, my emphasis)

> [Kosma turned red and started shouting. Ass-fucker!, he shouted. Should I cut you open? Huh? Should we cut you open, you asshole? Perverted pig, spy, murderer! Cut his ass up/open. Bite his balls off.]

After an insult in which he accuses Abel of being an "Arschficker," Kosma threatens to cut him open as punishment for partaking in perverse sexual practices, with "Arsch" now functioning as synecdoche for the pervert himself. In the next sentence, however, "Arsch" ceases to function synecdochally and, as indicated by the possessive pronoun preceding it, signifies Abel's "Arsch" rather than Abel himself. The transition to the third person possessive pronoun also suggests a transition on the level of narrative enunciation from a heterodiegetic narrator recounting direct speech to focalized narration; "Seinen Arsch aufschlitzen. Seine Eier abbeißen" would thereby not belong to Kosma's chain of shouted expletives, but rather Kosma's unvoiced thoughts, a reading supported by the shift from question and exclamation marks to full stops. Mora seems to be suggesting here that the desire to kill the man who is thought to have anal sex with other men mingles with an unconscious desire to symbolically assume the position of the penetrative partner in gay male sex; Kosma's desire to cut the perverse gay man up (by cutting the ass which synechdochally represents him open) is suggested to exist in a close proximity to some not-so-innocent sexual desires of his own, namely to cut open—and penetrate[48]—that same man's ass.

I have explored this passage in this depth because its subtle complexity suggests a detailed attention on Mora's part to the psychic processes that undergird fear or hatred towards deviant sexualities. This is mirrored by an attention to the presence of homophobia and its effects within migrant communities. Danko's abuse at the hands of his father, for example, who beats and strips him after Danko is seen walking with Abel, appears to be motivated by the same homophobia explored in the passage above: just as in Kosma's diatribe, the word "Arsch" appears as a slippery signifier in the father's tirade,[49] who accuses his son of being a "kleiner Stricher" (*AT* 203; little rent-boy) before threatening that "wenn du schwul wirst, kleines Schwein, bringe ich dich um" (ibid.; if you turn gay, you little pig, I'll kill you). Later in the novel, Abel is shown to also have been subjected to similar homophobic violence by his mother (*AT* 300). Clearly the heteronormative family, which Distefano presents as the lost object of desire hidden behind Abel's attraction to *Knaben*, and which provides the temporal template through which Erpenbeck attempts to positively reframe the refugees of *Gehen, Ging, Gegangen*, is suggested in *Alle Tage* to be anything but a safe haven for queer subjects.

Once we consider Mora's depiction of migrant communities as saturated by homophobia, a new significance emerges for the "Klapsmühle," the queer night- and sex-club where Abel spends days at a time. Biendarra groups the club together with the other heterotopia of migration of the novel "where time seems neutralized,"[50] but this description falls short. The club is no pure utopia; those having sex in the club are more interested in being seen by others than in their sexual partners (*AT* 191) and treat sex like a type of shift-work (*AT* 310). Despite this, it is significantly the only space with which Abel professes to have a strong connection; not only it is described by Abel as "paradise,"[51] but is the only place where he professes to feel *at home*: "Wer hätte das gedacht. Dass ausgerechnet so ein Ort das Anheimelndste sein würde" (*AT* 191; Who would have thought, that, of all places, that type of place would feel the most like home). In a roundtable discussion on queer temporalities, Halberstam stated that "queer time for me is the dark nightclub, the perverse turn away from the *narrative coherence*" of heteronormative frames of intelligibility.[52] Of the many articles examining *Alle Tage* from the perspective of displacement and the consequences of losing one's home(land), none makes any mention of Abel's claim of feeling at home in the *Klapsmühle*;[53] a fitting example of the invisibility that can result from the "perverse" turn away from the narrative coherence of frames of cultural intelligibility.

Conclusion

By way of conclusion, then, let us turn to the conclusions of the novels themselves. By the close of *Gehen, Ging, Gegangen,* all but twelve of the 476 residents of the Oranienplatz camp have their applications for asylum in Germany rejected (*GGG* 331). The novel ends with Richard's birthday celebrations at his home, which he now shares with several refugees, attended by refugees and old East German friends. At this point in the narrative, the refugees' hopes to achieve a sense of belonging and community within Germany have been thwarted by the state. One German man's mention of his wife's illness, however, sparks a sense of unity between the two groups in the form of a collective remembrance:

> Ein Mann denkt jetzt daran, wie die Frau ihm immer auf die Augen geküsst hat.
> Ein Mann denkt daran, wie die Frau so gut in seine Umarmung gepasst hat.
> Ein Mann denkt daran, wie die Frau ihm mit der Hand durchs Haar fuhr.
> [. . .]
> Ein Mann denkt daran, wie der Körper der Frau geglänzt hat, wenn sie sich zu ihm gelegt hat.
> Ein Mann denkt daran, wie sich die Lippen der Frau angefühlt haben.
> [. . .]
> Alle miteinander denken einen Moment lang an Frauen, die sie geliebt haben und von denen sie einmal geliebt worden sind. (*GGG* 343–44)

> [A man now thinks about how the woman always kissed him on his eyes.
> A man thinks about how well the woman fit into his embrace.

A man thinks about how the women ran her fingers through his hair.
[. . .]
A man thinks about how the woman's body shone when she laid
down beside him.
A man thinks about how the woman's lips felt.
[. . .]
All together they think for a moment about the women that they
have loved and by whom they were once loved.]

In this passage, separated from the surrounding narration by the page
setting and the obtrusive use of anaphora, (heterosexual) desire and love
appear as that which is capable of establishing communality between these
men, momentarily clearing away the wedge placed by the state between
the groups to create a communal "alle miteinander"—but this is only to
last a moment, as the communal remembrance of loves past gives way to
a discussion about the impossibility, for the refugees, of loves to come,
as they claim that they have no chance of finding a wife in Germany. The
German state's rejection of the refugees' asylum applications, presented
as the foreclosure of a future for the refugees, is thereby presented as
being coterminous with the impossibility of marrying and having children
(*GGG* 345).

The foregrounding of the foreclosure of this heterosexual future at
the novel's end inadvertently recalls another future foreseen within the
text, namely that "düstere Zukunft" (dark future) that Richard imagines
when remembering the body of the queer at the refugees' protest (*GGG*
273–74), a body that is marked within the text, by dint of its public align-
ment with queer politics and the "Sympathisanten," as a foreign body,
embodying political concerns putatively inimical to those of refugees. The
collateral damage in this process is of course those "foreign" migrant subjects for whom queer concerns are anything but extraneous; the queer
migrants whose existence is hereby erased.

It is also with an erasure of queerness that *Alle Tage* ends; Kosma
and his gang's attack causes Abel considerable brain damage, leaving him
with partial aphasia and total amnesia. The sham marriage he entered to
secure a visa seems, however, to become "real," as the final pages show
him sitting in a park watching Mercedes's son and their shared daughter
playing together. Married with children, Abel thus seems to be living the
unreachable life dreamt of by the refugees in *Gehen, Ging, Gegangen*, a
life that, within the frame of bourgeois heteronormativity, is recognizable as the good, even "viably human,"[54] life. Indeed, many critics put
forward such a reading themselves; Cornelia Anna Maul describes the
closing scene as Abel's "salvation," as he appears "glücklich in [dem]
locus amoenus einer familiären Parkidylle" (happy in the *locus amoenus*
of an idyllic family scene in the park),[55] while Markus May reads it as

presenting a "neue, globalisierte, heilige Patchwork-Familie" (a new, glo-
balized, holy patchwork-family).[56] Ironically, the affirmative stance taken
by these critics towards the novel's ending mirrors the affirmative stance
to which Abel is reduced after the attack, which leaves him almost unable
to say anything other than "Es ist gut" (*AT* 430; It is good).

While many critics seemingly take Abel's affirmation at face value, I
propose that we read it another way: against the voices of critics who present the (homophobic) attack on Abel as retribution for the lack of feeling
with which Abel has treated the women who loved him,[57] and against
the voices of novelists who attempt to humanize refugees by presenting
them as undyingly attached to the "order" of "work/home/marriage/
children" (*GGG* 345) while implicitly or explicitly suggesting queer refugees to be non-existent, the gormlessness and insistence with which Abel
affirms his situation seems like a parodic parroting of the heteronormative assumptions expressed by these voices. This is a parroting, however,
whose effects differ from the voices that it imitates; while the latter erase
the existence of queer refugees, Abel's parroting at the end of *Alle Tage*
directs our attention to that erasure and to the violence inherent within it,
bringing into our field of vision the damage done by the epistemological
frames that make such subjects invisible.

Notes

[1] The distinction between migrant and refugee is a contentious and difficult one.
Katharina Inhetveen argues in her essay "Der Flüchtling," in *Diven, Hacker,
Spekulanten: Sozialfiguren der Gegenwart*, ed. Stephan Moebius et al. (Berlin:
Suhrkamp 2010), 148–60, that while there is a marked legal difference between
the two categories, they exist as a muddled amalgamation in the public imaginary.
I differentiate here between refugee and migrant based on the status enjoyed by
that figure within the respective novel, using the phrase "undocumented migrant"
either to describe figures who came to Germany as refugees and stayed once their
application for asylum was denied/the conflict driving them to flee was ended, or
those who came to the country through "illegal" means.

[2] Fatima El-Tayeb, "Time Travelers and Queer Heterotopias: Narratives from the
Muslim Underground," *The Germanic Review* 88, no. 3 (2013): 305–19, here
307.

[3] Two well-known examples of films which explore the experience of queer
migrants (of various "generations") and/or refugees in Germany are Angelina
Maccarone's *Fremde Haut* (Unveiled, 2005) and Kutluğ Ataman's *Lola und Bilidikid* (Lola and Billidikid, 1999). The latter of these two films focused primarily on transgender and gay members of Germany's Turkish community, as did
Nurkan Erpulat and Tunçay Kulaoğlu's groundbreaking 2008 play *Jenseits—Bist
du schwul oder bist du Türke?* (Beyond—Are You Gay or Are You a Turk?). Aside
from the texts analyzed in this essay, other recent novels that explore queerness
and migration include Olga Grasjnowa's *Die juristische Unschärfe einer Ehe* (The

Legal Haziness of a Marriage, 2015) and Abas Khider's *Ohrfeige* (Slap, 2016), narrated by an intersex refugee from Iraq.

[4] Jenny Erpenbeck, *Gehen, Ging, Gegangen* (Munich: Knaus, 2015); Terézia Mora, *Alle Tage* (Munich: btb, 2006). Subsequent references to these are texts are cited in the text as *GGG* and *AT* respectively. All translations from the German are my own.

[5] *Judith Butler: From Norms to Politics* (Cambridge: Polity Press, 2007), 134.

[6] Judith Butler, *Undoing Gender* (London: Routledge, 2004), 17.

[7] Ibid., 2.

[8] Judith Butler, *Frames of War: When Is Life Grievable?* (London: Verso, 2016), 3.

[9] Ibid., 25.

[10] Butler, *Undoing Gender*, 226.

[11] Robert J. C. Young, "Postcolonial Remains," *New Literary History* 43, no. 1 (2012): 19–42, here 23.

[12] Ibid., 26.

[13] Ibid., 27; "Often without papers or documentation, they are denied the basic rights of the nation-state and are left only with the interminable inaccessibility of the dream of self-emancipation."

[14] See Klaus J. Bade, "Von Unworten zu Untaten: Kulturängste, Populismus und politische Feindbilder in der deutschen Migrations- und Asyldiskussion zwischen 'Gastarbeiterfrage' und 'Flüchtlingskrise'," *IMIS-Beiträge* 48 (2016): 35–171. Bade's study of the links between the discourse surrounding migration and anti-migrant violence in Germany can be read as an exemplification of Butler's claim that "on the level of discourse, certain lives are not considered as lives at all, they cannot be humanized; they fit no dominant frame for the human, and their dehumanization occurs first, at this level. This level then gives rise to a physical violence that in some sense delivers the message of dehumanization which is already at work in the culture." *Undoing Gender*, 24.

[15] See http://mut-gegen-rechte-gewalt.de/service/chronik-vorfaelle for a regularly updated list of attacks.

[16] The term was coined by Jasbir K. Puar in her monograph, *Terrorist Assemblages: Homonationalism in Queer Times* (Durham, NC: Duke University Press, 2007). Although still the seminal text on the topic, it is not without its shortcomings, particularly in its account of "Pinkwashing" and the Israeli state. For a more nuanced exploration of the workings of homonationalism, see Nikita Dhawan, "Homonationalism and State-Phobia: The Postcolonial Predicament of Queering Modernities," in *Queering Narratives of Modernity*, ed. Manuela Lavinas Picq (Oxford: Peter Lang, 2015), 51–68.

[17] See Andreas Kraß, "Einführung: Historische Intersektionalitätsforschung als kulturwissenschaftliches Projekt," in *Durchkreuzte Helden: Das "Nibelungenlied" und Fritz Langs Film "Die Nibelungen" im Licht der Intersektionalitätsforschung*, ed. Andreas Kraß et al. (Transcript: Bielefeld, 2014), 7–48, here 10.

[18] Eithne Luibheid, "Heteronormativity and Immigration Scholarship: A Call for Change," *GLQ* 10, no. 2 (2004): 227–35, here 227.

[19] Kira Kosnick, "Sexuality and Migration Studies: The Invisible, the Oxymoronic and Heteronormative Othering," in *Framing Intersectionality: Debates on a Multi-Faceted Concept in Gender Studies*, ed. Helma Lutz et al. (Farnham: Ashgate, 2011), 121–35, here 127.

[20] For more information on the camp, see Olivia Landry, "'Wir sind alle Oranienplatz!': Space for Refugees and Social Justice in Berlin," *Seminar* 51, no. 4 (2015): 398–413.

[21] "'Stuck in the Middle': Waiting and Uncertainty in Immigration Detention," *Time & Society* 25, no. 1 (2016): 61–79.

[22] Ibid., 71.

[23] Michel Foucault, "Of Other Spaces," trans. Jay Miskowiec, *Diacritics* 16, no. 1 (1986): 22–27, here 24.

[24] Ibid., 25.

[25] Ibid., 26.

[26] "Terézia Mora, *Alle Tage*: Transnational Traumas," in *Emerging German-Language Novelists of the Twenty-First Century*, ed. Lyn Marven and Stuart Taberner (Rochester, NY: Camden House, 2011), 46–61, here 56.

[27] Foucault, "Of Other Spaces," 25.

[28] See *GGG* 66–70, 73–83, 106–14, 123–28, 135–45, 184–87, 236–41.

[29] In an interview with the *B.Z.* she suggests that some of Awad's story is taken verbatim from a conversation with a refugee from the Oranienplatz: *B.Z. Online*, accessed September 12, 2016, http://www.bz-berlin.de/kultur/literatur/jenny-erpenbeck-fluechtlinge-sind-zu-freunden-geworden. Erpenbeck insists that the novel is largely loyal to fact, and at an event at the Literaturforum im Brechthaus on December 8, 2015, Erpenbeck agreed with Sigrid Löffler's description of *GGG* as a "Tatsachenroman" (novel of facts).

[30] Kosnick, "Sexuality and Migration Studies," 127.

[31] Jack Halberstam, *In a Queer Time and Place: Transgender Bodies, Subcultural Lives* (London: New York University Press, 2005), 152.

[32] Ibid., 5.

[33] Butler, *Undoing Gender*, 17.

[34] Terézia Mora, *Nicht sterben: Frankfurter Poetikvorlesungen* (Frankfurt am Main: Fischer, 2014), 76.

[35] E.g., *AT* 369, 376, 402.

[36] E.g., *AT* 391.

[37] Mora claims that she intended the reader only to have the impression that he is *perhaps* into boys. *Nicht Sterben*, 42.

[38] During his hallucination, Abel admits to having invited a boy back to his flat, but only to spend twenty-four hours resting his head on his shoulder (*AT* 369).

[39] It is implied that Abel leaves a dinner party with Simon, an openly gay actor, after the latter suggestively whispers into Abel's ear (*AT* 110).

[40] "'Ich bin genauso deutsch wie Kafka': German Linguistic Identity in the Novels of Terézia Mora," *German Life and Letters* 68, no. 2 (2015): 211–28, here 214.

[41] "Terézia Moras Winterreise: Über den Roman *Alle Tage* und die Poetik der Fremde," in *Literatur und Migration,* ed. Heinz Ludwig Arnold (Munich: edition text + kritik, 2010), 211–21, here 215.

[42] Aurora Distefano, "Körper und Geschlecht—Überlegungen zur Identitätsproblematik in Terézia Moras Roman *Alle Tage,*" in *Genderstudies in den Geisteswissenschaften: Beiträge aus den Literatur-, Film- und Sprachwissenschaften,* ed. Corinna Schlicht (Duisburg: Universitätsverlag Rhein-Ruhr, 2010), 89–104.

[43] Ibid., 90.

[44] Ibid., 95.

[45] Ibid., 90, 95.

[46] Ibid., 100.

[47] To my knowledge, the attack upon Abel has not been described as a gay-bashing in the secondary literature. Many critics' tendency to read the attack allegorically has even produced somewhat homophobic readings. Eszter Probst, for example, suggests that the attack "ist nur die physische Aushandlung der Gefühllosigkeit und Rohheit, mit der er früher die ihn Liebenden behandelt hat" ("is simply the physical negotiation of the crude and emotionless way that he treated those who loved him"). *Be-Deutung und Identität: Zur Konstruktion von Identität in Werken von Agota Kristof und Terézia Mora* (Würzburg: Königshausen & Neumann, 2012), 134.

[48] "Aufschlitzen" implies an "Einschnitt," or penetration. *Duden: Die deutsche Rechtschreibung,* accessed November 3, 2016, http://www.duden.de/rechtschreibung/aufschlitzen. It is also semantically and phonetically adjacent to "aufschließen," a vulgar term for taking someone's virginity.

[49] "Was?! Was ist das für ein Arsch?! Ha?!" (*AT* 203; What?! What kind of ass are you then, huh?!).

[50] "Terézia Mora, *Alle Tage,*" 56.

[51] "Außerdem [. . .] braucht mir keiner zu erklären, wie es im Paradies ist. Ich bin seit Jahren Stammkunde dort" (*AT* 375; Apart from that, no one needs to explain to me what it's like in Paradise, I've been a regular customer there for years).

[52] Carolyn Dinshaw et al., "Theorizing Queer Temporalities: A Roundtable Discussion," *GLQ* 13, no. 2/3 (2007): 177–96, here 182; my emphasis.

[53] Markus May, for example, describes the club only as a "schlecht beleumdeter, heruntergekommener Club, am Ende einer Sackgasse gelegen, der vor allem von Schwulen frequentiert wird" (a poorly lit, run-down club at the end of a cul-de-sac that is primarily visited by gay men) in his essay "'Der Krieg wird nicht mehr erklärt, sondern fortgesetzt': Fremdheit, Migration, und Gewalt in Terézia Moras *Alle Tage* (2004)," in *Phänomene der Fremdheit—Fremdheit als Phänomen,* ed. Simone Broders et al. (Würzburg: Königshausen & Neumann, 2012), 51–68, here 56.

[54] Butler, *Frames of War,* 3.

55 "'Mein neues Vaterland: die Scham.': Transdifferente Identitätsinszenierungen in Terézia Moras *Alle Tage*," in *Intermedialität und Alterität, Migration und Emigration: Tendenzen der deutschsprachigen Literatur*, ed. Olivia C. Diaz Perez et al. (Tübingen: Stauffenberg, 2014) 219–30, here 229. Italics in original.

56 May, "'Der Krieg wird nicht mehr erklärt, sondern fortgesetzt'," 65.

57 See note 47.

The Transgressive Representations of Gender and Queerness in Fatih Akin's *Auf der anderen Seite*

Sarra Kassem

I
N A RECENT STUDY, Melanie Kohnen argues that during the 1990s there was an explosion of gay and lesbian visibility in American popular culture and that cinema started to dissociate non-normative sexualities from the problem-oriented discourses that proliferated in earlier films that cast homosexual characters.[1] Notwithstanding the increase of queer characters on screen, cinematic constructions of queerness remain limited and ultimately limiting, observes Kohnen, meaning that only certain queer identities are rendered visible, while a whole range of others are either underrepresented or totally overlooked.[2] In Kohnen's view, it is white gay and lesbian identities that have found their way to mainstream representation.

Kohnen's observations regarding the elusive cinematic representation of queer subjects are asserted by a study conducted by Gayatri Gopinath.[3] Focusing particularly on films about the Asian diaspora, Gopinath engages critically with the absence of diasporic queer female subjectivities from cinematic texts. Her argument is that the figure of "woman" as a pure and unsullied sexual being is so central to dominant articulations of nation and diaspora that queer female subjects are rendered impossible. In Gopinath's view, female sexuality "is a crucial site of surveillance, as it is through women's bodies that the borders and boundaries of communal identities are formed," and in this context normative heterosexuality is regarded as the only kind of sexuality that diasporic women are allowed to practice.[4] Because the inclusion of queer diasporic subjects challenges the idea of non-Western sexualities as premodern and disrupts those narratives that imagine and consolidate the nation in terms of organic heterosexuality, as Gopinath argues, the representation of diasporic queer female subjectivities deserves more attention.

This essay explores how queer subjects are constructed in Fatih Akin's *Auf der anderen Seite* (On the Other Side, 2007; in English as *The Edge of Heaven*, 2007), focusing primarily on how queerness is played out in relation to non-Western female identity. While the term "queer" is routinely used to refer to homosexual, bisexual, and transgender people, it is also a term that intimates the wide range of subjectivities that resist rigid categorization and are oppositional to the norm. As David Halperin puts it, "queer is by definition *whatever* is at odds with the normal, the legitimate, the dominant."[5] Even though this essay engages mostly with queer lesbian subjectivity, other forms of queerness are incorporated into the film's narrative. The asexual oriental masculinity, the sex worker, and the single parent are all embodiments of queerness.

Representation is key to determining which lives are to be valued the most and count as human, asserts Judith Butler.[6] Certain human lives, she argues, tend to be valued more highly than others in the same way that certain lives are more vulnerable than others. Certain lives are often exposed to violence in the context of the normative notion of the human. Their dehumanization occurs first and then "this gives rise to a physical violence that in some sense delivers the message of dehumanization that is already at work in the culture."[7] Specifically, she explains that those who are granted access to representation "have a better chance of being humanized, and those who have no chance to represent themselves run a greater risk of being treated as less than human, regarded as less than human, or indeed, not regarded at all."[8]

Drawing upon Butler's arguments and building upon the foundations laid by Gopinath, I aim to demonstrate why the inclusion of a lesbian couple in the migratory narrative upon which Akin's film draws deserves attention, regardless of the marginal role same-sex desire plays in driving the story forward. This is because the lesbian refugee is a subject position that is habitually excluded from cinematic texts. Specifically, the few films about homosexual ethnic minority characters center mostly on gay men.[9] This does not mean that non-Western lesbians are totally absent from films. Yet they are a social group that rarely appears on screen.[10]

While the focus of this essay is the politics of sexuality, an analysis of the representations of gender cannot be omitted from the discussion. This is because representations of sexuality are nearly always negotiated in relation to constructions of gender, and in the case of *Auf der anderen Seite* it could be argued that the inclusion of lesbian subjects in the narrative is both a symptom and a cause of Akin's interest in introducing portrayals of gender relations and subjectivities that are not strictly informed by binaries. In what follows, I will argue that the gendered identities of the female characters are presented as multidimensional, constructed outside of any essentialism.

This points to the theoretical writings of Butler as suitable heuristic tools for framing the discussion. Butler's concept of performativity, in particular, is key to understanding the politics of gender and sexuality articulated in the film.[11] Performativity as a concept was set out in detail in Butler's book *Gender Trouble* and further elaborated on *Bodies That*

Matter to incorporate the influences of ethnicity in determining the range of possibilities available for doing gendered identity. According to Butler, gender is in no way a fixed or stable identity. Rather it is an identity constituted through a stylized repetition of acts. Gender in that sense is always performative, and this enables its possible subversion. She acknowledges that although there are several ways of acting out a gendered identity, what one does or does not do is clearly not an individual matter. Cultural norms operate as a regulatory regime shutting down alternative ways of doing gender and sexuality. Taking up Butler's arguments regarding the prevalence of such norms that regulate how a gendered body can act, this analysis begins by looking at how the film narrates the experience of four women whose lives and existences are shaped by both subverting and adhering to normative regimes in multiple, intersecting, and simultaneously diverse ways, before engaging more explicitly with the representation of lesbian sexuality in relation primarily to a non-Western female position.

Auf der anderen Seite

Auf der anderen Seite is Akin's fifth feature film and the second part of his trilogy Love, Death and the Devil (*Liebe, Tod und Teufel*). Utilizing a multi-strand narrative, the film tells the stories of six people whose lives are interconnected. The film is divided into three chapters. The first chapter, "Yeter's Death" (Yeters Tod), is set in the Northern German town of Bremen. The opening sequence follows Ali, a Turkish widower, as he walks through a peaceful May Day demonstration on his way to the red light district. There he meets Yeter, a widowed prostitute of Kurdish origin. Ali offers her a monthly payment to move in with him. Yeter does not accept immediately, yet she reconsiders his proposal when one night she gets threatened by two Turkish fundamentalists who call on her to repent for disregarding her Muslim identity and becoming a prostitute. Ali introduces Yeter to his son Nejat, who is a man in his thirties living in Hamburg and working as a university professor of German literature. The same night Ali suffers a stroke that sends him to hospital. Upon his discharge he has changed. Out of jealousy towards the bond Nejat and Yeter develop in his absence, he becomes more possessive towards Yeter, aggressively calling on her to perform her professional duties for him and in the process accidentally killing her. Ali is sent to prison. Disgraced by his father's deeds, Nejat travels to Turkey to track down Yeter's daughter in order to finance her studies, now that her mother can no longer support her. There he comes across a German bookstore for sale, which he decides to acquire, settling in Istanbul for a while.

Aiming to suggest simultaneity and to underscore the activist politics that underpin the narrative, the second chapter, "Lotte's Death" (Lottes

Tod), begins on the exact same day, yet this time capturing the May Day demonstrations in Istanbul. In a violent confrontation between the demonstrators and the police, a police officer loses his gun. A demonstrator grabs it and runs through the crowd, managing to hide it on the rooftop of a building and to escape the police. The demonstrator is Yeter's daughter, Ayten, an activist involved in a militant organization. Alerted by the arrest of her comrades, Ayten takes up a new identity and flees to Germany in search of her mother. At first she finds shelter at the house of one of her fellow militants, yet her hot-tempered personality leads to an argument, resulting in her finding herself homeless. With no place to go, she spends the night at the university campus, where on the following morning she meets Lotte, a middle-class German student who has recently returned from her travels in India. Moved by Ayten's story, Lotte takes her back to the home she shares with her divorced mother, Susanne, a former idealist, who has retreated into the comforts of a bourgeois life. A sexual relationship sparks between the two women. A few days later Ayten is arrested by the police at a random traffic stop and is sent to a detention center. When her asylum appeal is rejected by the German authorities, she is deported to Turkey where she is then imprisoned. To help her troubled girlfriend, Lotte travels to Istanbul. There, she rents a room from Nejat, whom she meets randomly at his bookstore. Nejat and Lotte never realize that they are trying to help the same person, because, as advised by Ayten's lawyers, Lotte does not reveal to him the real name of her girlfriend, referring to her as Gül. Lotte visits Ayten in prison and Ayten asks her to retrieve the gun she had earlier stolen from the police officer. Lotte follows her instructions but her bag is then stolen by a group of street kids. She chases them until one of them fires the gun, killing her.

The third chapter, which gave the film its title, *On the other Side* (*Auf der anderen Seite*), opens at Istanbul airport at the point of Susanne and Ali's arrival in Turkey; Susanne is there to retrieve Lotte's body, and Ali has been deported upon his release from prison. On her first night in Istanbul Susanne mourns the loss of her deceased daughter. The following day she meets with Nejat and asks him if she can spend the night in the room Lotte has been renting from him. During the night she reads Lotte's diary and then dreams of her. This is when she decides to take over her daughter's mission and help Ayten. Susanne's visit to prison prompts Ayten to use her legal right to repent, after which she is released (repentance in Islamic cultures refers to confessing having committed a sin and calling for Allah's forgiveness). In the meantime, a casual conversation with Susanne triggers Nejat's decision to forgive his father and to attempt to find him. He travels to Trapzon, the fishing village on the Black Sea coast where Ali had settled upon his return to Turkey. The film finishes with Nejat looking out to sea, waiting for his father, who had gone fishing, to return.

Beyond the Female Victimization Trope

Representations of gender in Western films about ethnic minorities have largely drawn upon images of young and beautiful women as victims in need of rescue from oppressive men, perpetuating the rape-and-rescue trope by which white (and sometimes dark) women are rescued from dark men.[12] Such narratives are inspired by popular fantasies that developed within the frameworks of colonial discourse in order to propose the superiority of the West over the uncivilized "orient," and, as Guido Rings notes, to emphasize "the Western duty to intervene in order to protect the victims of that other culture," a practice which in turn legitimized colonial rule.[13] Narratives of female victimization have informed representations of Turkish women in German cinema as well. As Katherine Pratt Ewing notes, "the young woman who is deprived of her freedom and rights by her family was a central figure in the limited repertoire of images constructed by filmmakers in the 1980s."[14] Tefvik Başer's film *40 Quadratmeter Deutschland* (40 Square Meters of Germany, 1986), which tells the story of Turna, a victim of a forced marriage who was brought to Germany by her husband only to be imprisoned in a cluttered apartment, is an example of this popular trope. Although the 1990s saw the release of numerous films that produced alternative representations of Turkish women, narratives of rescue have not yet disappeared. Feo Aladag's *Die Fremde* (The Foreigner, 2010, in English as *When We Leave*, 2010), a film possibly inspired by the "honor killing" of 23-year-old Hatin Sürücü that took place in Berlin in 2005, is one such example, as is Fatih Akin's *Gegen die Wand* (Against the Wall, 2004, in English as *Head-on*, 2004) which tells the story of Sibel, a woman of Turkish descent who struggles to liberate herself from patriarchal oppression in order to live out her sexuality in ways that are not available to her in the traditional Turkish context in which she was raised.

Auf der anderen Seite also draws upon scenarios of female victimization, albeit in ways that are less schematic in comparison to most "orientalist" texts.[15] Subverting the trope of brown women being rescued by white men, when Yeter is threatened she looks for shelter at the home of a fellow Turk. Later on though, her savior becomes her victimizer. The fact that she dies from an act of violence at the hands of Ali echoes stereotypical representations that demonize oriental masculinities. Ali does not, however, resemble the prevailing image of a domineering patriarch. His violent reaction that results in Yeter's death is somehow inconsistent with the representation of the caring father that he otherwise embodies. The scene of their fight unveils the disenfranchised position of both characters. Yeter is killed while trying to resist a sexual assault, and is therefore punished for not conforming to the subordinate female role of an oriental spouse who is expected to submit to her husband. Ali's attempt to assert his power over her is an act born out of frustration reflecting his insecurity about his masculinity.

Ayten's story in a way also taps upon a plot of rescue, even though she is not presented as a victim of patriarchal authoritarianism. Ayten flees Turkey when her comrades get arrested because she fears that if she gets caught she might face the death penalty due to her involvement with a militant organization. Lotte is not simply becoming her lover. She is also acting as her rescuer, as she is helping her with asylum application and tries to save her from a regime that, according to Ayten, is ready to violate human rights. On the one hand, there is a degree of stereotyping in the erotic relationship between the two women in *Auf der anderen Seite*. Desiring a troubled ethnic Other is irrevocably intertwined with Western fantasies of rescue. Helping Ayten becomes an act of empowerment for Lotte. Such a reading is sustained by Lotte's depiction as a romantic idealist in search of a purpose in life. Her statement "Mum, for the first time my life has a purpose. For the first time I am needed" (Mama, zum ersten Mal hat das was ich tue einen Sinn. Zum ersten Mal in meinem Leben habe ich das Gefühl gebraucht zu werden) shows how her feelings for Ayten are also conflated with a humanitarian mission. The film's reworking of the rescue trope, however, is more complex.

Ayten deviates from clichéd representations of an oppressed femininity, struggling to liberate herself and becoming powerful in the process. Introduced as a political activist, from the start she appears as a strong, liberated woman and, although she does turn into an exotic beauty in need of rescue, the audience witnesses her resistance against conforming to the role of a victim or seeing herself as such. By capturing her participation in physical confrontations with Turkish police and her recurring outbursts, Akin's film contests her vulnerability. Her persona is generally constructed in ways that associate her with a toughness that contradicts dominant notions of femininity, especially oriental femininity. The representation of her rescuers is also subversive. Lotte and Susanne are middle class and German and therefore belong to the hegemonic culture, but the fact that Ayten is rescued by the woman who becomes her lesbian lover and her mother, who is a single parent, is a representation that deserves unpacking. Assigning the role of the rescuer not only to female characters, but to characters whose female subjectivities are also transgressive, contributes to dismantling the power relations inflicted by gender hierarchies. Even though the film sustains the structures of domination and Western superiority to some degree, it does not schematically reproduce the binary logic imbued in orientalist texts. Moreover, it is implied that without Susanne's support Lotte cannot rescue Ayten. Susanne's comment "And who will pay for that? Do you know what your girlfriend has cost me? Did you ever ask yourself that? For a whole year I paid her solicitor fees. And we lost!" (Und wer bitte soll das bezahlen? Weißt du eigentlich was mir deine

Freundin gekostet hat. Hast du dir das jemals gefragt? Ein Jahr habe ich die Anwaltskosten bezahlt, und wir haben verloren) stresses that Susanne is the one covering the legal expenses of Ayten's case. Lotte's struggle to help Ayten is in vain, and it is only when Susanne decides to get actively involved that Ayten is set free. This draws attention to the mother figure that Susanne represents, and which is perhaps more critical to her role as a rescuer than her Germanness or her social status.

The lesbian identity ascribed to Ayten's character further unsettles the concept of a passive femininity upon which tropes of rescue are based. Her sexuality marks a point of divergence from the archaic femininities that govern orientalist texts, and even though her character is constructed much more in relation to the revolutionary politics she endorses than to her gender or cultural background (although her affinity with Kurdistan's armed struggle is inextricable from her Kurdish descent), the fact that she is a lesbian is key to demarcating her difference from the protagonists of diasporic and migrant cinema, who are perpetually depicted as heterosexual victims of patriarchal oppression.[16] In that sense, although queer politics and lesbian desire are peripheral to the story of rescuing Ayten, they form a subtext that contributes to disrupting the clichéd narrative of vulnerable women in need of rescue that underpins popular constructions of non-Western femininities.

The Multiple Female Subjectivities

One of the film's key points of divergence from reactionary representations of gender and sexuality is its repudiation of a collective female identity. Even though there are many ambiguities in the way the film's female characters are constructed, which makes it difficult to reach any conclusion regarding its approach to the politics of gender and sexuality, the multiple, fluid, and at times conflicting identities that the women in the film inhabit illustrate how gender can be lived out in various ways, within and outside the axes of heteronormativity. Along with the representation of the four women, which, as I will demonstrate, is informed by an understanding of gender as a contextualized identity that is performative in the sense that Butler sets out, the idea of multiplicity is teased out in the different names appropriated by the characters. Yeter is initially introduced with the Western name Jessie, which signals her appropriation of a Western femininity. Ayten takes up a new identity under the name Gül, and even if Lotte introduces herself as Lotte, Ayten tells her that she prefers to call her by her full name, Charlotte. Ayten's and Lotte's use of different names is not symbolically charged to the same degree as is Yeter's adoption of a different name. Nonetheless, it is a detail that unsettles notions of identity as a fixed entity, underscoring instead the multiple layers of the characters' subjectivities.

Yeter is assigned a deviant female role, that of a prostitute, and a very conventional one, that of a mother. Coupling two female identities traditionally regarded as incompatible, her portrayal challenges typical dichotomies between deviant and normative as well as passive and active female roles. Yeter in that sense is queer despite being heterosexual. Her queerness is multiply constructed. She is a sex worker, a single parent, and, most importantly, a mother and a prostitute at the same time (although the way the multiple facets of her identity are portrayed is less flexible than it first seems). While her profession initially seems to signal her power to exercise control over her sexualized body, her powerlessness is gradually evidenced. In a world dominated by men, Yeter exploits her body to fulfill a traditionally male role, that of provider for the family. Because Yeter's sex-working is bound with providing for her daughter, the very idea of her having the freedom to practice her sexuality in non-normative ways is contested, revealing in fact the limited opportunities available to her as a migrant woman. When her sexuality renders her the subject of harassment, she turns to Ali, and although initially she appears to be using him in the pursuit of safety and financial prosperity, the scene of their argument that leads to her death lays bare her powerlessness. Regardless of her illusion that she in control of her body and sexuality, she realizes that her self-determination is limited. While the film grants her some degree of agency, ultimately it proposes that the "oriental" femininity she personifies cannot be lived outside the boundaries set in place by her culture.

Ayten and Yeter share the same cultural background, yet their representation is very different. This could be simply read as a symptom of generational differences or of the different geopolitical contexts within which the two women have been socialized. Nevertheless, it also contributes to deconstructing the myth of a universally shared female experience. If, through Yeter's story, the film underscores the pressure upon Turkish (or as a matter of fact Kurdish) women to conform to certain ways of living out their gendered subjectivity, Ayten's character documents the possibility of subverting the moral underpinnings of the heteronormative system by which gender and sexuality are regulated. Portraying the lives of the two women in markedly different terms, the film contests what Butler refers to as a narrativized myth of origins, by which women's experiences are shared.[17] Instead, the film acknowledges the way in which personal histories feed into how different women may live out their gendered identity in ways that are unique and not solely defined by their cultural background. Such an acknowledgment of the diversity that characterizes the experience of female subjects echoes Butler, who engages critically with feminist theories and psychoanalytical models of theorizing gender when she states that the very notion of a common identity upon which these theories draw is inadequate because "it becomes normative in character and, hence, exclusionary in principle."[18] She proposes that "by grounding the metanarratives in a myth of the origin the psychoanalytic description of gender identity confers a false sense of legitimacy and universality to a culturally specific and in some contexts, culturally oppressive version of gender identity."[19] *Auf der anderen Seite* is not silent about the culturally imposed boundaries that constrain how a gendered body can act. Using the example of Yeter to demonstrate how those who fail to correspond to socially established gender norms are often treated with hostility offers a poignant critique of regulatory regimes. Yet it also asserts that there is at least some degree of flexibility, given that these boundaries are not presented as impermeable.

The film's departure from essentialist understandings of gender is even more forcefully made manifest through the shifts in how the female characters act out their gender at different moments during the film. Such shifts expose how gender is not natural but a social construct, or performative, as Butler puts it, and can be done differently depending on the context. Yeter, for example, is introduced to the narrative as Jessie, wearing a blond wig, a revealing red latex jumpsuit and black vinyl thigh-high boots. The outfit produces the effect of a hypersexualized female identity, while the yellow, red, and black colors, being the colors of the German flag, may be interpreted as a way of coding Germanness. This represents a form of drag, where a woman with a migration background imitates a Western femininity. Yeter's cultural crossdressing evinces how both gender and cultural identity are constructs that draw upon certain codes to produce their effect. Furthermore, it is an act through which cultural boundaries are exposed and simultaneously called into question. To impersonate a hypersexualized identity, Yeter models herself on an identity that is visually marked as German. And yet she also makes her ethnicity manifest; Gülden Karaböcek's song that she is listening to when Ali enters the room becomes a trigger for her ethnic background to be revealed. The multiple ways Yeter relates to her gendered body are also expressed in the scene of her first encounter with Ali, when her comment "can be" (kann sein) in response to his question whether she is Turkish indicates that she does not shy away from assuming multiple subject positions.

Following the bullying she experiences and her disclosure to Nejat that she is prostituting herself to finance her daughter's studies, her representation is de-eroticized. Once the film assigns to her the role of a mother, her femininity is no longer constructed with reference to her sexuality. Her portrayal switches to modest outfits and more "traditional" behaviors that underpin a conventional female role, such as cooking for her partner. In that respect, the shift in Yeter's representation reinforces the normative regimes that limit the possibilities available to her. The film's entrapment in thinking of gender roles through normative categories is also evinced by its apparent reluctance to allow the spectator to experience her as sex worker and mother at the same time.

That gendered identities are treated as constructs in the film is also imprinted in Ayten's representation. Her body language and mannerisms often contribute to defeminizing her character. While this might appear to be a means of reproducing an image of her that audiences could recognize as a representation of a lesbian, in reality there is more complexity at work. Her defeminization occurs in the scenes of her encounters with her comrades, with the police, and with Susanne, whereas when she is with Lotte her portrayal adheres to notions of conventional femininity. By showing her gender as acted out differently depending on the context, the film disrupts an understanding of gender as a fixed category, and reconfigures it as contextualized subjectivity instead.

As has been established already, Ayten is constructed as an activist whose life and identity are delineated by her political affiliations more than they are by her sexuality. This is also reinforced in the scene of the two girls going through Lotte's wardrobe to find clothes for Ayten. This scene exemplifies that social identities are constructs that find expression through the stylization of the body, as Butler asserts.[20] The t-shirt Ayten refuses to wear is one with a Nike logo printed on it. "I don't like American marka," she states (apparently trying to use the German word "Marken," or brands). This short scene, which is insignificant to the plot, is key to the construction of Ayten's identity, reflecting how the anticapitalist and antiglobalization ideals she endorses are expressed through her appearance as much as they are through her actions.

However, on a closer inspection the multiple and contextualized gender identities Ayten acts out do not reflect a freedom to switch between different subject positions, but in fact underscore the social boundaries that restrict her freedom. The masculinized identity she plays out in front of others lays bare her understanding of the disenfranchised positions available to her as a woman in a world of gender inequality. Furthermore, the film's references to the absence of her parents contribute to reinforcing her vulnerability; Ayten's sense of her self reflects an awareness of her vulnerability as a female and an orphan. The wildness inscribed in her character may therefore be read as a mechanism of coping and surviving or of undoing her vulnerability, which in her mind would have been increased had she been conventionally feminine. To assert her power within and in relation to typically male institutions (namely the militant organization to which she belongs and the police respectively) and to survive within a society where women are often regarded as subordinate, she feels that she has to act in ways that contest the vulnerability and fragility associated with femininity, which for her translates to disregarding her female identity and mimicking masculinity. This is also supported by the representation of her female comrades, who are also constructed in the same terms. In this context, the masculinization of female characters does not connote flexibility in how a gendered body can act. Dissociating the masculinization of Ayten's representation from sexuality and reading it in relation to other facets of her identity instead brings to the fore a critique of the power structures inflicted by gender hierarchies. Thus the film comments on how certain institutions are still closed to integrating conventional femininity. Having Ayten perform masculinity in order to integrate herself into the organization whose ideological frameworks she endorses and to cope with the hostility of a world that she as a female and an orphan is subject to, the film reaffirms the subaltern position reserved for women in Turkey, constructing femininity as fixed within hierarchically defined social positions. Put differently, non-Western female subjects in the film are envisaged as able to transcend social boundaries, but to do so they must disregard their femininity. In that sense, the film authorizes an understanding of non-Western femininity as a subjectivity locked into its subordinate status, This has to do not only with social expectations, but the internalization of these norms by female subjects too.

As already noted, Ayten is portrayed in more feminine terms when she is with Lotte. Such a reconfiguration of her representation is possibly assumed to be essential, in the film's terms, to her construction as an object of desire or an exotic beauty in need of rescue. It may also illustrate an intention to satisfy the spectators' gaze, providing them with the pleasure of looking at an intimate relationship between two young and beautiful women. Most importantly, it contributes to deconstructing the masculinization of Ayten's character, exposing the imitative nature of gender and illustrating the multiple layers of her gendered identity. Performing masculinity becomes an act of empowerment for Ayten within the masculine world she inhabits, yet her sexuality is not lived out as a masculine female.

In Susanne's case the performative nature of gender is not marked directly in the film. It is the star persona of Hanna Schygulla, who plays her, that brings it to the fore. Schygulla was Reiner Werner Fassbinder's muse and one of the most renowned actresses of the New German Cinema. As Johannes von Moltke demonstrates, from the beginning of her collaboration with Fassbinder, "Schygulla's performance is marked by an emphasis on a highly stylized type rather than a realistically motivated individual."[21] During the 1970s and 1980s she epitomized a kind of glamorous femininity and a parodic femme fatale. In stark contrast to that, Akin ascribes to her the role of mother. Such a palpable change in Schygulla's impersonation of femininity also encourages the audience to reflect on how gendered identities are fabricated.

The inclusion of a lesbian couple in the narrative also contributes to offering more flexible and diverse representations that challenge the binary logic that often governs constructions of gendered subjectivities in cinematic texts, especially those about ethnic minority groups living in diaspora. Strikingly, it reflects a divergence not only from earlier films of that same tradition, but also from how gender relations have been conceived in Akin's previous films, which draw on scenarios that are strictly heterosexual and affirmative of conventional modes of desiring. As critical as *Gegen die Wand* may seem towards heteronormative and other regulatory regimes that constrain gender and sexuality, its characters' inability to live out their sexualized identities in viable ways outside conventional relationship models lays bare the film's entrapment in a rigid binary gender order. References to homosexuality are not absent from the film, yet their function is to reinforce the heterosexual economy.[22] With *Auf der anderen Seite*, Akin breaks new ground in his engagement with the politics of sexuality and desire. Unlike *Gegen die Wand*, which denies any form of transgression of the female subject, *Auf der anderen Seite* shows multiple ways of doing sexuality and a female identity. The film does not depict the two women's lives and identities as entirely defined by their sexuality. In fact, their sexuality is not explicitly thematized. Yet, as I will demonstrate in what follows, it is precisely the fact that their queerness stays in the background of narrative developments that reveals that there is much complexity to its representation.

Contesting Secrecy and Invisibility

The cinematic representation of same-sex desire has often been narrativized through the coming-out trope, drawing upon a gay or lesbian character's struggle to come to terms with his or her non-normative sexuality and/or the tensions inflicted with publicly proclaiming his or her queer identity. The lesbian romance in *Auf der anderen Seite* is not constructed through narratives of secrecy and invisibility, and this disrupts the Otherness by which queer sexualities are often demarcated. Homosexuality is explicitly dissociated from a problem-oriented discourse. The struggles of coming out, or living as a lesbian in societies where heterosexuality has been established as the norm, are not negotiated. The characters' affirmation of their identity as lesbians occurs off-screen and is not presented as a source of tension. What makes the film very different from most films casting queer characters in leading roles is that sexuality is largely irrelevant to the narrative. In this sense, the film appears to be taking for granted the integration of non-normative sexualities within the dominant social fabric. This is evident not only in the scenario through which lesbian sexuality is played out, but also in the way the relationship of the queer subjects with space is imagined (even though it is important to acknowledge that homosexuality is framed differently in the parts of the film set in a German context and those set in a Turkish context).

Of particular interest is the scene of Lotte and Ayten kissing. The sequence that leads to the kiss opens up in the low-lit space of a bar's dance floor. The camera captures them drinking, laughing, and dancing. The proximity of their bodies in the frame, combined with the close-up shots of their faces filmed in slow motion, reinforces a lesbian reading. The scene is sonically embellished with Shantel's "Inel inel de aur" ("Bucovina Dub"), a song that, together with the dark red illumination, feeds into the scene's erotic atmosphere and, in line with its "oriental" instrumentation, into the exoticism that permeates Ayten's representation too. The kiss is not filmed in a close-up, which would be a typical way of framing an intimate moment between two lovers. Starting with a long shot, the camera gradually zooms in through the crowd that surrounds them. This marks the filmmaker's intention to signify visibility. The point of view the camera offers is not that of the two lovers. Placing the two women together in the same frame, the camera presents them as a couple and, offering a perspective other than theirs, it establishes that they are being looked at (importantly, though, they are not looked at by the others in the club; they are not an object of spectacle to anybody but the film's audience).

The love affair between the two women emerges at the bar and then is consummated in Susanne's home. This is a representation that is charged with meaning. Gopinath argues that the concept of home is key to the construction of female subjectivities in texts about diasporic communities, and is usually envisaged as a site that is marked by patriarchal gender and sexual arrangements, including heteronormativity.[23] The ways in which home and sexuality are negotiated in *Auf der anderen Seite* simultaneously contest and reaffirm the patriarchal heteronormative logic with which the concept of home is typically charged. The emphasis placed on Ayten's homelessness not only serves the representation of displacement that she experiences as a fugitive upon her arrival in Germany, but also contributes to dissociating her character from the domestic sphere. This could be interpreted as a way of suggesting that her non-normative sexuality can only be practiced in the non-spaces in which she wanders. Such a reading is sustained by Ayten's construction as an orphan. According to cinematic texts, the normative upbringing of the daughter (in non-Western cultures) is a duty carried out by the family, and ensuring her conformity to culturally conditioned gender norms is part of this process.[24] In that respect, the lack of a paternal figure and the absence of Ayten's mother, who herself does not practice her gendered subjectivity in accordance with conventional gender norms, somewhat limit the film's subversive potential because Ayten's sexuality is not treated as as acceptable as it may seem at first. It can be argued that she is able to subvert traditional Turkish norms regarding gender roles and sexuality because she does not have a family to regulate how her sexualized identity will be lived out. These very ideas, which are reflected in Ayten's representation as an orphan, are contrasted with the portrayal of Lotte's relationship to her mother, with whom she lives, and whose active involvement in her daughter's life is at no point questioned. Susanne's tolerance of her daughter's non-normative sexuality and the construction of the familial home as a site that can accommodate same-sex desire are significant because they counteract understandings of queer sexualities as a threat to the family and discard representations that cement the queer subjects' non-belonging. Importantly, though, this representation is not as radical as it may appear, because it is informed by cultural differences to some degree: it takes place in Germany and not in Turkey.

The way lesbians are integrated within the film's German public sphere marks a departure from spaces of invisibility. Queer narratives are often staged in sites associated with a subcultural queer milieu, such as gay bars or urban gay districts. Much as these sites contribute to producing the idea of a community, their appropriateness to a progressive staging of queer narratives needs to be questioned. This is because even though they belong to the public domain, such sites signify invisibility and social isolation, reaffirming that those who deviate from socially established gender and sexuality norms are not supposed to venture far from the subcultural milieus reserved for them within the societies they inhabit. In other words, while these are spaces where queer subjects have the freedom to express their sexualized identity in ways that perhaps are not available to them in mainstream society, they also legitimize ghettoization, reaffirming that non-normative sexualities are confined within tightly inscribed geographical (and social) boundaries. The absence of such spaces in *Auf der anderen Seite* is therefore noteworthy. Mapping a lesbian relationship onto public spaces that are not delineated as queer, the film dismantles popular assumptions of same-sex desire as belonging to the margins and unsettles the heteronormative logic that mainstream society is intent on maintaining. Allowing what is often regarded as deviant to enter the public realm, the film offers a perhaps utopian and yet optimistic representation of tolerance where public spaces are constructed as sites of belonging for subjectivities that have perpetually been imagined as marginalized. Strikingly though, there are no public displays of affection in the parts of the film set in Turkey, where the characters' sexuality remains invisible to those around them. This reinforces a different degree of openness towards non-normative sexualities in the two countries, which reveals how the representation of queerness is informed, to some degree at least, by cultural differences and binaries.

Downplaying Alterity

The depiction of same-sex desire that the film offers repudiates narratives of secrecy, suggesting the possibility of the inclusion of habitually marginalized subjectivities, at least when it comes to Germany. The way lesbians are constructed, however, can be subject to multiple and perhaps competing readings, and this makes it harder to discern to what extent room is allowed for subverting hegemonic norms of gender roles and sexuality. While it is true that *Auf der anderen Seite* offers nuanced representations of homosexuality, it is not clear to what degree it breaks social taboos, just as it is ambiguous whether it deconstructs some of the most popular stereotypes of lesbianism or in fact adheres to dominant mediated portrayals of femininity.

Chris Holmlund in his study of cinematic representations of gender in Hollywood films asserts that lesbians are a female identity that has been subject to selective representation, meaning that certain types of lesbian identity, specifically those of *femme* lesbians that adhere to notions of conventional femininity and beauty, dominate cinematic texts.[25] In Holmlund's opinion, such enactments of lesbianism that are only subtly different from hegemonic norms of femininity, undercutting therefore the threat that images of same-sex desire pose to the heteronormative status quo. This could be argued of *Auf der anderen Seite*, and most clearly in relation to the *femme* lesbian subjectivities Ayten and Lotte personify. Both are feminine and conventionally attractive. Lotte is young, tall, and slim; she wears skirts and dresses, and even though she has short hair, she can easily pass as straight. Ayten's appearance also adheres to conventional notions of female beauty, even though her mannerisms are more obviously coded as masculine in comparison to Lotte's. As established earlier, however, it can be difficult to evaluate to what extent the masculine traits imprinted in her behavior underpin the portrayal of a masculine female (or a butch lesbian for that matter). Put differently, it is unclear whether her "defeminization" is indicative of her sexual orientation or is intended to reflect the failure of the male-dominated revolutionary milieu with which she identifies to include women that are conventionally feminine.

As Joan Nestle notes, *femmes* are recognized as lesbians by their place next to their butch lovers.[26] Because both Ayten and Lotte are envisaged as *femmes*, although arguably not in the flamboyant manner described by Nestle, the film deconstructs the *femme*-butch binary, challenges the lesbian stereotype, and establishes a critical distance from a rigid framework in which gender identity determines modes of desiring or vice versa. Alternative interpretations, however, are also viable. Specifically, the portrayal of lesbians that the film offers may also be a symptom of mainstream media's construction of femininity. As Jamie Stuart argues, "women need to adhere to a particular standard of feminine beauty" and the cinematic representation of queer female subjects, influenced, as it is, by social constructions of femininity, in most cases adheres to these standards.[27] Images of lesbians that contradict conventional standards of beauty rarely appear on screen. Problematic as this may be, it is hardly surprising, given that cinema has historically privileged certain images of femininity and masculinity, while excluding a whole range of others.

Furthermore, the very idea of subversion is downplayed in the film by the fact that the portrayal of Ayten and Lotte's relationship is allusive. Its erotic nature is mostly made manifest through the intimacy imprinted in their gazes and the way they touch each other, which is erotically charged. The two of them are filmed in bed, yet the lesbian relationship is sexually consummated off-screen. The lack of lovemaking scenes is ambiguous in its function because, much as it may signal resistance to providing a representation that would legitimize a commodification of lesbian sexuality as a spectacle to satisfy the spectator's gaze, in a way it also renders the couple's sexuality invisible. The kind of lesbian identity the characters inhabit is equally ambiguous. Even though queer subjects are shown to enjoy a freedom to express their sexuality outside subcultural spaces, both women are constructed in conventionally feminine ways, which may be read as a way of deconstructing the lesbian stereotype but also as a way of aligning the characters with existing gender norms and therefore taming the threat that their sexuality poses to the heteronormative system.

Conclusion

Auf der anderen Seite counters the representation of femininity as a homogeneous experience that applies generically to all women, and acknowledges the complexity of gender and sexual identity formations. The multiple enactments of femininity that are displayed repudiate essentialist understandings of gender, treating it instead as a construct that is performatively constituted. Non-normative sexualities are presented in the film in ways that are multifaceted. While this essay has analyzed the representation of queerness primarily against the backdrop of the lesbian relationship, the two mothers are also queer in a way. Their portrayal as single mothers (and a sex-worker in Yeter's case) defies hegemonic heteronormative gender-role categories.

By negotiating lesbianism via an interracial relationship, Akin's film contests the fantasies of heteronormativity and cultural purity. The queer non-Western female subjectivity that is brought into representation unsettles the binary of modernity/tradition that informs the portrayal of "oriental" femininities as articulated by migrant or diasporic cinematic texts. Ayten's subsequent alienation is not pinned down to sexual orientation or cultural background. Because the film draws primarily on her political affiliations to produce her Otherness and does not foreground ethnicity or sexuality, her representation is transgressive, eschewing representational clichés of subaltern migrant women as victims of patriarchal authoritarianism. Her non-belonging is constructed in multiple ways and negotiated in a way that is nuanced and more socially engaged in comparison to plots that simply evolve around cultural difference.

While non-Western female characters in the film are shown to be coerced into maneuvering through the rigid boundaries set in place to regulate gender roles and sexuality much more than Western women have to, these boundaries appear to be somewhat permeable. The subversion of patriarchal heterosexual norms is particularly significant insofar as alternative ways of desiring and being desired have been treated as impossible by most cinematic texts, particularly for female subjects in Islamic societies. In that sense, the image of a non-Western female character that is a lesbian is significant, especially because it challenges cultural differences as they have been disseminated by the orientalist discourse, which perpetually viewed non-Western sexualities as archaic, in contrast to the openness of the West.

Lesbians are not typecast in the film. Refraining from casting the sexuality of the two women as determining the conditions of their existence, it produces a representation that does not reduce them to their sexualized bodies. Non-normative sexualities are not explicitly thematized, and ultimately very little is said about the lesbian experience in Germany or in Turkey. Despite the fact that, the relevance of sexuality to the film's thematic agenda is downplayed, or perhaps because it is downplayed, the (German) society in which the narrative is set appears to be more inclusive. *Auf der anderen Seite* makes the possibility of alternative modes of being and desiring imaginable in ways that plots which foreground struggle and non-belonging perhaps do not. It does so by offering a representation that allows for the possibility of repudiating normative categories and achieving social integration.

Notes

1 E. S. Melanie Kohnen, *Queer Representation, Visibility, and Race in American Film and Television: Screening the Closet* (London: Routledge, 2015).

2 This is also a symptom of the term "queer" being so broad in its scope, referring to a such a huge range of sexual and gender possibilities that even to define it limits its potential. See M. David Halperin, *Saint Foucault: Towards a Gay Hagiography* (New York: Oxford University Press, 1995).

3 Gayatri Gopinath, *Impossible Desires: Queer Diasporas and South Asian Public Cultures* (Durham, NC: Duke University Press, 2005).

4 Gopinath, *Impossible Desires*, 9.

5 Halperin, *Saint Foucault*, 62.

6 Judith Butler, *Precarious Life: The Powers of Mourning and Violence* (London: Verso: 2006).

7 Butler, *Precarious Life*, 34.

8 Butler, *Precarious Life*, 141.

9 See, for example, Stephen Frears's *My Beautiful Laundrette* (1985), Mehdi Charef's *Miss Mona* (1987), Kutluğ Ataman's *Lola und Bilidikid* (Lola and Billy the

Kid, 1999), Ayse Polat's *Auslandtournee* (Tour Abroad, 2000), Olivier Ducastel's and Jacques Martineus's *Drôle de Félix* (The Adventures of Felix, 2000) or Merzak Allouache's *Chouchou* (2002).

[10] *Fremde Haut* (Foreign Skin, in English as *Unveiled*, 2005) and *Nina's Heavenly Delights* (2006) are examples of films about non-Western lesbians.

[11] Judith Butler, *Gender Trouble: Feminism and the Subversion of Identity* (New York: Routledge, 1990) and *Bodies That Matter: On the Discursive Limits of "Sex"* (New York: Routledge, 1993).

[12] See Ella Shohat, and Robert Stam, *Unthinking Eurocentrism: Multiculturalism and the Media* (London: Routledge, 1994) and Ania Loomba, *Colonialism/Postcolonialism* (London: Routledge, 2005).

[13] Guido Rings, "Blurring or shifting Boundaries? Concepts of Culture in Turkish-German Migrant Cinema," *German as a Foreign Language* 1 (2008): 6–39, here 17.

[14] Katherine Ewing Pratt, "Between Cinema and Social Work: Diasporic Turkish Women and the (Dis)pleasures of Hybridity," *Cultural Anthropology* 21, no. 2 (2006): 265–94, here 272.

[15] "Orientalism" is a term coined by Edward Said, who argues that a problem with the representation of the "orient" is that it is always constructed in line with the West's image of it. Said suggests that this is largely attributable to the fact that discourses about the orient are often produced by representatives of the West who interpret Eastern cultures in relation to their own experiences as Westerners, and this perpetuates an unrepresentative image of the Eastern world. See Edward Said, *Orientalism* (London: Routledge, 1978).

[16] Diasporic cinema refers to films by and about ethnic minorities that have settled in the West. See Hamid Naficy, "Phobic Spaces and Liminal Panics: Independent Transnational Film Genre," *East-West Film Journal* 8, no. 2 (1994): 1–30. Along with its wide use in the academic literature to designate the works of "hyphenated" filmmakers, "hyphenated" here meaning filmmakers like Fatih Akin with a migration background (in his case the hyphenated descriptor is "Turkish-German"), it is also used to describe films about refugees, migrants, and narratives of exile. Distinguishing between diasporic, migration, or exilic cinema is important, as these are quite different and can be indicative of the different biographies of the authors. While the term diasporic cinema is not fully expressive of the diversity that characterizes the different types of films it is used to describe, it is still useful as a category of inquiry and a term that is inextricable from discussions about the representation of ethnic minorities in European cinema.

[17] Judith Butler, "Gender Trouble, Feminist Theory and Psychoanalytic Discourse," in *Feminism/Postmodernism*, edited by Linda J. Nicholson (London: Routledge, 1990), 324–40.

[18] Butler, "Gender Trouble, Feminist Theory and Psychoanalytic Discourse," 325.

[19] Butler, "Gender Trouble, Feminist Theory and Psychoanalytic Discourse," 330.

20 Butler argues that "the effect of gender is produced through the stylization of the body and, hence, must be understood as the mundane way in which bodily gestures, movements and styles of various kinds constitute the illusion of an abiding gendered self." Butler, *Gender Trouble*, 140.

21 Johannes von Moltke, *No Place Like Home: Locations of Heimat in German Cinema* (Berkeley: University of California Press, 2005), 94.

22 In the opening scenes of *Gegen die Wand*, Cahit smashes a chair on another man who has called his masculinity into question by asking him "are you gay or what?" (Bist du ein Schwuler, oder was?), while later on, Sibel uses the Turkish derogatory term for homosexual, *ibneler* to insult the three men who attack her in Istanbul. As Petek observes, "homoeroticism is hardly an unspoken subtext in Akin's film; in fact, homosexuality is quite frequently invoked in *Gegen die Wand*, however, always as a means of disparagement." *Gegen die Wand* not only celebrates heteronormativity but in fact proposes a very conventional version of heterosexuality as the route to happiness. See Polona Petek. "Enabling Collisions: Re-thinking Multiculturalism through Fatih Akin's *Gegen die Wand/Head On*," *Studies of European Cinema* 4, no. 3 (2007): 177–85; here 181; Joanne Leal and Klaus-Dieter Rossade, "Negotiating Gender, Sexuality and Ethnicity in Fatih Akın's and Thomas Arslan's Urban Spaces," *German as a Foreign Language* 3 (2008): 59–87; Victoria Fincham, "Violence, Sexuality and the Family: Identity within and beyond Turkish-German Parameters in Fatih Akin's *Gegen die Wand*, Kutluğ Ataman's *Lola+Bilidikid* and Anno Saul's *Kebab Connection*." *German as a Foreign Language* 1 (2008): 40–72.

23 Gopinath, *Impossible Desires*, 14.

24 See, for example, *Gegen die Wand*, *Die Fremde*, or Hark Bohm's *Yasemin* (1988).

25 Holmlund argues that during the 1980s a hybrid subgenre of the woman's film and the lesbian drama began to flourish. These films merge lesbian sexuality with female friendship, casting a set of characters that could be read as either lovers or just friends. In such films lesbians are constructed as *femmes*, and references to sexuality are allusive. Eluding an indisputable reading on whether the relationships represented are friendship-based or erotic, such enactments of lesbian identity undercut the threat that images of same-sex desire posed to the heteronormative status quo. See Chris Holmlund, *Impossible Bodies: Femininity and Masculinity at the Movies* (London: Routledge, 2002).

26 Joan Nestle, *The Persistent Desire: A Femme-Butch Reader* (Boston: Alyson, 1992).

27 L. Jamie Stuart, *Performing Queer Female Identity on Screen: A Critical Analysis of Five Recent Films* (Jefferson, NC: McFarland & Company, Inc., 2008), 14.

Part III.

Queering the Normativity

Bitter Tears and Pretty Excess in Fassbinder's *Die bitteren Tränen der Petra von Kant* (1972) and *Die Sehnsucht der Veronika Voss* (1982)

Lauren Pilcher, University of Florida

R AINER WERNER FASSBINDER is one of the most important yet controversial figures in the history of queer German cinema. His films often depict sexualized bodies and aesthetics, debatably to the point of fetishism, without affirming an explicit LGBTQ politics. This essay proposes that Fassbinder's depiction of gender performativity is key to understanding and assessing the queerness of his oeuvre's engagement with representations of otherness and visual pleasure. Linking feminist and queer theory, I examine how the New German Cinema director emphasizes a stylized femininity acted out by female characters in *Die bitteren Tränen der Petra von Kant* (The Bitter Tears of Petra von Kant, 1972) and *Die Sehnsucht der Veronika Voss* (Veronika Voss, 1982). These female-focused films, I argue, speak to the ways in which he draws attention, throughout his body of work, to Western cinema's interest in performativities of difference, not only of gender but intersecting aesthetics of race, class, and queer sexualities. As he focuses on women as they manipulate feminized clothing, gestures, and objects to perform an ever-doubling representation of female difference, Fassbinder reveals that cinema eroticizes aesthetic and bodily imitations of otherness that can never be fully contained within a gender binary or within the cinematic frame.

Cinematic Subjectivity and Queer Excess

Fassbinder's films often explore the relationship between cinematic images of sexual otherness—which engage bodily and aesthetic performativities of gender, race, class, and sexuality—and visual pleasure. This is due in part to the artistic and sociohistorical context in which his films were produced. As a key filmmaker in New German Cinema, a movement that emerged in West Germany in the 1960s, he, along with his counterparts, unsettled notions of German identity, film authorship, and cinematic identification. The movement gained much of its momentum from state initiatives aiming to revitalize German film culture following a period of American control over the country's film markets after the Second World War.[1] As a result, a small number of independent-minded, mostly male directors utilized government sponsorship to establish themselves as art cinema auteurs in Europe and the United States.[2] In describing the movement near its end in 1980, Thomas Elsaesser concluded that "the Germans are beginning to love their own cinema because it has been endorsed, confirmed, and benevolently looked at by someone else: for the German cinema to exist, it first had to be seen by non-Germans. It enacts, as a national cinema, now in explicitly economic and cultural terms, yet another form of self-estranged exhibitionism."[3] John Davidson critiques Elsaesser's reading of the movement in his *Deterritorializing the New German Cinema*, as he argues that "what is sutured over in this ambivalent stereotype of German cinema within the West" in his conceptualization of New German Cinema, "is the *non-Western*, the 'other' both inside and outside the community of the West . . . And there are Others who have not even become a matter of concern."[4] For Fassbinder, an ambivalence about German identity is evident in his attention to the ways in which cinema depicts otherness for pleasure at the level of form, or as Elsaesser argues, "His very concept of film form is inflected by the problem of otherness and the Other, regardless of whether his films deal, for instance, directly with homosexuality (usually not)."[5]

In analyses of his films, scholars tend to assess Fassbinder's approach to cinematic subjectivity and visual pleasure in relation to either his gay politics or his status as an art cinema auteur. For example, in his 1976 analysis of Fassbinder's use of camp, film scholar Richard Dyer argues, "I feel I want to defend his involvement in camp even while acknowledging its problems. The latter include the extreme ambivalence of his/ camp's depiction of women, of which Christiane Maybach/Hedwig (Franz' sister in *Fox*) is the clearest instance. Are we to enjoy her strength and commonsense, her warmth, her unabashed vulgarity, or is it her fleshly physicality, her streaked, peroxided hair and slobbering lips?—either way she is too much and camp enjoins us to *both* aspects."[6] Dyer struggles here to categorize Fassbinder's images of female characters as camp because he creates a subject/spectator position that resists identification with Hedwig's character to focus on her "physicality." Ultimately, for Dyer, the director's representation of women does not go far enough to undermine the "vocabulary of straight society."[7] In an analysis of Fassbinder's auteur style, film scholar Brigitte Peucker argues that he often cites other works of art by contextualizing them primarily within a collection of objects. She notes the role of pleasure in this process as she concludes, "Fassbinder film citations are cropped, like Poussin's painting in *Bitter Tears*—torn from their context, or unframed—then re-framed as part of a collection. From this perspective, citations 'extend subjectivity through investment in a series of objects.' Are these fetishsized? Perhaps."[8] For Peucker, Fassbinder objectifies art in a potentially fetishistic manner, as his collected "citations" crop but do not empty out textual meaning.[9] Despite their differing disciplinary aims, both Dyer and Peucker locate in the director's films a potentially fetishistic pleasure at play in his cinematic framing.

Explicating the relationship between subjectivity and pleasure in Fassbinder's films necessitates assessing the ways in which gender has shaped cinema's illusion of looking. Narrative cinema, Laura Mulvey posited in her 1975 "Visual Pleasure and Narrative Cinema," constructs pleasure via "looking" at women. Employing psychoanalysis, Mulvey argues that narrative continuity privileges the looks of characters at each other over the camera's view of recorded action and the audience's view of the screen, which minimizes male anxiety concerning the presumed "lack" represented by the female body.[10] The woman's "lack of a penis" leaves the "male unconscious," she concludes, "two avenues of escape from this castration anxiety: preoccupation with the re-enactment of the original trauma (investigating the woman, demystifying her mystery), counterbalanced by the devaluation, punishment or saving of the guilty object (an avenue typified by the concerns of the *film noir*); or else complete disavowal of the castration by the substitution of a fetish object or turning the represented figure itself into a fetish so that it becomes reassuring rather than dangerous (hence over-valuation, the cult of the female star)."[11] For Mulvey, narrative cinema reinforces patriarchal subjectivity by either demystifying or fetishizing the female in order to signify and fix sexual difference in the image, a visual construction of pleasure that perpetuates the oppression of women.

In many of his films, Fassbinder's construction of cinematic subjectivity exposes the performativity of gender in ways that destabilize patriarchal visual pleasure. Thomas Elsaesser argues that, in his films, Fassbinder repeatedly creates "a masochistic identification with an idealised oppressor" yet a "masochistic pleasure" that proves "unpalatable, ambiguous, queasy" because it "is not rationalised by a unified and privileged perspective that the spectator is allowed to project on a character—as, say, in the masochistic males usually playing opposite Marlene Dietrich in Josef von Sternberg's films."[12] Fassbinder, he argues, positions the audience as "voyeurs, but only because the characters are so manifestly exhibitionist. Substantiality is denied to both characters and audience, they de-realize each other, as all relations polarise themselves in terms of seeing and being seen."[13] Judith Mayne argues similarly that in Fassbinder's *Angst Essen Seele Auf* (Ali: Fear Eats the Soul), a film that follows an unexpected sexual relationship between a middle-aged German woman and a younger Moroccan man, "The spectacle is a relation between observer and observed where the object of vision is rigidified, reduced to one-dimensionality. Yet, the seeming power of the observer's gaze [. . .] is illusory; like the observed, she/he is locked into the spectacle *relationship* as a form of power."[14] She concludes that Fassbinder, "by stripping cinematic continuity down to its bare essentials of looking, of vision, simultaneously lays bare the totality of the spectacle as social form."[15] Gender plays an explicit role in this process, Kaja Silverman argues, because "Fassbinder's cinema does more than exteriorize the gaze; it also separates it from its usual support, the look, a dislocation which has extreme consequences for sexual difference. No character within that cinema, male or female, is ever represented as possessing the gaze, regardless of how central his or her look happens to be to the articulation of the visual field."[16] Fassbinder, as Elsaesser, Mayne, and Silverman shed light on, resists establishing a patriarchal subject position that unifies the view of the camera with that of the characters to simulate possession of and separation from the object of vision. In doing so, his films denaturalize visual pleasure as they expose cinema's attempt to authenticate sexual difference via the illusion of looking.

In the years since Mulvey's seminal piece, feminist theory has evolved to address the conflation of gender and sexual difference in ways that inform her conceptualization of cinema's male gaze. Judith Butler, in her 1988 "Performative Acts and Gender Constitution," argues that "Gender reality is performative which means, quite simply, that it is real only to the extent that it is performed."[17] In challenging the idea of "essential sex" and "true and abiding masculinity and femininity," she concludes, "gender is not passively scripted on the body, and neither is it determined by nature, language, the symbolic, or the overwhelming history of patriarchy. Gender is what is put on, invariably, under constraint, daily and incessantly, with anxiety and pleasure."[18] Butler goes on to argue that "gender is a kind of imitation for which there is no original; in fact, it is the kind of imitation that produces the very notion of an original as an effect and consequence of the imitation itself."[19] Teresa de Lauretis, in her 1987 "The Technology of Gender," argues that "the representation of gender *is* its construction—and in the simplest sense it can be said that all of Western Art and high culture is the engraving of the history of that construction."[20] Butler and de Lauretis's emphasis on the constructed rather than essential relationship between gender and sexual difference expands the possibilities at play in Mulvey's male gaze. Western narrative cinema's structuring of masculine/active/subject versus feminine/passive/object consists of a set of acts made to visualize notions of female sexual difference and male heterosexual desire. Yet, these gendered acts resist stable notions of sexual difference precisely because they are "imitations" without an original, to use Butler's term, and "the effect of representation but also its excess, what remains outside discourse as a potential trauma which can rupture or destabilize, if not contained, by any representation" to use de Lauretis's language.[21]

In films like *Petra von Kant* and *Veronika Voss*, Fassbinder's destabilized looking relations emphasize the performativity of theatrical femininity. Queer film scholars in recent years have drawn attention to the ways in which gender performativity challenges the patriarchal logic of cinematic subjectivity. Edward R. O'Neill argues that film theory has neglected to acknowledge the ways in which gay spectators view female stars via *"performative identification* or identification with performative agency itself, with the power to perform."[22] He argues that stylized Hollywood divas are "a marker in the Hollywood text of a site for gay subjectivity," but also "the very moment of stylization within the text becomes a point of identification as labor and as style and taste (which can never be the 'property' of gays or of anyone else), and it is not yet clear to what extent this stylization evokes desire."[23] Rosalind Galt challenges the patriarchal values that govern cinematic looking as she maps the politics of "pretty" aesthetics: feminized forms, bodies, and décor read as too stylized. The politics of "the pretty," she argues, is "always engaged in a critique of gender, sexuality, and race as these terms have been imagined and codified through visual culture. The bodily politics of the pretty, as entirely formal constructions of aesthetic value, are usefully distinct from identitarian categories: the persistent denigration of decorative images in the languages of femininity, perversion, or orientalism enables us to think beyond a politics of representation and to see histories of bodily exclusion instead as underwriting the structuring principles of cinematic value."[24] Galt concludes that "pretty" aesthetics in cinema—the malleable forms of performative femininity that intersect racialized and sexualized aesthetics of otherness and have been devalued as superficial decorations and deceptions of the image—trace the patriarchy's "histories of bodily exclusion."[25] Following from Galt and O'Neill, Fassbinder's emphasis on feminine performativity in films such as *Petra von Kant* and *Veronika Voss* exposes the ways in which the conventional construction of cinematic looking stifles alternate subjectivities within filmic texts and denigrates the gendered acts by which they construct pleasure. He focuses on femininity as a stylized act and imitation of difference central to visual pleasure and to cinema's larger project of delimiting otherness within the image.

Re-framing Femininity in *Die bitteren Tränen der Petra von Kant* and *Die Sehnsucht der Veronika Voss*

Petra von Kant and *Veronika Voss*, two films made ten years apart in Fassbinder's career, can be described as "pretty" in comparison to his other work. Though the films differ greatly in cast, narrative, and setting,

both depict female lead characters that act out performative femininities as they manipulate clothing, gestures, and objects. Fassbinder queers
conventional cinematic looking relations in each by repetitively doubling their aesthetic figures and stylized gestures. Read in relation to one
another, the two films shed light on Fassbinder's approach to visual pleasure: in both, femininity is always already performative and detached from
the interiority of the female characters, and, as such, is an imitation of
sexual difference whose pleasure comes from its reproduction rather than
its authentic presence in the cinematic image.

Based on a Fassbinder play, *Petra von Kant* is divided into five
sequences set in the bedroom of fashion designer Petra von Kant. The all-
female film, which features six cast members, centers on both a romantic
relationship between Petra and Karin, a younger woman whom the fashion designer meets through her cousin Sidonie, and a masochistic relationship between Petra and her assistant Marlene. Throughout the film, the
characters move very little around the bedroom and often appear poised
in front of a wallpaper reproduction of a Nicolas Poussin painting, *Midas
Giving Thanks to Bacchus*, and amidst several female mannequins, various
mirrors, and dolls positioned throughout the room.[26] These static images
and objects, which are often stripped of clothing and laid bare, frequently
double the decorative figures of Petra and Karin within the camera's frame.
Marlene, a voyeur always at the edge of the action, calls attention to the
camera's subjective point of view, which remains detached from her own
gaze and its role in the romance that develops between Petra and Karin. As
Fassbinder resists unifying the assistant's look with that of the camera, in
tandem with repetitive doubling of Petra and Karin, he draws attention to a
performative femininity that cinema cannot possess or authenticate.

Veronika Voss, the second film in Fassbinder's BRD trilogy, was
inspired by Billy Wilder's film noir *Sunset Boulevard* (1950). It was shot
in black and white and focuses on Veronika, a former actress for UFA, the
German film production company active from 1917 through the Second
World War. She has fallen out of the limelight due to controversy over her
relationship with Joseph Goebbels, the Reich Minister of Propaganda of
Nazi Germany, and is both addicted to morphine and consumed by her
screen performances. In meeting sports reporter Robert Krohn, Veronika
acts out the role of femme fatale, the mysterious and seductive woman
who lures and deceives the male protagonist in the American film noir of
the 1940s and 1950s, in the various on- and off-screen spaces within the
diegesis of the film. Krohn is drawn to and deeply affected by his relationship with the former actress as he attempts, unsuccessfully, to save her
from her addiction, which is abetted by Dr. Katz. Throughout the film,
Veronika's femininity is performative on and off screen as she manipulates
her surroundings and blurs the lines between reality and acting in the narrative of the film.

She Sees Everything, Hears Everything, Knows Everything

In *Petra von Kant*, Fassbinder sets up Petra's femininity as a self-representation that she configures in relation to the collection of arty objects and looking relations in her bedroom, which doubles as a design studio. As she uses slow, subtle gestures and dons decorative outfits throughout the film, the mannequins posed in the room and wallpaper's nude figures loom behind her, mirroring her stylized presence. Brigitte Peucker argues that the wallpaper, as a "citation" of the original Poussin painting, disperses within Fassbinder's framing in ways that speak to his approach to artistic authorship, "the spilling over of Poussin's tableau into the theatrical space of actor interaction—and into spectatorial space [. . .]—mirrors the citational nature of authorial 'identity,' one that colors narrative and *mise-en-scène* alike."[27] Beyond the notion of authorial identity, Fassbinder frames the wallpaper—a reproduction of the original painting that depicts several nude men and other men who look at them—in juxtaposition to the "pretty" aesthetics in the room.[28] The film's opening shot reveals this juxtaposition as the camera moves slowly to survey the wallpaper and the arty décor of Petra's bedroom. As Marlene enters to wake the fashion designer, a discontinuous shot from across the room pans over various dolls and mannequins to re-frame the two women against the wallpaper as Marlene brings a telephone to Petra's bedside. Moments later, the camera moves toward Petra as she pauses her phone call to command Marlene to begin work on the "Skizze" (sketch), and, as the shot continues to circle the fashion designer and turn away from the painting, Marlene becomes visible at the easel in the background. A cut to a close-up shot over the shoulder of Marlene re-frames Petra adjacent to her sketch, still in bed as if a model for the drawing. The movement of the camera here situates the women within the wallpaper, as representations of sexual difference posed in juxtaposition to the male body, then reframes the image to reveal their roles as designer and model of femininity as Marlene sketches new fashions at Petra's command.

As the plot develops, Marlene's muted presence in the film further reveals the performativity of Petra's stylized femininity. Marlene, whose bland dress suits and cropped hair read as more masculine than the fashion designer, who dresses in decorative gowns and wigs, references Fassbinder's role as director as she sets the film's stage by waking Petra and ends the narrative as she leaves the apartment in the final moments. The assistant is also a voyeur who complicates the camera's point of view throughout the film: as she responds to Petra's commands in the periphery of, or moving through, the frame, she calls attention to the camera's subjective position within the room and challenges the authenticity of its view as she hears and sees Petra's actions equipped with knowledge not granted to viewers of the film. For example, in a scene in which Petra's cousin Sidonie visits, the fashion designer tells her to ignore Marlene's presence as they talk intimately about Petra's recent divorce. In a close-up shot, Petra puts on makeup using a small mirror to the right side of the frame, Sidonie sits next to her on her bed on the left side of the frame, and Marlene, working at the easel in the background, is positioned between the two women. Petra explains, "Marlene ist seit drei Jahren bei mir. Marlene hört alles, sieht alles, weiß alles. Auf Marlene muß man keine Rücksicht nehmen" (Marlene's been with me for three years. Marlene hears everything, sees everything, knows everything. You do not need to be considerate of Marlene). During the course of the conversation, Marlene's mannerisms suggest that she is listening in, and at one point a close-up reveals a tear on her cheek. The scene provides ambiguous information about Marlene's involvement with Petra and her role in her fashion design. By telling Sidonie to ignore Marelene's presence, Petra downplays the potentially erotic relationship between the two and the effect that Marlene's voyeurism has on her behavior. Yet, throughout the film, brief pans and cutaways to Marlene as she hears and sees Petra's interactions hint at the influence her restrained interest in and history with the fashion designer have on her masochistic obedience to her constant demands. Using these techniques, Fassbinder establishes Marlene as an implied subject that influences Petra's stylized persona and behavior throughout, yet he separates her point of view from the camera's view. In doing so, he disrupts the continuity of the conventional cinematic gaze—which attempts to authenticate femininity by unifying the views of the camera, spectators, and characters—as he draws attention to a subjectivity that is not fully contained in the frame or narrative yet is crucial to the fashion designer's gender performativity.

Fassbinder also doubles Petra in relation to the objects in the design workspace within her bedroom and links her femininity with her fashion design. After leaving her bed in the opening moments, Petra stands and dresses slowly in an ornate white gown with fur fringe and decorative beading. Cigarette in hand, she plays a vinyl record as she puts on a wig and adjusts it using a hand-held mirror, while a nude mannequin posed in the work area mirrors her figure in the background of the medium shot, as if the fashion designer is dressing herself as she would the life-size doll. Soon, Marlene walks past to continue working on the sketch, but Petra subtly grabs her hand and pulls her toward her to dance in a posed manner. The two dance briefly before Petra commands Marlene "So, jetzt beeil dich" (hurry up) to finish the drawing. Here, the way Petra awakens and adorns herself with attire and mannerisms stereotypically befitting a fashion designer, is an act she puts on for herself, Marlene, and presumably the other women who later enter her bedroom and design studio. As she pulls Marlene aside momentarily, their dance symbolizes the way in which the assistant participates in Petra's self-representation by sketching the designer's fashions at her demand and, later in the film, modeling them on the same mannequins. The two women, dancing briefly at the edge of both the bedroom and workspace, blur the distinction between designer and model, and visualize femininity as a bodily and aesthetic representation that can be recreated but never original.

As Petra meets Karin, Fassbinder utilizes mirrors and Marlene's presence to double the figures of the women and to disrupt the camera's gaze by drawing attention to the ways in which they look at themselves and one another in performing femininity. When Karin arrives for dinner at Petra's invitation, she wears a sequined dress reminiscent of classic Hollywood's ornate costuming of its female stars. As she walks into Petra's bedroom to wait for her host to come downstairs, the camera pans to follow Karin, again passing over mannequins and dolls that obstruct the view, and frames her as she looks at herself in a mirror off screen. A close-up shot shows Petra, also in a fantastical and provocative dress, enter the room from the stairwell and pause; after several moments, the shot pans quickly as the two women turn to face one another, revealing the earlier image of Petra to be a reflection in the mirror. The pan exposes the shot as Karin's view of herself and Petra as she looks in the mirror and catches the fashion designer's eye in the reflected image of their decorative bodies. Throughout the scene, Fassbinder continues to frame mirrors that reflect and double the decorative figures of Petra and Karin as they converse on Petra's bed, yet as they talk, Marlene disrupts the continuity of the scene as she can be heard throughout, typing feverishly off screen. Present in the room but omitted from the frame, she is, as Elsaesser argues, "virtually outside or at the edge of the fiction" and

> offered to the spectator not as a figure of projection, but merely as an increasingly uncanny awareness of a double. To perceive this manoeuvre also makes the viewer realize that Marlene only appears to be the puppeteer who holds the strings to the mechanism called "Petra von Kant." As soon as we recognise our double, we become aware of the "narrator," and in an attempt to gain control over the film, we need to phantasmatise an author, another instance of control, controlling us. We are plunged into the abyss of the en-abyme construction which the film opens like a trap.[29]

Marlene again renders the limits of the subjective position of the camera explicit as her off-screen presence implies that Petra and Karin act in relation to her voyeurism and vice versa. Her proximal position to Petra and Karin, as Elsaesser argues, does not reveal the assistant to be the "puppeteer" controlling Petra as a "mechanism." Similar to the doubling of the mirrors, the assistant's off-screen looking position refracts the camera's view of Petra and Karin's femininity and de-realizes cinema's illusion of a subjectivity that can contain their performativity as an object, or image, of visual pleasure.

The film's final sequences draw further attention to the inability of the camera, and the looks of the characters, to contain femininity within the frame and narrative. After Petra confesses her love to Karin in the dinner sequence, Fassbinder omits the course of their relationship and picks it up again as it comes to an end. In the scene, which also takes place on Petra's bed, the fashion designer wears a wig, dress, and makeup that appear more stylized, less sexualized, and almost doll-like in comparison to the earlier scene in which they begin their relationship. Karin, now one of Petra's top models, lies in pajamas in bed, her hair slightly messy. As she reads a magazine, she hardly looks at her lover, who presses for attention and reprimands her. Growing more irritated, Karin tells Petra she slept with a black man the night before—the spectator cannot know if this is true—with the seeming awareness that her fetishizing of the lover will anger Petra. Petra pushes for more information, yet grows angry as she learns that Karin's behavior does not match her perception of her lover. Karin soon receives a call from her husband, from whom she has been separated for some time, and upon realizing he is in Zurich, she agrees to meet him in Frankfurt that afternoon. Despite Petra's pleading and insults, Karin prepares to leave. In a long shot that resembles Karin's earlier entrance for dinner, she, Marlene, and Petra pause in the frame as Karin confirms that she is leaving the fashion designer. Petra's back is turned toward the camera and is only partially visible at the periphery of the frame, Karin stands at the door in the middle ground, and Marlene, dressed in black, stands in shadows on the stairwell. Here, Marlene's look at Petra and Karin is explicit rather than implied from off screen, and, on the entry stairwell, she symbolizes the aesthetics of otherness always refracted in cinematic depictions of women. As she doubles Petra's gaze at her lover, she exposes the myriad looks at Karin in the frame and their inability to fix her as a model of femininity possessed solely by Petra, Fassbinder, or the audience. Femininity, though shaped by looking, is a bodily and aesthetic act that moves and changes in relation to other aesthetics of difference.

The closing scenes reveal the way in which gender performativity, as an aesthetic and bodily imitation of sexual difference, creates an excess of femininity that is neither fully erased nor rendered invisible in patriarchal looking relations. Distraught over Karin's departure, Petra vacillates between idealizing her former lover's beauty and deeming her a "Hure" (whore), and, in doing so, enacts ambivalently the boundaries of a model femininity to make sense of her desire. The fashion designer then tests these limits herself when her family visits for her birthday; upset that Karin has not telephoned, she sheds her postured mannerisms as she stands on the white fur carpet of her bedroom in a vibrant dress and shatters a tea set by stomping on it in high heels and yelling insults at her mother and daughter. After sleeping off the episode and removing her stylized attire, Petra admits to her mother that she has learned that she cannot "besitizen" (possess) Karin. She attempts to apologize to Marlene, and when the assistant complies by offering her hand, Petra rejects the gesture and asks Marlene to tell her about herself. Without hesitation, Marlene grabs and quickly packs a suitcase in the middle of the bedroom floor. She stows in it an array of objects from the apartment, including two of Petra's records, a gun, and a doll that resembles Karin. Her reaction—packing various items collected in Petra's bedroom as part of her performance—is a refusal of the notion that a more authentic form of their relationship, predicated on getting to know one another, is possible or pleasurable. Marlene's exit, which ends the film, suggests that Petra's femininity, as well as her own, is a performance of otherness designed and recreated for pleasure in relation to looking but can never be authentically possessed.

She Needs Music and Light

In *Veronika Voss*, Fassbinder again destabilizes the film's gaze at a female character, this time as Veronika acts out her former screen roles within the narrative of the film. Where in *Petra von Kant* Marlene's voyeurism disrupts the camera's view of Petra, Veronika's manipulation of the theatrical personas she performs confuse the temporal and narrative continuity of the film. The opening shot of the film frames a movie playing on a theater screen, and a cut reveals that the view of the screen belongs to Veronika, who sits in the theater dressed as if starring in the film she is watching. Within moments, we realize that she is watching a film in which she acted earlier in her career. Making a cameo appearance, Fassbinder is seated behind her in the theater. In this opening scene, the camera doubles Veronika as a feminine star on screen and a spectator in the audience of her own film. Fassbinder's brief appearance in this scene suggests that as he, as director, is not orchestrating the doubling but is caught in the same blending of reality and performance as he watches Veronika on screen. He resists establishing a clear distinction in the film between Veronika's on- and off-screen personas, as well as his own. As the former actress watches her acted role being replayed as if present in the diegesis of the film, she shuts her eyes and recalls a former movie set. In the imagined scene, Veronika emerges from the bright lights of the set amid congratulations on her "erschüttert" (marvelous) performance, and she soon confesses her love to the film's screenwriter, her future husband. The stylized lighting and melodrama of the romantic moment suggest that Veronika's recollection may be a nostalgic imagining of her past stardom that she entertains while watching herself on screen. By rendering the flashback's content ambiguous, Fassbinder refuses to authenticate an off-screen identity for Veronika and instead blurs the line between her acted femininity and her character within the film.

As the plot develops, the distinction between Veronika's screen portrayals and her self-representation of femininity in the plot of the film becomes increasingly blurred. As the former actress leaves the movie theater, she walks hurriedly and in tears through the rain and soon runs into sportswriter Robert Krohn, who offers his umbrella to her, whereupon her emotional state shifts immediately. Moments later, the two run playfully through the rain to meet a trolley car, and the music suggests that romance is abloom. Once on the trolley, however, Veronika explains that she must avoid being seen by other passengers and exits abruptly, leaving Krohn behind. Given the opening's ambiguity about Veronika's off-screen identity and history, it is unclear whether or not her behavior with Krohn is an acting out her of screen role in another attempt to reimagine her past in the present. Similar to the opening flashback, Fassbinder constructs a theatrical *mise-en-scène* and narrative that establishes Veronika's performativity as both act and reality in the film.

As Veronika and Krohn develop a relationship, the former actress manipulates the *mise-en-scène* and narrative in ways that suggest that her she performs *noir* femininity by appealing to both authenticity and theatricality. After Veronika and Krohn's first encounter, she calls his home in the middle of the night to request that they meet again. She meets the sports reporter for dinner dressed in a decorative outfit that resembles the attire she wears on the movie set in the first flashback. The music that accompanies the scene invites a melodramatic affect similar to the couple's initial meeting in the rain, further confusing Veronika's acted role and off-screen persona. Veronika soon explains to Krohn that after he did not recognize her as Veronika Voss during their first encounter, "Endlich, endlich war ich wieder ein Mensch" (Finally, finally I was a human again); her statement suggests, that she can be herself with him but also implies that Krohn experiences the authenticity of her theatrical persona. Krohn replies that he does not go to see movies, because they are not real, yet he is caught in the actress's allure as she orchestrates the *mise-en-scène* around them. Veronika soon directs the waiter to adjust the lighting, lights a cigarette, and persuades the reporter to give her three hundred marks to buy a brooch. As Veronika returns with the brooch she has purchased in a nearby jewelry store, Fassbinder frames her in relation to a pastoral landscape painting that she passes by as she walks up a flight of stairs. The static painting, a framed representation of masculine exploration and conquering of land and reason, juxtaposes her fluid and theatrical femininity. The painting mirrors Krohn's stiff, stereotypically mannish mannerisms as Veronika returns to dinner and greets him from behind by covering his eyes before, once again, leaving suddenly. The flirtatious gesture draws attention to Krohn's willingness to blindly experience her performativity as reality, not unlike the film spectator who suspends their disbelief when looking at the screen.

Krohn's intoxication with Veronika's theatrical femininity increases throughout the film, even though he grows more aware of her controversial past as an actress. Showing up at his apartment as he and his girlfriend return from a date, Veronika tells him that she would like to spend the night with him. At her command, he drives her to the mansion where she used to live, which now resembles an abandoned movie set. Amid furniture covered with sheets to protect against dust, Veronika stages a romantic candlelit night. She and Krohn soon sleep together, a scene that Fassbinder elides, and afterward Veronika does not remember who he is. Whether this loss of memory is staged or sincere, whether it is brought on by her addiction to morphine or triggered by the memory of her husband, she secures Krohn's affection as he holds her close before taking her, at her request, to Doctor Katz. Kate Leadbetter argues:

> In this scene, Voss attempts to create her own *mise-en-scène*, through manipulation of music, costume, lighting and her own stilted performance as a *film noir* seductress. Her desire to have her own image returned to her and repeated failure of this impulse is the force behind the scene's visual dynamics. The use of movement, lighting, and costume all contribute to towards undermining this attempted self-assertion. Voss' body appears in terms of its failed synthesis with the surrounding environment. In the vacant house, her possessions all shrouded by dustsheets, Voss appears as a relic among the relics, illuminated only by candlelight. It is made clear earlier in the film that this is her preferred lighting condition, as though she herself is aware of the fragility of her persona and appearance.[30]

Leadbetter claims that Veronika's "body," as it appears among her "shrouded" possessions, reflects her failure to perform the role of *film noir* seductress in the abandoned home. When read with an eye toward Veronika's feminine performativity, the scene resists Leadbetter's reading; though the former star can no longer portray women on screen, her abandoned home and possessions are now blank canvases for her recreating herself as femme fatale with Krohn. As she secures his erotic interest and empathy by manipulating the *mise-en-scène* of her past, she recreates her cinematic persona in the present reality of the film.

By omitting the sex scene between Veronika and Krohn, Fassbinder not only speaks to his own desire to re-create Billy Wilder's *noir* film by imitating the Motion Picture Production Code's censorship of sexual intercourse, he also disrupts the temporality of the film with another flashback of Veronika. The scene, which again reflects Veronika's imagining of her past, begins as a shot of Krohn turning on the radio cuts to Veronika and her husband as he turns on the same radio in their former home. Bright lighting again mixes with dark shadows as she asks her husband, several times, to turn the radio broadcast of war news to music and to adjust the lights, again attempting to control the space around her as if the stage of set. He replies: "Immer musst du was machen. Immer must du was herstellen. Können wir nicht einfach so sein, wie wir sind?" (You always have to do something. You always have to create something. Can't we just be the way we are?"). Veronika, seated on the sofa and not returning the eye contact of her husband, who stands above her, replies by questioning why he does not understand that "Wenn ein Schauspielerin eine Frau spielt, die einem Mann gefallen will, dann versucht sie natürlich alle Frauen in dieser Welt in einer zu sein. Und dann braucht sie Musik und Licht" (When an actress plays a woman who wants to please a man, then she tries to be all the women in the world rolled into one. And then she needs music and light.) Disinterested, her husband tells her that she drinks to make herself "groß, schön, verführerisch, einmalig" (big, beautiful, seductive, unique). The flashback ends here in an abrupt cut, reminiscent of *noir* editing, to Veronika in bed after having presumably slept with Krohn. This flashback, whether Veronika's imagined memory or background context provided by Fassbinder, replaces the sexual encounter between the couple. The omission suggests that Veronika continues to recreate herself as an image of all women to please a man, implying that the representation of femininity is the reality of sexual difference.

In the climax of the film, Veronika thwarts Krohn's attempt to rescue her from her morphine addiction, yet Fassbinder resists characterizing her femininity as deceptive performance masking darker motives. As Krohn and the police interrogate Dr. Katz, the doctor who supplies patients with morphine as a way to con them out of their money, Veronika enters the scene from her bedroom as if already acting on a movie set. She stands at her door, hands on either side of the doorframe, with a cigarette in hand. Krohn pleads with her to tell the police that Dr. Katz has been exploiting her patient's addictions in order to take possession of their finances after they die. Smiling, Veronika instead tells the police officers her own name. As they recognize her, they are caught in the appeal of her fame and abandon any investigative questions concerning Dr. Katz. Veronika explains to the policemen that she barely knows Krohn as she turns toward Dr. Katz and puts her arm seductively around her, suggesting that their relationship is also erotic. As the police and Krohn leave, Veronika embraces Dr. Katz and breaks down in tears. Katz comforts her and thanks her, saying "Du hast nur getan, was getan warden mußte" (You only did what had to be done). In the scene, Fassbinder again resists revealing what is true about Veronika and what is performed as Krohn's efforts prove trivial and her relationship with Katz appears more complex than one based solely on her morphine addiction.

In the film's final moments, Veronika's demeanor de-realizes the genre conventions shaping her role as femme fatale within the film. At her farewell party in her former mansion, which is now lively and filled with people rather than covered in sheets, she realizes that Dr. Katz has locked her in a room with a fatal dose of morphine. In a particularly striking close-up, she looks at the camera in a satirical manner as her facial expression implies that she is fully aware of the femme fatale act she stages and is about to end in the diegesis of the film. The shot suggests that both her seductive mysteriousness throughout and the drama of the tragic conclusion are cinematic constructs, which the former actress acknowledges playfully as she breaks the fourth wall by looking at the camera and addressing the audience. Fassbinder avoids, here and throughout, setting up Veronika's theatrical femininity as a mask for deceptive intentions revealed in her downfall and instead emphasizes her death as a reproduction of a *noir* performance that she acts out with self-awareness made visible to the audience in the final moments. As her femininity blurs the lines between reality and theatricality, the director draws attention to *film noir* conventions that aim to authenticate Veronika's sexual difference yet cannot demystify her gender performativity.

Conclusion

In both *Die bitteren Tränen der Petra von Kant* and *Die Sehnsucht der Veronika Voss*, Fassbinder constructs and deconstructs Western cinema's gaze at women, which unifies the look of characters, camera, and spectator to reinforce a patriarchal subjectivity that attempts to delimit sexual difference in the image for pleasure. In these two films, he frames female characters as they play with the aesthetic and bodily forms that signify femininity on screen, yet he refuses to provide a continuous subjectivity that simulates the camera and spectator's possession of these women as erotic objects. In both films, performative femininity undermines the patriarchal logic of cinematic looking by diffusing a strict division between subject and object, and a hierarchic gender binary, at the level of form. These two female-centered films model Fassbinder's broader approach to images of difference, both sexual and social, as they queer the filmic conventions that sustain the illusion of a patriarchal subject position that has the power to determine, devalue, and take pleasure in otherness. In avoiding an explicit politics of LGBTQ representation in *Die bitteren Tränen der Petra von Kant*, *Die Sehnsucht der Veronika Voss*, and other films, Fassbinder exposes Western cinema's exploitation of performativities of difference and traces bodies, forms, and desires subjected to cinema's gaze but never fixed in the film image.

Notes

[1] For more information on New German Cinema, see Thomas Elsaesser, *New German Cinema: A History* (New Brunswick: Rutgers University Press, 1989); Timothy Corrigan, *New German Film: The Displaced Image* (Bloomington: Indiana University Press, 1983); John E. Davidson, *Deterritorializing the New German Cinema* (Minneapolis: University of Minnesota Press, 1999); and Julia Knight, *Women and the New German Cinema* (New York: Verso, 1992).

[2] Much of the scholarship on New German Cinema focuses on a limited number of male filmmakers. For more on the history and films of female German filmmakers working in this period, see Julia Knight, *Women and the New German Cinema* (New York: Verso, 1992).

[3] Thomas Elsaesser, "Primary Identification and the Historical Subject: Fassbinder and Germany," *Cinè-tracts: A Journal of Film and Cultural Studies* 3, no. 3 (1980): 52.

[4] Davidson, *Deterritorializing the New German Cinema*, 20.

[5] Elsaesser, *New German Cinema: A History*, 140.

[6] Richard Dyer, "Reading Fassbinder's Sexual Politics," in *Fassbinder*, ed. Tony Rayns (New York: British Film Institute, 1980), 62.

[7] Dyer, "Reading Fassbinder's Sexual Politics," 62.

[8] Brigitte Peucker, "Un-framing the Image: The Artificiality and the Art World of *Bitter Tears*," in *A Companion to Rainer Werner Fassbinder*, ed. Brigitte Peucker (Malden, MA: Blackwell, 2012), 368.

[9] Ibid., 368.

[10] Laura Mulvey, "Visual Pleasure and Narrative Cinema," *Screen* 16, no. 3 (1975): 17.

[11] Ibid., 13–14.

[12] Elsaesser, *New German Cinema: A History*, 139.

[13] Ibid., "Primary Identification and the Historical Subject: Fassbinder and Germany," 47.

[14] Judith Mayne, "Fassbinder and Spectatorship," *New German Critique* 12 (1977): 74.

[15] Ibid.

[16] Kaja Silverman, "Fassbinder and Lacan: A Reconsideration of Gaze, Look, and Image," *Camera Obscura* 19 (1989): 59.

[17] Judith Butler, "Performative Acts and Gender Constitution: An Essay in Phenomenology and Feminist Theory," *Theatre Journal* 40, no. 4 (1988): 527.

[18] Ibid., 531.

[19] Judith Butler, "Imitation and Gender Insubordination," in *Lesbian and Gay Studies Reader*, ed. Henry Abelove, Michelle Aina Barale, and David M. Halperin (New York: Routledge, 1993), 313.

[20] Teresa de Lauretis, "The Technology of Gender," in *The Technologies of Gender: Essays on Film, Theory, and Fiction* (Bloomington: Indiana University Press, 1987), 4.

[21] Ibid., 3.

[22] Edward R. O'Neill, "The M-m-mama of Us All: Divas and the Cultural Logic of Late Ca(m)pitalism," *Camera Obscura* 65 (2007): 16.

[23] Ibid., 15.

[24] Rosalind Galt, *Pretty: Film and the Decorative Image* (New York: Columbia University Press, 2011), 20–21.

[25] Ibid.

[26] For more on Poussin's painting, see Peucker, "Un-framing the Image," 353–57.

[27] Peucker, "Un-framing the Image," 368.

[28] See Galt, *Pretty: Film and the Decorative Image*.

[29] Elsaesser, *Fassbinder's Germany: History Identity Subject* (Amsterdam: Amsterdam University Press, 1996), 86–87.

[30] Kate Leadbetter, "Fugitive Physicality and Female Performance in Rainer Werner Fassbinder's *The Marriage of Maria Braun, Veronika Voss,* and *Lola*," *Movie: A Journal of Film Criticism* 1 (2010): 6.

Mothers, Masculinities, and Queer Potentials: Jonathan Franzen's Rereading of Thomas Brussig and Phillip Roth

Gary Schmidt, Coastal Carolina University

I N RECENT DECADES, the increasing fluidity, overlap, and ambiguity of sex-gender identities has been accompanied by, if not actually brought about, a reevaluation of hegemonic masculinity both as an analytic concept and as cultural practice; we see an increasing complexity and ambiguity in performances and representations of masculinity—used ever more often now in the plural form "masculinities"—in the public sphere. A careful analysis of such trends in German-speaking Europe must account for the influence of Anglo-American popular culture, media, and literature without assuming that their meaning and function are maintained without alteration when transferred to a different linguistic and cultural setting.

The complexity of cultural adaptation and the impossibility of ever just appropriating cultural forms without altering them can be illustrated using an episode from one of the three texts examined in this essay: Thomas Brussig's 1995 novel *Helden wie wir* (*Heroes Like Us*, 1997), in which protagonist Klaus Uhltzscht comes across a copy of John Irving's 1978 novel *The World according to Garp* (or rather, a German translation entitled *Wie Garp die Welt sah*) while breaking into the apartment of an individual under surveillance by the Stasi. The title immediately attracts the attention of Klaus's colleague Gerd Grabs, who steals the book with the intent to prove to the *Standesamt* (registry office) that Garp is a common first name. Grabs, who has given all his children one-syllable names that start with G, is excited about the possibility of naming his next son Garp, but ultimately he fails in his efforts to get the *Standesamt* to recognize the name. In this fashion, Brussig hints at his American literary influences, even suggesting that he has stolen from them, but also points out the impossibility of simply reusing the American source material unchanged if it is to be recognizable to a German-speaking readership.

This essay examines *Helden wie wir* as part of an intertextual and intercultural semiotic web in which gendered meanings are spun for the psychosexual development of young males, of adolescents who become men in their respective societies. I situate Brussig's novel in the center of the web, which looks backward chronologically to Phillip Roth's novel *Portnoy's Complaint* (1969) and forward to Jonathan Franzen's novel *Purity* (2015). At stake in the literary texts is the meaning and valorization of masculinity and manhood, which are always renegotiated in relationship to femininity and non-hegemonic forms of masculinity. The female Other in all three novels is the mother, whereas non-hegemonic masculinity is represented most frequently by the male homosexual. The relationship of Roth's Alexander Portnoy, Brussig's Klaus Uhltzscht, and Franzen's Andreas Wolf to their overbearing mothers is a striking if not surprising commonality in all three texts. In addition, Franzen's novel explicitly plays upon Brussig's East German setting, with a protagonist who, like Brussig's, grew up under the SED regime but now, in the twenty-first century, is an infamous leaker and irrepressible Don Juan. All three texts contain elements that, to a certain degree, can be interpreted as undermining the strident sexism and phallocentrism of their narrators and/or protagonists: an association of hypersexual heterosexual masculinity with mental illness or perversion, elements of self-deprecation and/or irony, and finally, oblique references to homosexuality that bring heterosexual masculinity into proximity with queerness in a broad sense, that is, as the kind of sex-gender fluidity and indeterminacy mentioned above.

Texts such as those by Roth, Brussig, and Franzen, which seem to focus far more on heterosexual masculinity while disavowing queer moments, can be productively analyzed for how the relationship between hegemonic, that is, heterosexual masculinity, has evolved as non-heterosexual masculinities have become increasingly visible culturally, and to a degree, socially accepted. As heterosexual masculinity itself has come under scrutiny, its unquestioned status as a normative, non-queer identity has been increasingly challenged. What Eve Sedgwick wrote over thirty years ago in her seminal study *Between Men* can still serve as a guide for our assessment of the situation today. Defining "male homosocial desire" as a continuum that encompasses a whole range of possible ways to structure relationships between men from homophobic forms of male-bonding to openly homoerotic relations, Sedgwick's analysis insists on analyzing "the shapes of sexuality, and what *counts* as sexuality" as dependent on "historical power relationships."[1] Power is certainly a productive force, in the Foucauldian sense, of the sexuality of Alexander Portnoy, Klaus Uhltzscht, and Andreas Wolf. In all three, masculine power is associated with violence directed primarily against the maternal figure, but also against fathers. And contrary to Klaus Theweleit's understanding of proto-fascist masculinity as an armored body steeled against the threats of engulfment by feminine forces, insecure masculinity and misogyny go hand in hand with progressive liberalism for Alexander Portnoy, an irreverent albeit self-celebratory anti-authoritarianism for Klaus Uhltzscht, and a rebellious anarchism for leaker Andreas Wolf. In particular, Franzen's novel, by giving Wolf an alter ego called "The Killer," breaks a facile political association of problematic masculinity with fascism and also suggests that sexual liberation for the heterosexual male in the form of an endless cycle of female conquests might be read as nothing more than a *Wiederholungszwang*, a compulsive heterosexual promiscuity that is a symptom of a deeper trauma: the removal of maternal love and the boy's *nachträgliche* consciousness of his mother's repeated infidelity to his ostensible father.

Yet the renegotiation of heterosexual masculinity in these texts is also a renegotiation of the boundary between homosocial and homosexual desire, a boundary that Theweleit himself attempted to describe in political terms when he contrasted the "inauthentic homosexual acts" of the proto-fascist militias to the deterritorialization of the anus theorized by Guy Hocquenghem.[2] Significantly, Franzen's novel makes it clear how shifts in the continuum of homosocial desire affect and are affected by shifts along the axis measuring cultural representation of gender, at one end of which we would find an understanding of gender as the result of an autonomous choice of role—a form of performativity based entirely on free will and hence subject to immediate boundless permutations—and at the other end the belief that one's gender is entirely predetermined by one's biological sex. Of course, most positions are somewhere in the middle of this spectrum, with Butlerian performativity, for example, cutting the bond between biological sex and gender by denying the objective reality of the former while describing the latter more as a set of parameters in which intelligible performances of identity are possible.[3] Hence, to understand the degree to which contemporary literary representations of masculinity have become "queer," we must address how they situate non-hegemonic expressions of both gender (i.e., masculinity, manhood, or manliness and femininity or womanhood) and sexual orientation (gay, straight, bisexual, or something more amorphous) in relation to one another.

A common thread we see in all three novels is, unsurprisingly, psychoanalysis. Specifically Freudian psychoanalysis, and to a lesser degree, Lacanian, continues to inform the narratives that describe the sexual maturation of males. Whether or not these literary narrativizations of Freudian paradigms can truly expand our understanding of masculinity and open up spaces for new, non-hegemonic or queer masculinities remains up for debate. Thus, for a queer project it is imperative to address to what extent these literary texts remain invested in heteronormative developmental paradigms or whether or not they offer alternatives to these.

Tim Dean provides another way of thinking about the queer potential of psychoanalytic theory that we may also apply to literary narrative that is steeped in such theory. Emphasizing the disruptive productivity of retaining a notion of the unconscious that is transindividual and historical, Dean foregrounds the anti-normative potential of psychoanalysis as well as the necessity of continuing to excavate this potential: "One has only to consult contemporary humanistic discourse or, further down the cultural food chain, peruse the self-help section at the bookstore—or, further yet, turn on the television to one of the many talk shows glutting the airwaves—to confirm that Freudian concepts have become almost completely 'deadened by routine use.'"[4]

Dean's disruptive-productive project regarding psychoanalysis can be applied to literary texts when we examine whether these invoke psychoanalytic concepts and narratives in a way that brings new life to them rather than re-inscribing worn out clichés. This, of course, begs the question as to why psychoanalytic paradigms should not be eschewed altogether and whether novelists who use them do so because they are unable to imagine another framework through which to describe and analyze psychosexual development. Arguing with Dean, we would state that we must continue to work with Freudian paradigms because we have not yet come to a point historically at which "erotic desire would have been fully disarticulated from personhood" (BS 21) Dean argues that such a disarticulation would actually be the culmination of what started with Freud, and while certain anti-identitarian strains of queer theory would also presuppose this as the endpoint for a queer social-political-cultural project, here my focus will be on Dean's approach: I will examine the three literary texts to see where they might possibly lie along an imagined axis that moves into a potential future where ego maintenance and the preservation of gendered personhood fade and textual readings that refuse understanding and systematization become not only possible but productive.[5]

Mirjam Gebauer has identified several important parallels between *Portnoy's Complaint* and *Helden wie wir*, including the similar narrative situation: both narrator-protagonists are looking back from adulthood on their childhood and adolescence. While Klaus narrates to a New York reporter with a Jewish-sounding name, Portnoy recounts his woes to a psychotherapist named Dr. Spielvogel; both narrators allude to Sigmund Freund; the central frame of reference for both is the mother and, to a lesser degree, the father.[6] In a certain sense, in all three novels, sons and husbands become victims of their mothers and wives, who emasculate them. As Susan Bordo notes in her study *The Male Body*, Alexander Portnoy's father gets a greater degree of sympathy and respect than his mother: "I am less struck by the portrait of Sophie Portnoy than I am by Alex/Roth's ambivalence about his kindly, anxious, powerless Jewish father, whose forever constipated bowels are 'doomed to be obstructd by this Holy Protestant Empire' but whose manly member has miraculously escaped cultural castration."[7]

If there is little sympathy or admiration directed by Brussig's Klaus Uhltzscht or Franzen's Andreas Wolf towards their fathers, they nevertheless take up far less space in the narrative than their mothers. Yet Klaus's extreme detestation for his father should not go unmentioned: his father becomes not only an object of hatred but also the very emblem of the abject. Reminiscent of Portnoy's father's constipation, Klaus's father's body fills up with feces, and Klaus, rather than eulogizing his father's testicles, as does Alexander, describes instead how he took them in his hand and crushed them: "Ich konnte für zwanzig Sekunden seine Eier quetschen. Er hat meine zwanzig Jahre gequetscht, so wie sie aussehen./ Es gibt Dinge, die ich getan habe und heute am liebsten ungeschehen machen würde. / Das nicht." (I squeezed his balls for twenty seconds. He'd squeezed mine for twenty years, from the look of them. / There are certain things I've done that I'd sooner not have done, but that isn't one of them.)[8]

As Gebauer notes, the similarity between the two mothers in spite of the shift in milieu suggests that Brussig took Roth's Jewish mother as a model for his GDR-mother; one can further add that the references to Freud function as a justification in both novels for the universalizing of mother-son conflict centered around the absolute necessity of boys to rebel against their mothers (even murderously) in order to become men. In *Portnoy's Complaint,* Alexander recalls kicking his mother when he was a little boy and then being made to feel like a monster by her. Franzen may have had this episode in mind when he describes how Andreas Wolf kicked his own mother as a child, resulting not in a series of endless reprimands but in her withdrawal into a coma-like state. Andreas's mother remains a distant but beautiful object that he can never obtain.

Klaus Uhltzscht, in contrast, envisions killing both his parents in order to complete his sexual liberation, perhaps a logical fantasy for a young man who envisions a sexuality devoid of people but focused primarily on objects of all kinds, animate and inanimate: "Wann werden sie begreifen [. . .] dass es mein Schwanz ist und meine Angelegenheit, wo ich ihn reinstecke und was dranklebt, wenn ich ihn rausziehe. Muss ich sie erst erschiessen, um endlich Ruhe zu haben?" (*Hww* 123) (When would they grasp [. . .] that it was *my* dick and *my* business what I inserted it in and what adhered to it when I extracted it? Would I have to shoot them both before they left me in peace?) (*HLU* 109) Yet the impersonal orientation of Klaus's sexuality—whether he is penetrating objects or speaking of phallic penetration of the vagina as if it were an object removed from a female body or person—is nonetheless personal in another sense: it is phallocentric: the liberation of Klaus's penis becomes the vehicle for his narcissistic self-love. In this sense, all other individuals are valuable merely to the extent that they reflect his hyperbolic sense of himself as the savior of East Germany. The instability of this phallocentric self-image is, however, recognizable in his obsessive need for repetition and assertion of his own virility and heroism vis-à-vis his interlocutor.

Franzen's *Purity* complicates Brussig's traditional gender coding by representing phallic rebellion not only in the aggression of Andreas Wolf against his GDR-complicit mother but also in the resentment of the eponymous Purity (nicknamed Pip), against her extreme left-wing, vegan, feminist American mother who has actually hidden her father's identity from her and fabricated an elaborate story of abuse and victimization. Yet ultimately the conflicts between individuals (or rather, following Lacan, between fantasies of individuals) remain highly gendered, given that it is largely male-female relations that remain mired in endless cycles of miscommunication and misunderstanding; indeed the relationship between Tom Aberant and Anabel, Pip's mother, might be seen as a narrativization of Lacan's famous statement that "there is no sexual relation."[9] Significantly, while Franzen engages with the same themes of masculine development and mother-son conflict addressed by Roth and Brussig, he foregoes for the most part the first-person form, which is perhaps the single element of their two novels that produces the most potential irony and subversion of the narrator's own misogyny: as embodied narrators, Alexander Portnoy and Klaus Uhltzscht both speak in a voice that tends towards the hyperbolic: in short they are both melodramatic, unreliable narrators. Franzen's return to the third-person omniscient narrator resets the rules of the game, as it were, to the default narrative voice that masks the gendered subject position of the text itself.

One might argue that *Helden wie wir* puts male development, masculinity, and male sexuality on display in a manner perhaps unprecedented in German language literature, although one could just as easily argue that it does far more to veil all of these behind phallic imagery and hysterical misogyny. In spite of the fact that narrator Klaus Uhltzscht obsessively repeats the words for the male and female genitalia again and again, there is actually very little description of the male organ beyond its slang appellation. *Helden wie wir* provides an aesthetic of male genitalia that is reminiscent of Susan Bordo's definition of the phallus as a prosthetic penis in her study *The Male Body*. This becomes most evident in the novel's climax, when Klaus's surgically enlarged member is revealed to the East German border guard, leading to the penetration of the Berlin Wall. The wall opening could be interpreted homoerotically given the guard's fascination with what he sees and also given various other episodes in the narrative that, if read from a queer perspective, suggest a certain obsession of the narrator with male homosexuality that cannot be erased by his obsessive-compulsive repetition of various slang terms for the vagina as the correct place for his penis to be inserted.

Brussig's fictionalized border opening episode is itself an iteration of the phallus, which Bordo describes in her study of American popular culture and literature as "the penis that takes one's breath away—not merely because of length or thickness . . . but because of its *majesty*. Those who gaze upon it immediately feel themselves to be its subjects" (*MB* 87).

> Mit einem Grinsen zog ich meine Unterhose herunter—dass Grinsen dazugehört, wusste ich seit diesem Exhibitionisten, der mir mal in der S-Bahn begegnet war. Und während Aram Radomski mit klaren und engagierten Worten auf den Verantwortlichen einredete, ohne zu vermerken, was ich neben ihm tat, starrten die Grenzer wie gebannt auf das, was ich ihnen zeigte. Als alle Grenzer wie gelähmt am Tor standen, wandte ich mich an den Verantwortlichen, worauf seine Widerrede abrupt endete. (*Hww* 291)

> [Grinning, because I'd known that grinning was *de rigeuer* ever since encountering the flasher in the S-Bahn, I lowered my underpants. And, while Aram Radomski continued to argue with the man in charge in lucid and committed language, unaware of what I was doing beside him, the border guards stared spellbound at my display. When all of them were standing at the gate, transfixed, I turned to face the man in charge. His flow of argument ceased abruptly.] (*HLU* 258)

As Bordo notes, "The word 'fascinate' has its origin in the Latin word fascinum, which meant 'witchcraft,' and derived from the phallic god Fascinus, worshipped by Romans, who sometimes wore an image of an erect penis around the neck as an amulet or hung one on the walls of their houses" (*MB* 43). In subjecting the East German border guards to involuntary enchantment with his fascinating penis, Klaus is reversing a role that he played as a child, when as a gullible *Muttersöhnchen* (mama's boy) he unwittingly served as masturbatory aid to a classmate by wearing an ABBA T-Shirt backwards and sitting in front of the other boy who could thus do his business while gazing at the smiling face of Agnetha Fältskog. Klaus reverses the shame and humiliation he felt as a child, shame that was fueled by his mother's reprimands when she found out what happened, by repeating the act of exhibitionism and magnifying its significance exponentially. We can ratchet up the metaphor even more and say that Klaus is screwing the border guard, as it were, instead of it being done to him; he is the active penetrator rather than the one who is passive and penetrated. But Klaus has penetrated not just the guard but the wall itself.

One might find queer potential in interpreting Klaus's conquest of the wall as a homosexual act—or more precisely as an act that skirts the boundaries between homosocial and homosexual desire—and viewing the Berlin Wall as a kind of inflatable sex doll if the wall did not so clearly serve a phallic logic that reinforces narcissistic heteromasculinity. Yet it is also possible to find within the text itself, albeit at the margin, the magic word that breaks the ban of enchantment emanating from Klaus's enlarged organ. Significantly, Klaus refers to his penis repeatedly as his "dildo," which if taken literally emphasizes its artificiality as a fantasmatic superphallus that attests to "dildo envy." Dildo envy, the anxiety and resentment that arises when comparing the constant attributes of a prosthetic penis with the unreliability of its biological equivalent, according to Pat Califa, "inhabits the male unconscious more than penis envy torments women" (*MB* 48).

As Bordo argues, the increasing popularity of penile augmentation, penis enlargement, or so-called male enhancement cannot be attributed to heterosexual men's desire to give more pleasure to their female partners but rather to the need to one-up their male rivals and increase their performance quantitatively rather than qualitatively. Similarly, Klaus's superphallus is not at all an instrument of pleasure; in fact, other than in one brief sex scene describing Klaus's deflowering by a woman who infects him with gonorrhea—a trophy of war?—Klaus uses his penis primarily to penetrate inanimate objects; his use of the typical East German *Broiler* (roast chicken) for this purpose is not only a cultural adaptation of the piece of liver that Philip Roth's Alexander Portnoy defiled as an adolescent; the fact that he engages in sex with a piece of meat while already working (he believes at least) for the Stasi, rather than as a schoolboy, as did Roth's protagonist, might be interpreted as a device to emphasize his arrested development under the repressive East German regime. On the other hand, Klaus's effusive narration of such "perversions" is also a celebration of a polymorphous—and at least potentially queer sexuality that he embraces after the fact and in direct contradiction of his mother's vision of her son's unilinear development towards adult heterosexuality in her obsession with the figure skater Katarina Witt:

> Was Mama schon immer über 6[10] wissen wollte, aber bisher nie zu fragen wagte: Ob ich imstande wäre, Katarina Witt flachzumachen. Um das mal klarzustellen: davor würde ich nicht zurueckschrecken! Aber meine ideelle Lustgemeinde war unüberschaubar, also warum ausgerechnet nur Katarina! Als ob Sex nur durch junge, gutgebaute und oft abfotografierte Stars verkörpert wird [. . .]. (*Hww* 53–54)

> [Was this what Mama had always wanted to know about 6 but had never previously dared to ask: whether I felt like screwing Katarina Witt? Don't get me wrong: I wouldn't have spurned Katarina, but my imaginary harem was incalculably vast, so why single her out as if sex were personified exclusively by well-built, photogenic young figure-skating stars—as if I needed a double Lutz and a miniskirt to put me in mind of sexsexsex?] (*HLU* 46)

The comical episodes with Klaus's masturbatory exercises, with or without roast chickens, also allow the focus of the narrative to remain centered on Klaus and his penis while avoiding any actual interaction with women. This contrasts starkly with the protagonists of *Portnoy's Complaint* and *Purity*, whose sexual relations with actual women, or perhaps better said, with female genitalia, are central to the plot. It is perhaps because of the relative dearth of actual females that Klaus must obsessively repeat the incantation of "Möse" (pussy) as the correct receptacle for his "dildo." If there is any queer sexuality lurking behind Klaus's phallic narcissism, he is very eager to disavow it.

The protagonists in all three novels remain trapped in a love/hate relationship to the phallus that is literally embodied in their problematic relationships to their own penises. While narcissistic exhibitionism plays a role for all three protagonists—Alexander Portnoy masturbates on a bus next to a sleeping woman; Klaus Uhltzscht bares his giant organ to the East German border guards; Andreas Wolf brazenly tells his mother to leave him alone so he can go masturbate and at one point even asks her if she wants to watch—they also share in the embarrassment caused by the penis that has been described by Bordo elsewhere as a kind of foreign appendage that unmasks the male intellect as materially determined and hence emasculated, that is, feminized (*MB* 19–20). The great irony is that the sexual organ associated with quintessential masculinity is also the one that deconstructs itself through its uncontrollability and unpredictability. For Klaus Uhltzscht, this comes in the embarrassing moments at school when he gets erections; these erections were a secret that he believed he had kept hidden only to discover that all his schoolmates knew about it all along. For Alexander Portnoy, it appears in his self-consciousness regarding the discrepancy between his altruistic political ideals and his private pursuit of sexual conquests; and this is also true to a certain degree for Andreas Wolf. Yet in the cases of all three protagonists, any potential embarrassment does not prevent an endless textual production surrounding their penises and the sexuality that it signifies. This suggests that for these three authors, at least, an examination of masculinity needs to take a close look at the negotiation, even celebration, of male deviance, particularly in the form of exhibitionism—which, through its calling on the other to "look at my glorious phallus," can be linked with narcissism.

Narcissism was first mentioned by Freud in 1910 as an attribute of homosexual men. As Laplanche and Pontalis write, "The discovery of narcissism leads Freud—in the Schreber case [. . .] to posit the existence of a stage in sexual development between auto-erotism and object-love. The subject 'begins by taking himself, his own body, as his love-object,' which allows a first unification of the sexual instinct."[11] We might ask ourselves, to what degree does masculinity itself become queer in these texts, in spite of the best efforts of their authors to disavow any association with homosexuality? In *Portnoy's Complaint*, male homosexuality still functions largely as a specter of the abject, of the danger that he has narrowly escaped from by rebelling against his mother. In responding to her insistent desire that her son be a "nice young man," he proclaims, "The mystery is . . . that I'm not like all the nice young men I see strolling hand in hand in Bloomingdale's on Saturday morning. Mother, the beach at Fire Island is strewn with the bodies of nice Jewish boys."[12] And Portnoy goes even further, prefiguring Klaus Uhltzscht's defilement of broilers: "There is worse even that that—there are people who fuck chickens! There are men who screw stiffs! [. . .] So if I kicked you in the shins, Ma-ma, if I sunk [*sic*] my teeth into your wrist clear through the *bone*, count your blessings! For had I kept it *all* inside me, believe me, you too might have arrived home to find a pimply adolescent corpse swinging over the bathtub by his father's belt" (*PC* 126).

The gay male is also instrumentalized by Brussig for his ability to underscore Klaus's emasculation by his mother, with Klaus himself describing his first visit to summer camp as follows:

> Rückblickend kann ich mein Gefühl mit dem eines stockschwulen weissen Modemachers vergleichen, der mit einer farbigen Streetgang für eine Nacht die Zelle teilt. Diese Jungs waren mir irgendwie unheimlich. Sie machten sich nichts daraus, wenn man sie ihrer Mutter wegnahm. Wahrscheinlich sind sie schon vom Kindergarten daran gewöhnt. (*Hww* 44–45)

> [In retrospect, I can compare my feelings with those of a flamingly gay white fashion designer who is sharing a cell with a colored street gang for the night. Those boys somehow gave me the creeps. It was no big deal for them to be taken away from their mothers. Probably they were used to it since kindergarten.][13]

Yet, Klaus's rejection of his mother's prudery and the feeling of manhood that he experiences after his first time with a woman position him alongside male homosexuals insofar as she tells him he could have gotten infected with AIDS instead of just gonorrhea, and Klaus imagines himself as an invalid in a wheelchair marked by a sign stating, "Er wollte nur seinen Spass, ohne an die Folgen zu denken" (*Hww* 127; He had his fun, heedless of the consequences, *HLU* 112). This socialist denunciation of the individual's pursuit of pleasure resembles the rejection in American culture of what Tim Dean calls gay males' "noxious jouissance": "Its [homosexuality's] genital nonreciprocity with the opposite sex, together with its overt anti-utilitarian—that is, nonreproductive—pleasure, plus its association with fatality and self-destruction (for which AIDS is the

current, most intensified figure), makes homosexuality appear as an especially noxious form of the Other's *jouissance*" (*BS* 127).

Klaus Uhltzscht not only embraces narcissistic jouissance but also
perversion as what was necessary in East Germany to rebel against the
all-powerful state. Whereas Klaus celebrates his liberated manhood in
the form of endless arousals and penetrations, exulting in liberation not
only from maternal restrictions but also enjoying freedom from the need
even to have a partner, Franzen's novel draws back from this celebratory
approach towards narcissistic male sexuality. While Brussig references
Freud in passing, he makes no serious attempt to grapple with psychoanalytic paradigms; many of these allusions appear to be used more for their
comic effect than anything else. Indeed, too much seriousness is precisely
the critique that Brussig levies against the author Christa Wolf by having
her novel *Der geteilte Himmel* cure Klaus of his permanent erection.

While Brussig's narrator is sometimes a stand-up comic, sometimes
a ranting, hysterical drama queen, and sometimes a loudmouthed critic,
Franzen gives us the allegedly impartial third-person narrator. The character that most corresponds to Uhltzscht is Andreas Wolf, who grows
up as the privileged child of the Socialist Unity Party elite. Wolf's relationship to his mother is much more strongly Oedipal than Klaus's. Wolf
describes how beautiful his mother is, how much pain he felt at her withdrawal; he also recalls inflicting pain on her by kicking her—all of these
hearken back to Roth's protagonist. Like Portnoy, Wolf begins to masturbate compulsively in his adolescence; however, while Portnoy is able to
hide this activity from his invasive mother by physically blockading himself in the bathroom and feigning constipation, Wolf provocatively tells
his mother to leave him alone so that he can enter his "secret passageway
out of self-alienation, in the form of giving himself pleasure while also
receiving it [. . .]."[14] The very wording of this description suggests a fantasy of oneness beyond sex, gender, and sexuality, which in and of itself is
not necessarily narcissistic. Unlike for Klaus Uhltzscht, Wolf's penis-play
is not linked with megalomaniacal fantasies of matricide and revolution.
Instead, it is only through the intervention of his mother and a psycho-
analyst that Wolf begins to understand his excessive masturbation in a
different way. The therapist to whom his parents send him asks him provocatively, "Are you sure you're not drawing self-portraits?" and shortly
thereafter, "What about the boys in your school? Are you attracted to any
of them?" (*P* 119) Andreas firmly negates both of these questions, and
from this point on, as if in a conscious disavowal of both narcissism and
homosexuality, turns his attention away from masturbation to the conquest of actual female bodies.

The need for the adolescent Wolf to bring his self-sufficient sexuality
in line with heteronormative expectations explains how he himself can
interpret his promiscuous heterosexuality, his Don Juanism, as politically

subversive, such that he explicitly thematizes it in his attempts at literary expression, for example in a poem published in the premier East German academic journal on German literature, *Weimarer Beiträge*. The poem, published in both English and German, is however, merely a slightly sublimated form of exhibitionism. Entitled "Muttersprache/Mother Tongue" it is actually an ode to masturbation and nocturnal ejaculations. If one reads the first letter of each line only one gets the following in German and English: "Ich widme eurem Sozialismus den herrlichsten Samenerguss. / I dedicate the most glorious ejaculation to your social-ism" (*P* 124–25). Andreas suffers drastic consequences for this, as does the editor of *Weimarer Beiträge*. Yet with this act he also starts to become self-aware, to realize how he has been so fixated on himself that he never thought about the harm that he did to others. It is perhaps this feeling of guilt that the older Andreas, after he has become a world-renowned leaker, generalizes into a gender ethic that suggests men are by nature oppressors, which he expresses in an e-mail to Pip, attempting to encourage her to leave her domineering mother in California and join his group of leakers in South America: "It's true I'm male and have some power, but I never asked to be born male. Maybe being male is like being born a predator, and maybe the only right thing for the predator to do, if it sympathizes with smaller animals and won't accept that it was born to kill them, is to betray its nature and starve to death. But maybe it's like something else—like being born with more money than others. Then the right thing to do becomes a more interesting social question" (*P* 66). It is perhaps this "more interesting social question" that Wolf seeks to answer through his political activity, but as for both Portnoy and Uhltzscht, Wolf's sexuality cannot be separated from his political activity.

Renegotiating the parameters of homosocial desire appears to be one approach to Wolf's (and Franzen's) examination of male privilege; these explorations occur within a series of relationships with other men that are mediated by women, much as in the classical way described by Gayle Rubin as the "traffic in women," interpreted by Sedgwick as "the use of women as exchangeable, perhaps symbolic, property for the primary purpose of cementing the bonds of men with men" (*Between Men* 25–26). This is evident in two particular asymmetrical triangles: in the first of these triangles, a teenage girl named Annegret, provides Wolf with a target for his murderous lust in her mother's lover Horst, whose sexual exploitation of Annegret mirrors Wolf's own predatory phallocentrism. The other important male character of the novel is a reporter named Tom Aberant. As with Wolf's story, we learn about Tom's past life in a flashback incited by a major revelation in the present; what is important for the current analysis is the fact that Tom had a tumultuous marriage with Annabel (Pip's mother), who is portrayed as a woman without any intellectual or moral flexibility whom he eventually leaves. Shortly after the *Wende* he goes to Berlin and meets Andreas Wolf, who tells him a dark secret, the fact that he killed a man (Horst) whose body is still buried in the garden of his parents' dacha. This part of the novel has switched into the first person, and Tom remembers his tête-à-tête with Andreas tenderly: "I put my arm around his shoulders, and he turned to me and clung to me. [. . .] He cried for a long time, I stroked his head and held him close. If he'd been a woman, I would have kissed his hair. But strict limits to intimacy are the straight man's burden. He pulled away and composed himself" (*P* 423). A queer reading might interpret Aberant's reference to the "straight man's burden" as a disavowal of latent homosexual desire, but such a reading might also unpack the notion of the "straight man's burden" in terms of the homosocial/homosexual continuum. Where is the border between the fear of being perceived as gay and the specter of ego-shattering anality theorized by Leo Bersani in "Is the Rectum a Grave?," in which anal intercourse becomes a choice for masochism analogous to the predator's self-abnegating choice to starve to death?[15] Who enforces these boundaries and to what aim? One might understand the refusal of same-sex intimacy as choice for self-preservation at the character level or, at the textual level, as authorial interventions to foreclose potentially queer readings of such episodes.

Aberant's and Wolf's intimacy is, however, not consummated sexually, but in a different way: Aberant helps Wolf move the body of his victim and thus becomes an accomplice after the fact to the murder. In a role reversal of what Wolf did to many of his female lovers, he is then jilted by Aberant, who does not show up to a dinner date. It is then undoubtedly significant that Andreas Wolf ultimately occupies the space of Roth's abject suicide victim, who appeared in *Portnoy's Complaint* in such close textual proximity to the despised gay men's bodies strewn across Fire Island like flotsam and jetsam. Wolf commits suicide after being rejected yet again by Aberant, when the latter travels to Bolivia to confront him for having revealed to Pip that Aberant was her father. While a heteronormative reading of the plot climax would interpret Wolf's suicide as the result of his inability to have normal personal and sexual relations with women, a queer reading would explore the latent homosexuality in the asymmetrical triangle Wolf/Pip/Aberant. The murderous intimate physical proximity of the men suggests an intense desire for one another that is only superficially veiled by the spectral presence of the woman and remains after the female object is removed. Franzen's third-person narrator describes Wolf's final thoughts as follows:

> But this thought, the idea of being killed by Tom, was like the prospect of rain in a desert. Not a relief in itself but a reason to keep moving forward. Death by any means would put an end to his throttling fear of it; the precise means should have been a matter of

indifference. But to be killer and killed was arguably the closest form of human intimacy. In a sense, he's been more intimate with Horst Kleinholz than he'd been with any other person since he'd left his mother's womb. And to die knowing that Tom, too, was capable of killing—to exit the world feeling he hadn't been so alone in it after all—seemed like a kind of intimacy as well. (*P* 505)

Wolf's suicide seems to be the result of his inability to integrate his alter ego, "The Killer," with his self-image as someone who brings truth into the world and pursues "purity." In a sense, his final meeting with Aberant is an attempt for a kind of recognition that would have allowed him to repair his ego, but since Aberant refuses to grant him this, he instead settles for the very suicide that he once mentioned in an e-mail to Pip as the only way out for a predator. Yet just as he once killed another man, he fantasizes his own suicide as death at another man's hands, creating a fantasmatic masculinity of predator-victim, and a kind of male-male relation in which both men fully understand and inhabit their previously reversible but now fixed roles as perpetrator/victim (predator/prey).[16] Read this way, Wolf can only fully expel "The Killer" by becoming the one who is killed. Yet his fear of being killed, his irrational fear that Aberant will reveal his secret—stemming in part from his feeling of being "jilted"— leads Wolf to the very actions that provoke Aberant's retribution. This begs interpretation as an allusion to Freud's Schreber case, which as Segwick describes, "shows clearly that *the repression of homosexual desire* in a man who by any commonsense standard was heterosexual, occasioned paranoid psychosis [. . .]" (Sedgwick 20). This becomes explicit in the following passage:

> What he [Wolf] saw all at once: that Tom had glimpsed the Killer. In the light of dawn, in the Oder valley. The monster stiffy that hugging Tom had given him was not, as he'd supposed, the natural unleashing of the libido he'd suppressed since the night of the murder. Nor was it a gay man's stiffy, not in any meaningful sense. But it was nonetheless a stiffy *for Tom*. He had it for the same reason he'd had it for the fifteen-year-old Annagret: because Tom had made himself part of the murder. Man, woman—the Killer didn't trouble with such distinctions. (*P* 494–95)

And just as the victors write history, Aberant himself is the one who issues the official diagnosis to Wolf and hence to the reader before Wolf's suicide: "You're psychotic, and you can't see it because you're psychotic" (*P* 513).

From a textual perspective, Wolf's disappearance at the end is also an occasion for the disappearance of a sexuality associated with the death drive. Franzen's text seems to engage in an attempt to recover the ego by recovering recognition and coherence; Andreas Wolf's failure to do so results in paranoiac psychosis. The narrative ultimately offers a fantasy of ego recovery along with restoration of heterosexual bliss (the unlikely relationship between Pip and her boyfriend Jason), even as it negates this possibility for Tom and Anabel. If, as Dean asserts in his queer interpretation of Lacan, Lacan's famous statement that "there is no sexual relation" can actually be interpreted to apply to any relations between human beings regardless of sex, Franzen's novel seems nevertheless to make clear distinctions between the psychoanalytic function of heterosexual and homosocial/homosexual relationships. The failure of the pairing between Aberant and Wolf forecloses same-sex desire as a possibility for escaping Tom's tumultuous marriage or Wolf's obsessive-compulsive Don Juanism. The great contrast at the end of the novel is between the return to agonistic discourse between Tom and Anabel when they see each other for the first time in decades, and the blissful silence of Pip and Jason, whose budding romance appears to be outside of language and provides, using Dean's words, "a fantasy of oneness . . . the illusion of identity, as well as reassurance that the traumatic real of sex can be rehabilitated to a sexual *relation*—a fantasy image of sexual completion, the copulatory couple" (*BS* 109).

The endless production of discourse in the older couple is set explicitly against the non-symbolic oneness of the younger one:

> Pip shut the door again, to block out the words, but even with the door closed she could hear the fighting. The people who'd bequeathed a broken world to her were shouting at each other viciously. Jason sighed and took her hand. She held it tightly. It had to be possible to do better than her parents, but she wasn't sure she would. Only when the skies opened again, the rain from the immense dark western ocean pounding on the car roof, the sound of love drowning out the other sound, did she believe that she might. (*P* 563)

What Dean describes in Lacanian terms as an S1, or master signifier, is both culturally inflected and political:

> The price of such identification with S1 in a master discourse is precisely the repression of division (S/ below the "bar"), the mechanism by which political discourse itself functions repressively and by which it displaces division to its outside in the form of externalized *agents* of division. Thus, for example, a certain concept of the nuclear family functions in contemporary Anglo-American political discourse as an S1, operating as the fundamental social unit to which political discourse addresses itself. Like the Holy Family (and the doctrine of the Trinity) that still sanctions it, this mythic family is sacred; as a unit

denoting unity, oneness, it figures the social bond by repressing divisions of gender, sexuality, and the sexual nonrelation, while giving rise to the routine domestic violences of incest, rape, and battering as symptomatic returns of the repressed. (*BS* 109)

The final passage of *Purity* contains all the elements of S1: attribution of division to an external source—"the broken world bequeathed to them"—and the repression of division through the fantasy of a sexual relation. And, as with any fantasy of heterosexual wholeness, there remains an outside: the mother/daughter dyad,[17] whose dysfunctionality is then definitively described by Aberant's sister Cynthia when describing Anabel to Pip: "She created you to be what no one else can be for her. I'm angry at the selfishness of that. I'm angry that she's the kind of 'feminist' who gives feminism a bad name. I feel like going over to Tom's right this minute and slapping him in the face. For enabling her fantasies" (*P* 539).

Although Anabel and Pip offer an extreme example of unhealthy dysfunction between parent and child, mothers in general appear to be vulnerable to creating their children "to be what no one else can be" for them. The son's need to rebel against his mother becomes overdetermined insofar as both Aberant and Wolf share the scars of their relationships with their GDR-complicit mothers. When read in the context of Brussig's portrayal of "Muttisozialismus," the link between ideology and mothers' psychic need for oneness with their children becomes evident.

Sexuality beyond personhood is also a clear specter of the abject that must be expelled from the fantasy of heterosexual bliss that concludes *Purity*; here the internet becomes the emblem of non-personhood and the death drive, the very factors that Dean celebrates in his interpretation of Lacanian jouissance as the "disarticulation of erotic desire from personhood." Wolf himself bewails his fate as a non-person: "[S]ince a person couldn't exist in two places at once, the more he existed as the Internet's image of him, the less he felt like he existed as a flesh-and-blood person. The Internet meant *death* [. . .]" (*P* 492).

Understanding the potential queerness of the masculinities negotiated in these novels is perhaps most productive in terms of the fantasmatic project of the novels themselves. Whereas *Helden wie wir* all but removes Woman's role of "being the Phallus" for the man, celebrating instead narcissistic exhibitionism literally and figuratively (the never-ending monologue of the narrator supersedes all developmental narrative and heterosexual romantic fulfillment),[18] *Purity* consistently describes the failure of heterosexual relationships while at the same time foregoing alternatives and fantasizing a return to a new non-discursive heterosexuality in Pip and Jason.

Notes

1 Eve Kosofsky Sedgwick, *Between Men: English Literature and Male Homosocial Desire* (New York: Columbia University Press, 1985), 2.

2 Klaus Theweleit, *Männerfantasien. Band 2: Männerkörper. Zur Psychoanalyse des weißen Terrors* (Munich: dtv, 1977/1978), 313–15. The main distinction here is between homosexuality as an act of self-preservation (Erhaltungsakt) representing the killing of desire that directs itself against the threatening feminine for those who have not "fully been born" (die Nicht-zu-Ende-Geborenenen) and homosexuality as the deliberate deterritorialization of a bodily region that has been excluded from the sexual: the anus.

3 "There is always a dimension of ourselves and our relation to others that we cannot know, and this not-knowing persists with us as a condition of existence and, indeed, of survivability. We are, to an extent, driven by what we do not know, and cannot know, and this 'drive' (*Trieb*) is precisely what is neither exclusively biological nor cultural, but always the site of their dense convergence." Judith Butler, *Undoing Gender* (New York: Routledge, 2004), 15.

4 Tim Dean, *Beyond Sexuality* (Chicago: University of Chicago Press, 2000), 23. Cited hereafter in text as *BS*.

5 As Annamarie Jagosie states in her early stocktaking of queer theory, the ideas of anti-identitarian theorists such as Butler, Halperin, Fuss, and others "critique the putatively causal relation between a secure identity and an effective politics" (Annamarie Jagosie, *Queer Theory: An Introduction* [New York: New York University Press, 1996], 93). Dean, however, seeks to overcome the theoretical impasse between essentialism and constructionism, the political counterpart of which lies in the conflict between a politics of identity versus a queer politics. He does so by exploring a Lacanian understanding of the unconscious that admits to an element of desire beyond language, which although always inaccessible and unknowable can nevertheless be productively theorized and made politically efficacious.

6 Mirjam Gebauer, "Milieuschilderungen zweier Verrückter Monologisten: Philip Roths Portnoy's Complaint als ein Vorbild für Thomas Brussigs 'Helden wie wir,'" *Orbis Litterarum: International Review of Literary Studies* 57, no. 3 (2002): 222–40, here 225.

7 Susan Bordo, *The Male Body* (New York: Farrar, Straus and Giroux, 1999), 52. Cited hereafter in text as *MB*.

8 Thomas Brussig, *Helden wie wir* (Hamburg: Spiegel Verlag, 2006/2007), 244. Cited hereafter in text as *Hww*. English translations are taken from Thomas Brussig, *Heroes Like Us*, trans. John Brownjohn (New York: Farrar, Straus, and Giroux, 1997), 217. Cited hereafter in text as *HLU*.

9 Tim Dean asserts that it is possible to move beyond a heteronormative interpretation of Lacan's statement: "Lacan's axiom [. . .] counters the heterosexist assumption of complementarity between genders; yet Lacan's explanations of this axiom are couched in terms of each gender's failure to relate to the other, rather than in terms of sexual relationality's failure as such, independent of gender" (*Beyond*, 27). Dean interprets this as Lacan's failure to use terminology that actually keeps up with the complex implications of his theoretical elaborations.

[10] Klaus uses the number "6" to refer to his mother's Germanicized pronunciation of the English word "sex" with a voiced initial consonant, making it a homophone of "sechs" (six).

[11] Jean Laplanche and J.-B Pontalis, *The Language of Psycho-Analysis*, trans. Donald Smith-Nicholson (London: Karnac Books, 1988), 255.

[12] Phillip Roth, *Portnoy's Complaint* (New York: Vintage International, 1994), 125. Cited hereafter in the text as *PC*.

[13] Significantly, this passage is omitted from John Brownjohn's translation (See *HLU* 38), so I have translated it myself.

[14] Jonathan Franzen, *Purity* (New York: Farrar, Straus and Giroux, 2015), 108. Cited hereafter in the text as *P*.

[15] Leo Bersani, "Is the Rectum a Grave?," in *Is the Rectum a Grave? And Other Essays* (Chicago: University of Chicago Press, 2010). Dean rightly points out that Bersani's framing of receptive rectal sex as "ego-shattering jouissance" (*BS* 130) can be read as a call for the male ego to redeem itself by self-abnegation, which appears problematic as a conscious choice. Yet, these precisely are the parameters that appear to limit the choices for Wolf and the other male characters in Franzen's novel; there appears to be no escape from the choice to be either victim or perpetrator—except madness.

[16] Aberant is doubly the winner/predator in the male-male agonistics of the novel, given that he also successfully woos a married woman, Leila, taking her away from her disabled husband.

[17] The treatment of the relations between women in *Purity* deserves an examination in its own right, but it is unfortunately beyond the scope of this article. Suffice it to state that Wolf is thwarted in his relationship with Annegret when she enters a relationship with a lesbian whom she meets at a women's center.

[18] Sebastian Peterson's film adaptation reverses this in its final scene, in which Klaus finds bliss with Yvonne in a field of tulips in Holland. (Sebastian Peterson, dir., *Helden wie wir*. 1999.)

Contributors

Leanne Dawson is Lecturer in German and Film Studies at the University of Edinburgh and Chair of the Scottish Queer International Film Festival. Her research focuses on the intersection of LGBTQ+ identities with class and ethnicity in film, literature, theater, and performance art. She is completing a monograph, *From Girls in Uniform to Men in Drag*, about queer femininities on the German screen from 1930 to the present day. Her publications include: *Queering European Film Festivals* (Taylor & Francis, 2018); *Queer European Cinema: Queering Cinematic Time and Space* (Routledge, 2017); and *The Other: Gender, Sexuality and Ethnicity in European Cinema and Beyond* (Taylor & Francis, 2014) as well as a range of article and book chapters considering a spectrum of queerness from monstrosity (vampires and ghosts) to normalization in European, US, and Asian cultures. She continually employs her academic research to create, promote, and support queer culture beyond the academy: she has worked as a consultant for theater; curated and introduced film seasons for cinemas; spoken about LGBTQ+ matters on the BBC; and is making a documentary, *Femmes on Film*, in which she interviews a spectrum of feminine-presenting queer women in the public eye about femme representation and socio-political reality.

Nicholas Courtman is in the second year of his PhD at Jesus College, Cambridge, where he holds the Schröder Scholarship in German Studies. After completing a BA (Hons) in Modern and Medieval Languages (French and German) at the University of Cambridge, he spent a year studying at the Humboldt-Universität zu Berlin with support from the DAAD before completing a MSt in German as a Clarendon Scholar at the University of Oxford in 2016. His PhD research addresses ideologies, histories, and representations of work and labor in German-language writing since the mid-1970s, focusing on works by Volker Braun, Rainald Goetz, Herta Müller, and Jenny Erpenbeck, among others. His research interests include twentieth- and twenty-first-century German literature, film, and thought.

Kyle Frackman is Assistant Professor of Germanic Studies at The University of British Columbia in Vancouver, where he is also Associate Faculty in the Institute for Gender, Race, Sexuality, and Social Justice and in the Centre for Cinema Studies. He is the author of *An Other*

Kind of Home: Gender-Sexual Abjection, Subjectivity, and the Uncanny in Literature and Film (2015) and co-editor of *Classical Music in the German Democratic Republic* (Camden House, 2015) and the forthcoming *Gender and Sexuality in East German Film* (also appearing with Camden House). His current research focuses on expressions of queerness in East German history and culture.

Sarra Kassem holds a PhD from Birkbeck, University of London (2015) on the representation of post-migrants in the films of Turkish-German filmmaker Fatih Akin. She did her undergraduate degree in Sociology at Panteion University, Athens, Greece and her MA in Criminology at Middlesex University, London. She has been working as a researcher for Euromonitor International since 2006, and is also involved in curating film events. Her research interests include German film, European cinema, transnational cinema, gender studies, migration studies, and social construction of deviance.

Lauren Pilcher is currently a PhD candidate at the University of Florida. Their research areas include depictions of gender, sexuality, and race in film and visual media and theories of queer and intersectional feminist representation. Their primary research focuses on documentary and marginal cinemas in the United States, with an additional, theoretical interest in the history and images of sexuality in twentieth-century German cinema. They have published on representations of gender and sexuality in German and American films.

John L. Plews is Professor of German at Saint Mary's University, Halifax, Canada. He is President of the Canadian Association of University Teachers of German (2016–18), President of the Halifax Languages Consortium, Director of the Canadian Summer School in Germany, and a DAAD Research Ambassador. His co-edited books include *Translation and Translating in German Studies* (2016), *Traditions and Transitions: Curricula for German Studies* (2013), *Intercultural Literacies and German in the Classroom* (2007), and *Queering the Canon: Defying Sights in German Literature and Culture* (1998). He has written on learner identities in study abroad, second-language teaching and learning, and various aspects of German literature and culture.

Gary Schmidt is Professor of German and Chair of the Department of Languages and Intercultural Studies at Coastal Carolina University. He is the author of *The Nazi Abduction of Ganymede: Representations of Male Homosexuality in Postwar German Literature* (2003), translator of Joachim Helfer's *What Makes a Man: Sex Talk in Beirut and Berlin* (2015), and co-editor of the volume *Thomas Mann: neue kulturwissenschaftliche*

Kulturen (2012). He has published articles and book chapters on sexuality and gender in the writings of Thomas Mann, W. G. Sebald, Leo Perutz, Christian Kracht, Lilian Faschinger, and Peter Henisch, as well as essays on the films of Florian Henckel von Donnersmarck, Wolfgang Becker, and Stephan Lacant.

CYD STURGESS currently holds a Wolfson Foundation doctoral fellowship at the University of Sheffield and is completing her thesis on discourses of queer feminine identity and desire in Berlin and Amsterdam between 1918 and 1933. She is currently the Early Career Representative for Women in German Studies in Great Britain and Ireland and previously held the position of Postgraduate Representative. She recently published a book chapter on literary engagements with sexological discourses in Josine Reuling's *Terug naar het eiland* (1937) and has published several articles on queer history in DIVA magazine.